COUNSELLING SKILLS AND THEORY
MARGARET HOUGH

Hodder & Stoughton

A MEMBER OF THE HODDER HEADLINE GROUP

To my aunt, Mary McElroy, for all her love and support

Order queries: please contact Bookpoint Ltd, 130 Milton Park, Abingdon, Oxon OX14 4SB. Telephone: (44) 01235 827720 , Fax: (44) 01235 400454. Lines are open from 9.00–6.00, Monday to Saturday, with a 24 hour message answering service.

A catalogue record for this title is available from The British Library

ISBN 0 340 70179 X

First published 1998
Impression number   10 9 8 7
Year   2003

Copyright © 1998 Margaret Hough

Cover illustration by Matthew Russell

Typeset by Fakenham Photosetting Ltd, Fakenham, Norfolk
Printed in Great Britain for Hodder & Stoughton Educational, a division of Hodder Headline, 338 Euston Road, London NW1 3BH by J. W. Arrowsmith Ltd., Bristol.

CONTENTS

Acknowledgements

The author would like to thank the following:

The European Association for Counselling for permission to quote their definition of counselling: The European Association for Counselling for permission to refer to the work of their Professional Training Standards Committee; The British Association for Counselling for permission to refer to their Code of Ethics and Practice for Counsellors, with special reference to Clause B.6.3.; Sue Beesley for typing the manuscript and providing diagrams and Josephine McCrea and Patricia Campbell Hughes for proof reading sections of the text.

The following publisher granted permission for use in the book:

Brooks/Cole Publishing Company in California for material from *The Skilled Helper* by Gerald Egan. Copyright © 1994, 1990, 1986, 1982, 1975
Brooks/Cole Publishing Company, Pacific Grove, CA 93950, a division of International Thomson Publishing Inc. By permission of the publisher.

All attempts have been made to contact publishers to gain permission to reproduce material.

Introduction

My purpose in writing this book is to provide a text which will be of practical value to students who are completing Foundation or Certificate level courses at college or university. The book is an introductory one which presents the main theoretical approaches to counselling and psychotherapy. These include the Psychodynamic, the Behavioural and the Humanistic approaches, along with the models of therapy which derive from these. The basic counselling skills which form an integral part of every model are presented and discussed, while the techniques and procedures characteristic of individual approaches to counselling are also described.

Chapter 9 is devoted to the subject of groupwork, including self-help and counselling groups. This important subject is included because of its increasing relevance within counselling and therapy generally. Group counselling may not be included on every training programme at present, but this is an omission which is, in my view, likely to be remedied in the near future. The benefits of groupwork are increasingly obvious to helpers in a wide spectrum of occupations, including youth work, nursing, social work and teaching. These benefits are not just related to issues of cost effectiveness and other practical consideration, but include certain therapeutic factors which are unique to groups. The development and extension of social skills is one example of such factors, so too is the enhanced self-confidence which clients experience as a result of helping themselves and others in groups.

Throughout the book I have tried to provide as many examples as possible of good counselling practice. The case material used is based largely on my own experience of working with clients and is included so that counselling theory can be set in context and linked to practice. However, any details which could possibly identify individual clients have been omitted or changed. My method of writing case material is a creative one, and involves selecting a range of problems seen in counselling and placing these in a slightly different context or background. Clients' names are changed to ensure confidentiality, and in some instances details relating to age, sex or occupation are altered too. The importance of the client/helper relationship is highlighted in each chapter dealing with theory, and the personal counsellor attributes necessary for effective therapy are highlighted too. The central place of good training and supervision is also addressed in a separate chapter.

In a book dealing with counselling skills and theory it is, I believe, important to consider the different situations in which counselling is used. It is also necessary to consider the many people who use counselling skills as part of their work. The ways in which various approaches can be applied, and their appropriateness to individual situations and needs have been addressed at various points in the text. There is a proliferation of counselling courses at the present time, and many professional people are keen to complete these. In addition, most professions now require employees to update their work skills on a regular basis, and counsellor training is often seen as a valuable extension to a personal CV. This is a trend which is likely to continue, because people are more aware of the need to enhance communication skills generally and members of the caring professions (for example nurses) now know that counselling is an integral part of their work. There is an emphasis on counselling skills within teaching too, and people who work for voluntary agencies also now identify counsellor training as essential to their work. Many voluntary agencies do provide their own specialist training, but it has been my experience that workers want general training as well.

Finally, many of the exercises included in the book can be used by students working alone, but are probably more effective when completed with the guidance of trainers. At the beginning of training students frequently need support when completing exercise assignments. This is because some of the tasks may evoke unexpected emotional responses, which necessitate follow-up discussion if insight is to be achieved. This kind of experiential learning is very important in counsellor training and can only be facilitated in the context of a well-planned, supportive and organised training programme.

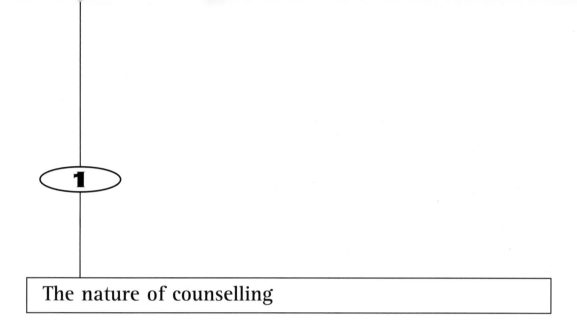

The nature of counselling

INTRODUCTION

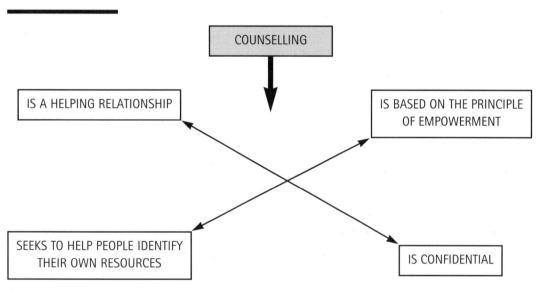

COUNSELLING

IS A HELPING RELATIONSHIP

IS BASED ON THE PRINCIPLE OF EMPOWERMENT

SEEKS TO HELP PEOPLE IDENTIFY THEIR OWN RESOURCES

IS CONFIDENTIAL

What is counselling? How does it differ from other helping activities? These are among the first questions which you, as students, may be asked to consider at the start of your training programme. A wide variety of ideas are likely to emerge in response to these questions, because there is no single answer which adequately defines counselling. One way of approaching the problem of definition is to work in small groups and generate as many answers as possible among the participants. A typical working group might produce results similar to the following list.

What is counselling?

◆ it is a relationship
◆ it is a special form of communication
◆ it involves listening
◆ one person helps another
◆ one person helps several other people in a group
◆ it is a confidential form of helping
◆ it is based on the principle of *empowerment*
◆ it means helping people to clarify and address their problems
◆ it is an activity carried out by trained people
◆ it is guided by theories about the causes of problems, and the methods needed to help

These are just some of the usual responses to the question, and in this first chapter we shall discuss them in turn, along with several other important issues relating to the nature of counselling. These include an examination of the difference between counselling skills and counselling theory, as well as an assessment of the uses of counselling in a wide range of professions. We shall also consider some of the situations in which counselling is used, and the kinds of problems which it addresses. Aspects of counsellor training will be highlighted, although aspects of this topic will be taken up and dealt with in more detail in Chapter 10. Before discussing any of these subjects however, it is useful to look at a list of the possible answers to the second question asked above:

How does it differ from other helping activities?

◆ some helping relationships involve giving advice, and counselling doesn't
◆ other helping relationships may not have the same kind of boundaries
◆ there may be a conflict of interests in other helping relationships
◆ there are some helping relationships in which the helper might be judgmental
◆ other helpers may offer sympathy rather than empathy
◆ other helpers may not be objective
◆ there is an absence of mutual expectations in counselling, which may not be true of other relationships
◆ counsellors do not impose conditions or expectations upon clients, while other helpers may expect their clients to behave in certain ways

Although these are not exhaustive lists, they do provide enough material for discussion purposes. However, it is worth making the point straight away, that counselling is not the mysterious or inscrutable activity which members of the public sometimes suspect it to be. Counsellors themselves occasionally contribute to an obscurantist view of their work, especially when they are reluctant to discuss it in terms which are accessible to the uninitiated. Many people use counselling skills every day in their work, although most of them would not describe themselves as counsellors. Additionally, there are many more people who have completed counsellor training yet do not describe themselves as counsellors either. These are some of the people whose roles and responsibilities we shall discuss later in the chapter.

EXERCISE — Response to Questions

Working individually, look at the answers given to the two questions asked above. Say how many of these apply to your own professional practice, or to your relationships with other people. Is your work based on the principle of client empowerment, for example? Discuss your ideas with other members of the training group.

SOME DEFINITIONS

All the responses to the questions raised in this chapter are, in fact, correct, though they do need some qualifying comments. Counselling is indeed a relationship, often between two people, but sometimes between a number of people and another person who is designated to act as counsellor for the group. Counselling, therefore, takes place both in individual and group settings, and in the latter context, two counsellors are occasionally present to work with members of the group. Regardless of the setting, however, the counselling relationship is a special form of communication, and this is true for a variety of reasons. One of the factors which makes it special is the quality of helper listening, which is developed as a result of training. This listening involves attending to what the client *means* to say, as well as what he is actually saying, and this will be discussed in some detail in the next chapter.

Confidentiality is another important component of the counsellor/client relationship which sets it apart from several other helping activities, although it should be noted that most professional helpers also regard it as essential to their work. Nevertheless, there are still some helping activities, like teaching – for example, where confidentiality towards pupils or students cannot be totally guaranteed. On the other hand, absolute confidentiality may not always be possible in counselling either, and these and other limitations will be addressed in Chapter 10.

Another important aspect of counselling is the concept of client empowerment. In simple terms, this indicates a confidence in the innate potential for self-determination which clients are believed to have. This capacity for self determination may not always be apparent to the client, and certainly in times of stress or emotional upheaval it may become blocked or temporarily obscured. Counselling can help by enabling clients to look more closely at their problems, and to clarify them. When this is achieved, ways of addressing these problems can be devised by clients themselves, and strategies for change can be implemented. The non-judgmental and empathic presence of a trained helper facilitates the processes just described, and the fact that counsellors do not expect any reciprocal help from clients (the kind of help which friends might expect from each other, for example) means that clients feel valued and respected in a way they may not have experienced before. Nor do counsellors impose conditions or expectations on the clients they help, and even when goals and objectives are an integral part of the counselling contract, these are freely negotiated between client and counsellor.

THERAPEUTIC COUNSELLING AND COUNSELLING SKILLS

Therapeutic counselling is an activity undertaken by people who are specifically trained in this field. It differs from many other occupations and areas of work which are often described as 'counselling' but, strictly speaking, are not. These other areas include, for example, career counselling, colour counselling, financial counselling, tourist counselling and horoscope counselling. In fact, there is a growing tendency to describe any occupation in which advice is given as 'counselling'. Therapeutic counselling does not include advice giving in its repertoire of skills, although it should be added that clients can hardly fail to be influenced by a counsellor's attitudes, even when these are not explicitly stated.

In therapeutic counselling, the relationship between helper and client is especially significant and based on the principle of equality. There is, moreover, no obvious conflict of interest in the relationship, and this is just one of the factors which set it apart from other working relationships. Teachers may, for example, need to discipline pupils, while nurses and social workers often give advice to the people they help. However, a distinction should be made here between the use of therapeutic counselling with clients, and the use of counselling skills by other professionals in a variety of work situations. As we noted earlier, there are many people who now undertake counsellor training, because they believe the skills they gain will prove useful in the work they do. Because of the training they receive, these people are well aware that they are not acting 'as counsellors' in their professional roles. Instead, they are using the interpersonal skills which they have developed and refined within their counsellor training. A range of interpersonal or counselling skills will also be discussed in Chapter 2 and in subsequent chapters throughout the book. Before looking at the differences between theory and skills, however, it is useful to consider the ways in which counselling has been defined by organisations which are directly linked to it. The following is a definition offered by the European Association for Counselling:

> Counselling is an interactive learning process contracted between counsellor(s) and client(s), be they individuals, families, groups or institutions, which approaches in a holistic way, social, cultural, economic and/or emotional issues. Counselling may be concerned with addressing and resolving specific problems, making decisions, coping with crisis, improving relationships, developmental issues, promoting and developing personal awareness, working with feelings, thoughts, perceptions and internal or external conflict. The overall aim is to provide clients with opportunities to work in self defined ways, towards living in more satisfyig and resourceful ways as individuals and as members of the broader society.'

(European Association for Counselling News Letter, January 1996)

EXERCISE —— Some differences ——————

Working in groups of three or four, compile a list of the ways in which the counselling relationship differs from other helping relationships. These other relationships might include nursing, social work, medicine and church ministry, though there are probably others you can think of. What are the conflicts of interest which might exist within any of these other relationships? How might counselling skills training help people in these professional roles?

COUNSELLING SKILLS AND COUNSELLING THEORY

It is important to make a distinction between theory and skills in the context of counsellor training. At a basic level, the word 'skills' refers to the interpersonal tools which counsellors need to possess or acquire in order to communicate effectively with clients. These essential tools or skills include those of

◆ listening

◆ paraphrasing

◆ summarising

◆ asking questions

◆ encouraging clients to be specific

◆ reflecting their feelings

◆ helping them to clarify their thoughts

◆ encouraging them to focus on key issues

◆ offering forms of challenge and confrontation when needed

In addition to these, however, there are other skills which are applicable to the actual organisation of counselling sessions. These basic skills will be discussed in some detail in Chapter 2, along with examples of the way they are used with clients.

Counselling theory, on the other hand, deals with assumptions and hypotheses about the process of human development. The problems and difficulties which can arise at various stages throughout our lifespan, as a result of environmental or other influences, are also considered under the heading of counselling theory. The ways in which different forms of therapy and counselling approach these problems, as well as their individual methods of helping clients, have evolved alongside theories about human development and the acquisition of helpful and unhelpful behaviours. A summary of the three main approaches to counselling theory will be given in Chapter 2. Individual theories will be described in more detail in subsequent chapters.

People who use counselling skills in their work

We have already noted that many people, including doctors, nurses, ministers of religion and teachers, use some counselling skills as part of their work. Doctors, for example, listen to their patients, and they usually try to understand the complex messages which people in distress often wish to convey. There is a growing emphasis on the need for interpersonal skills training among health professionals, but even when this is undertaken, doctors and others cannot devote the necessary listening time to individual patients. In addition to this, doctors frequently tell their patients what to do, and the central focus in doctor/patient encounters tends towards the factual rather than the emotional aspects of problems presented. This last point is applicable to people working in other areas of health care too. Despite the limitations just described, however, it is still the case that many health professionals, carers and others, use what have come to be known as counselling skills in their daily work. A list of professions in this category would include the following:

◆ teaching
◆ nursing
◆ occupational therapy
◆ physiotherapy
◆ medicine
◆ social work
◆ church ministry
◆ speech therapy
◆ midwifery
◆ health visiting
◆ voluntary work
◆ youth work

This represents only a selection of the many areas of work in which some counselling skills form an integral part of the professional's role. All of these people are likely to benefit from further training. The reason for this is that even when their interpersonal skills are quite well developed, professional people gain a great deal from further skills training and the process of *self-development*, which is a fundamental part of counsellor training. These counsellor skills and attributes will be the subject of Chapter 2.

CASE STUDY — Mrs Feltmann

Mrs Feltmann was a sixty-eight year-old patient who attended her central GP surgery suffering from chest pains. She had a history of chronic obstructive airway disease, as well as a long-standing history of anxiety which had worsened over the previous six months. This heightened anxiety was associated with her recent move to the area, and was further exacerbated by the experience of chest pains and profound worries about her health generally. Mrs Feltmann's doctor ensured that all aspects of her physical problems were investigated and treated. He referred her to a consultant chest physician, who suggested that she might benefit from stress counselling or some other form of psychological assistance. Mrs Feltmann tended to become tearful during visits to her GP and although he was sympathetic and attentive, he could not give her the time and the quality of support she obviously needed. When the subject of counselling was raised, Mrs Feltmann was enthusiastic about it, and an appointment was made with one of the counsellors who worked at the practice. During her first session with the counsellor, Mrs Feltmann talked at length about her health worries, and about the sequence of events which had led to her state of anxiety. She also cried a great deal, and seemed relieved to express the pent-up emotions she had tried to ignore in the past.

CLIENT: I never really wanted to move here. It was my husband's idea. He always wanted to come here. I just went along with it and never said how I really feel.

COUNSELLOR: You didn't state your true feelings ...

CLIENT: He never gave me a chance ... him and the kids. Every time I went to say something they just took the line ... 'Oh you'll love it. It's a lovely place, and it will help your chest.'

COUNSELLOR: So you felt you were never properly consulted ... that nobody really listened.

CLIENT: That's right. Now I'm here and I don't know a soul. I feel trapped.

COUNSELLOR: Not able to talk to the family ... nor to anyone else either.

CLIENT: The neighbours are not friendly. I have tried to be sociable, but the fact that I can't get out much ... I can't drive and my chest is bad ... means that I'm isolated. This is the first real talk I've had with anyone.

COUNSELLOR: The first time you have been able to say what you really feel.

CLIENT: Yes.

One reason for including this case study is that it highlights the difficulties which exist for many professionals in relation to their patients/clients. Mrs Feltmann's GP, for example, understood that she needed more time than he could possibly give her. He had other patients to see, though he was aware of her emotional needs and suggested counselling to address these.

Another reason for describing Mrs Feltmann's problems is that it illustrates the close link between physical and emotional conditions. In her case the link was quite marked, and she seemed aware of this herself, since she readily agreed to counselling when it was suggested to her. This last point is an important one, because clients who feel under pressure to accept counselling seldom achieve a great deal as a result of it. In other words, counselling should be an option which clients are free to accept or decline according to their individual needs and wishes. In Chapter 2 we shall look at other case studies which illustrate the use of various counselling skills. However, an important point to make here is that the counsellor who helped Mrs Feltmann was able to give her *time*, something which the doctor could not offer because of his other commitments. Lack of time may also be an inhibiting factor in many of the other professional roles mentioned earlier. Nevertheless, there are some professional roles in which the time factor is a built-in consideration, and Health Visiting is an example of this. Health Visitors who work closely with young mothers are very aware of the potential emotional problems which can affect their clients, so they ensure that sufficient time is devoted to the exploration of these problems. The following exchange between a young mother named Louise, and her health visitor named Lesley, illustrates this point:

LOUISE: I get a bit uptight about housework ... I really worry about it.

LESLEY: All the new commitments you have now, especially the baby ... that's a very new experience and responsibility.

LOUISE: [starting to cry] It seems endless ... and I'm so tired. Sometimes I can hardly get out of bed.

LESLEY: Sit down for a moment and let's talk about this. Just tell me exactly the way you feel.

Lesley, the Health Visitor, was concerned to help Louise express her feelings and gave her sufficient time to do so. As part of her work Lesley used a range of counselling skills, including listening, paraphrasing, reflecting back feelings, and the skill of asking relevant questions. However, Lesley's job also included giving advice, which was entirely appropriate and necessary in this instance, since Louise needed it in order to identify and seek help for the post-natal depression she suffered. Advice giving would not be appropriate in therapeutic counselling though, because the focus there is on helping clients to identify what it is they want and need.

PROBLEMS OF ADVICE

Many clients seek counselling in the hope they will be told what to do. Others hope for advice about the best ways to tackle their personal problems. Advice is not given in therapeutic counselling, however, and there are many good reasons for withholding it. Perhaps one of the most important reasons is one which Amada (1995) identifies. He refers to the experiences of young children who are given frequent and copious advice, and who harbour deep feelings of resentment on account of it. These feelings do not disappear, but are carried into adult life and operate at an unconscious level thereafter. Advice, therefore, is not always valued in the way that advisers would like to believe. Nevertheless, there are some people who might be quite willing to follow any advice in a slavish and uncritical way. These people tend to view all helpers as experts, but in the context of therapeutic counselling they can be helped to look more closely at this aspect of their thinking and identify the reasons such expectations exist. If a client in therapy is willing to believe and follow everything a counsellor says, it is likely that he responds in a similar way to other significant people in his life. These ways of responding should be discussed between counsellor and client: if they are not, the client will have gained little as a result of therapy.

Clients who habitually invite or expect the control of others, or those who acquiesce to the views of other people, are in danger of losing sight of their own capabilities and resources. Counsellors can help their clients to locate and identify these resources, but in order to do this they need to be honest in relation to the subject of advice and its distorting influence. Clients are helped much more when they gain some understanding of the insecurities which impel them to seek advice in the first place. When clients develop greater understanding of their emotional problems, they tend to become more self-directed as a consequence, and the opinions and views of others are considered in a more detached way. This represents a real shift towards personal development and empowerment.

Advice or information?

We have seen that advice is a necessary component of some helping relationships. Patients expect and need advice from their doctors, for example, and practical help is often given too. Psychological and emotional conflicts cannot be approached in this utilitarian way, however, since it is only clients themselves who are aware of the complex dimensions of their own problems. The ways in which counsellors can help clients to identify and clarify their problems will be discussed in subsequent chapters. Meanwhile, an important caveat should be added in this section dealing with advice: this concerns certain emergency situations in which clients seem incapable of acting in autonomous ways to protect themselves against harm or danger. In these situations the counsellor may find it necessary to intervene by suggesting alternative courses of action. A client who is deeply depressed or suicidal, for example, may lack the psychological strength to make a constructive or informed decision about effective and available treatments which might be of benefit. Giving information to clients is, of course, not quite the same thing as giving advice, although a distinction between the two is sometimes hard to detect. The skill of information giving will be discussed in Chapter 2.

PROBLEMS WHICH BRING PEOPLE TO COUNSELLING

People seek counselling for a wide variety of problems. Sometimes these are problems which have become unmanageable, while at other times they may simply present as feelings of dissatisfaction or unhappiness with life in general. People frequently find themselves locked in repeated self-destructive relationships, and just as often fail to anticipate the consequences of the actions they take. Many people are, as Amada (1995) so succinctly puts it, 'confounded by their own behaviour'. In spite of a genuine desire to change and to engage in more satisfying relationships, these goals remain elusive for some people. There are many reasons for this inability to change, but perhaps the most significant of these is a lack of self-awareness and personal insight. Other people seek counselling when they are troubled by physical symptoms which fail to respond to medical investigation or remedy. Psychosomatic problems may include skin problems, tension headaches, sleep disorders, tiredness, stomach problems and many other equally debilitating symptoms. Sometimes people are propelled towards counselling when they lack motivation or direction. Academic under-achievement, difficulties at work, lack of assertiveness and low self-esteem are also reasons which prompt people to ask for help through counselling. Addictions and phobias are problematic for many people, while others are troubled with anxiety, feelings of worth-lessness, and often the conviction that they will fall apart or break down if help is not obtained. The following is an outline of some of the reasons which may prompt clients to seek counselling:

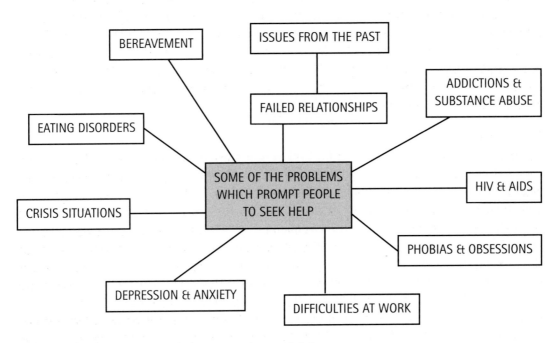

BEREAVEMENT

ISSUES FROM THE PAST

ADDICTIONS &
SUBSTANCE ABUSE

FAILED RELATIONSHIPS

EATING DISORDERS

SOME OF THE PROBLEMS
WHICH PROMPT PEOPLE
TO SEEK HELP

HIV & AIDS

CRISIS SITUATIONS

PHOBIAS & OBSESSIONS

DEPRESSION & ANXIETY

DIFFICULTIES AT WORK

Figure 1.1   *Some problems which prompt people to seek help*

◆ Repetition of destructive relationships

Relationship problems are high on the list of factors which prompt clients to seek coun-selling. As I have already indicated, people are often perplexed by their own behaviour and their inability to establish and maintain enjoyable and healthy relationships. This does not imply that counsellors are relationship experts, since clearly this is not the case. Counsellors, like everyone else, experience difficulties in their private lives, although with a background of proper training they should be aware at least of the importance of getting help. Clients who attempt to solve their own relationships problems often find themselves unable to do so. This is because of the unconscious element which frequently operates to sabotage all conscious efforts. The chapters dealing with psychodynamic counselling in this book provide more information about unconscious motivation, and the ways in which it is manifest. With the aid of a trained person (in this case the counsellor) clients can be helped to identify the factors which disturb their relationships.

◆ Crisis situations

The word 'crisis' can be used to describe a variety of situations which seem overwhelming at the time they are experienced. What is perceived as a crisis by one person may not be viewed as such by someone else. On the other hand, there are certain situations including sudden bereavement, assault, the discovery of serious illness, suicidal feelings, loss of employment and divorce which are likely to constitute a crisis for the majority of people. A sudden crisis may serve to re-activate long-forgotten traumas or emotional problems from the past. These may be factors which bring people into counselling for the first time. Telephone counselling is another context in which crisis situations are addressed. Both Childline and the Samaritans offer listening services for people in crisis, although these two services differ in the sense that Childline also offers practical, sometimes interventionist advice. Volunteers who work for The Samaritans do not describe themselves as counsellors, but nevertheless use counselling skills in their work. Like Cruse, both Childline and The Samaritans provide their own training for volunteers, though some do complete other general training programmes too.

◆ Bereavement

Bereavement is an experience which often brings people into counselling, and is also one which everyone is likely to have at some stage in life. Although many bereaved people would, in the past, have received help in the community – from either family, friends or both, this is not automatically the case today. However, even when bereaved people are supported by family and friends, there remain certain situations in which counselling has added benefits, and this is especially true when several members of a family have suffered the same loss. Counselling is also applicable in crisis bereavement, or in circumstances which are complicated in other ways. Children who have lost a parent or parents are especially vulnerable, and often need the added support which counselling can give. Bereavement counselling helps people to deal with the deep feelings of loss which may be experienced soon after a death, or indeed at any stage thereafter. Cruse is one organisation which offers its own training programme to helpers who wish to work in this area, but it is a specific form of training and many people who undertake it go on to further training.

◆ Issues from the past

There are some clients who seek counselling because of problems they experienced in childhood. These include sexual, emotional or physical abuse, or may be related to experiences of loss or abandonment. Unresolved problems which stem from the past often cause feelings of mental or even physical exhaustion. They may also cause lack of confidence, feelings of worthlessness, inability to enjoy life, deeply-felt grievances or an ongoing pattern of destructive relationships.

◆ Depression and anxiety

Depression and anxiety are common problems for many people who seek counselling. Both these conditions vary from very severe to bearable, but are usually sufficiently debilitating to disturb those clients who experience them. Depressive conditions often need medical as well a psychological support, and some of the clients who are seen in counselling may be referred by their GPs. Although some anxiety is unavoidable in everyday living, it can become problematic in certain situations and at certain stages of an individual's life. Anxiety attacks, or anxiety which cannot be controlled, often prompts clients to ask for help. In the same way, free-floating or vague anxiety may impel some people to seek help in identifying the underlying causes.

◆ Addictions and substance abuse

Occasionally clients are forced to seek help because they find themselves unable to deal effectively with their own addictive behaviour. Addictions and substance abuse include the more obvious examples of alcohol, drugs, and gambling, although there are other addictive problems which are less well publicised. These include addictions to shopping and casual sex, for example, and there are no doubt more which are less easily identified. Clients need to address the underlying causes of addiction and substance abuse, and counselling gives them the opportunity to do this. There are other forms of help available for these problems, including support groups and recovery programmes, which are sometimes used alongside counselling. In Chapter 9, we shall consider the advantages of group therapy for clients with a variety of problems.

◆ Phobias and obsessions

There is an almost infinite variety of phobias which people can suffer from. Perhaps the most common, or at least the best known, are phobias about animals, insects, meeting people, enclosed spaces, germs and flying. Different theoretical approaches to counselling offer varying explanations for the causes and development of phobias, and some of these ideas will be discussed in later chapters of the book.

◆ Work problems

Many relationship problems are experienced in the context of work, and employment stress or burn-out are often symptoms of the underlying difficulties which clients bring to counselling. Some companies now offer stress counselling to employees who need it, and even those who do not are increasingly aware of the importance of counselling support. People need to understand how they themselves contribute to the stress which they experience, and a focus of counselling is this identification of individual factors in stress maintenance. Clients are often surprised to discover that they sometimes collude in punishing themselves when they agree to every single request, no matter how unreasonable it seems. Stress counselling is effective in helping people to examine their own behaviour in the work place, and to adjust it when necessary.

◆ Personal growth

Sometimes people decide to seek counselling in order to assist the process of personal growth and development. These people could be described as 'worried, though well' and they are often prompted to ask for help when they reach a certain age (for example mid-life). In the past people in this category might have talked to a minister of religion, for example. Because of changing patterns of church attendance and the secularisation of society generally, such help is less often sought out and counselling is sometime used instead.

◆ Eating disorders

Anorexia Nervosa, Bulimia, Obesity and compulsive eating are all problems which some-times impel clients to seek counselling. Often clients are referred by their GPs, but occasionally they come into counselling for other reasons, such as depression, which are linked to the eating problem. Anorexia Nervosa in particular has been on the increase over the past two decades, and research has indicated that in North America girls as young as nine years suffer from the condition (Orbach, 1994). Eating problems can be very difficult to overcome, but most experts in the field acknowledge the importance of psychological support (often long-term) for those people who suffer from them. A focus of counselling is to help clients identify the underlying cause (or causes) of their conflicts in relation to food, and this is often a lengthy process. Counsellors who work in General Practice will usually communicate with the client's GP, although clients should know when this is happening. Many clients benefit from a feminist perspective in counselling. This is because of the sociological factors which are often implicated in appetite conditions.

◆ HIV and AIDS

Counselling for clients who are worried about HIV and AIDS is not, as Burnard (1994) points out, an area which can be described as totally homogenous. People who are concerned about their health in relation to HIV and AIDS include the relatives of clients who have been tested HIV Positive, as well as clients who have actually developed AIDS. These groups encompass, therefore, a fairly wide and varied range of people, which means that different approaches may be needed in order to help them (Burnard, 1994). Some of these approaches will be considered in later chapters.

◆ Other reasons for seeking counselling

It would be impossible to discuss all the reasons which bring clients into counselling, since they are obviously as varied and numerous as the people themselves. However, the follow-ing is a list of further reasons for seeking counselling and therapy.

- ◆ social problems
- ◆ bullying
- ◆ harassment at work
- ◆ chronic illness
- ◆ gambling
- ◆ job loss
- ◆ rape and assault
- ◆ developmental crises
- ◆ problems of sexual identity

In addition to the reasons for counselling, there is also a range of specific contexts in which counselling and therapy are actually used. Some of these (group counselling, for example) will be discussed in more detail in the subsequent chapters. Others include:

- couples counselling
- family therapy
- group counselling
- co-counselling
- telephone counselling
- counselling children

Most of these areas require their own specific training, and are usually undertaken by counsellors who are especially interested in them. There are also a number of backgrounds or settings in which counsellors may choose to work. These include:

- school, college and university counselling
- counselling in the work place
- counselling in general practice
- counselling in private practice
- counselling in hospices/hospitals
- counselling in voluntary work

EXERCISE — Common problems

Working in small groups, identify the most common problems which clients (in your area of work) tend to have. Afterwards, discuss your findings with members of the training group generally. What were the outstanding problems identified overall?

Self-development and self-awareness in counsellor training

One of the things you will become aware of quite early on in your training is that learning about counselling is not an entirely theoretical exercise. On the contrary, there is a substantial element of personal development which is integral to all training programmes. What this means in practice is that a great deal of what you learn throughout the course will be 'experiential' in nature. From the very beginning you will probably think much more about yourself, the experiences you have had, the opinions you hold, the prejudices of which you were previously unaware, your relationships of the past and present, and indeed any other significant factors of your personal and professional life. This experience is both rewarding and challenging, and no doubt your trainer/trainers will discuss it with the group. Your teacher or trainer may also establish a contract or working agreement with group members, and when this is the case a number of important 'ground rules' may form part of it. These ground rules obviously vary from one training establishment to another, but there are certain areas which are common to most of them. Once these rules have been discussed and agreed upon, group members tend to acquire a much clearer view of course structure and objectives. Areas which are usually discussed at the beginning of each course include the following:

◆ administration details and dates of course breaks
◆ attendance and time keeping
◆ confidentiality
◆ the role of the trainer/teacher
◆ respect for views expressed by all group members
◆ the importance of listening to what others say
◆ methods of teaching, learning and assessment criteria
◆ use of personal experience for skills practise and discussion
◆ tea-breaks (if any) and when they take place
◆ keeping a diary or journal

◆ Time keeping

In my experience, attendance and time keeping are central issues in counsellor training, especially at the level of introductory and foundation courses. It is sometimes difficult for trainees to understand the link between their behaviour on the course, and their behaviour and expectations in relation to the clients they work with (or hope to work with). It is useful to consider the word 'boundaries' in this context, since it refers to the parameters or guide-lines which govern the working relationship between counsellor and client. Clients need to know that counsellors are reliable, and reliability encompasses such areas as punctuality and good time keeping. If students are unable to come to training sessions on time, or if they frequently feel obliged to leave before sessions end, it is unlikely that a miraculous transformation of behaviour will occur late on. Another relevant point to make is that other students in a training group tend to resent the disruptive effect created when people arrive or depart at different times. Last, but not least, poor time keeping means that whole areas of both theoretical and practical experience are missed, and are never properly regained throughout training.

◆ Counselling practice and supervision

Other important issues central to counsellor training include experience of working with clients and supervision. However, both these topics should have been discussed with you before you enrolled for the course, and the requirements for the course generally should have been clarified with you. For fairly obvious reasons, most training establishments would expect their students to have ongoing experience of working with clients in a counselling context. Such experience is essential if real learning is to take place, although as Thorne and Dryden (1991) point out, it is understandable that some agencies are reluctant to allow trainees to counsel their clients or patients. Arrangements for supervision also need to be in place, though once again individual training courses will stipulate requirements for students on their courses. Many of you are probably working with clients already in your professional roles, and if this is the case, then regular supervision should be an inbuilt part of the work you do. In Chapter10 we will look in more detail at aspects of counsellor training, supervision, confidentiality and other ethical issues in counselling.

◆ Keeping a journal

Most trainers expect counselling students to keep a journal or diary throughout the course. This record may be either written- or verbal (recorded on tape), and its purpose is to enable trainees to reflect on the experiences they have and the personal development they have achieved, as a result of both professional practice and training. Keeping a journal is a valuable aid to self-exploration, and you should make a point of keeping entries up to date. One way of doing this is to ensure you make an entry as soon as possible after each training session. In this way, you are less likely to forget the relevant areas of theory and practice which have been covered each time. Some course trainers require their students to submit these diaries at the end of the course, while others regard them as confidential and for the student's use only. It is a good idea to record the number and dates of sessions at the beginning of each entry, and it is also useful to present the journal in loose-leaf format. A file with individual loose leaf pockets works well, and when journals are used for assessment purposes, relevant sections can be extracted as required. The structure of the journal should be clear, with sufficient space allowed for tutor comments if applicable. You need to show some evidence of reflection and thought, and this can, of course, prove difficult, especially at the beginning of a course when you are learning about a new subject. The following is a guide to recording sessions:

◆ record the content of the session
◆ what skills were practised?
◆ what topics were discussed?
◆ how were practice sessions organised?
◆ how did you respond to the work being done?
◆ how did other people in the group respond?
◆ record any feedback you received from other trainees
◆ record any significant group discussion which followed each session
◆ write an entry even when you were absent for a session. Say why you were absent, and how you felt about this. What areas of work were covered when you were away?
◆ record any connections you have made between work covered in sessions, and the experience of the client/counsellor relationship. Has anything happened, or has anything been discussed, which sheds some light on how clients might feel in certain situations, for example?
◆ say something about your reactions to particular theories discussed
◆ record any connections which you might have made between theory and practice
◆ record any significant insights you have gained
◆ refer to any relevant newspaper articles or books which you have read
◆ refer to lecture handouts and say how useful or otherwise these have been

This may seem like a fairly extensive list, but it is meant as a guide only. Most trainers discuss the content of journals with their students, and requirements are often clearly set out. The most important point to remember about journals, is that they should indicate evidence of developing self-awareness. They should also show that you are increasingly aware of the way other people think and feel. Both these areas of awareness (self-awareness and awareness of others) need then to be linked to the counselling context. Writing a journal throughout training is a valuable aid to self-understanding, and has some similarity with the therapeutic effects which are gained through talking in counselling. As Storr (1997) points out, both these activities are similar in the sense that they help increase insight, although it should be added that keeping a diary or journal does not provide the feeling of acceptance which is so important for clients in counselling. A well-kept journal also demonstrates your ability to record information, to collate material, and to present this material in a logical and clear form. It further demonstrates your ability to use skills gained on the course, in your personal and professional life. You may be required to submit your journal for assessment purposes, and when this is the case, it will be regarded as confidential between you, your course tutor and the moderator.

SKILLS TRAINING

Throughout your training you will probably be asked to work with other trainees in groups. Some courses incorporate Personal Development Groups (PDG) into their training programmes. These groups give students the opportunity to work closely together, and to explore personal issues and relationships in a safe and supportive environment. Counselling skills practice is another integral part of most training courses, and this is designed to give students the chance to demonstrate the use of a range of basic skills in an ongoing way throughout training. Skills practice may take the form of role play, or it may take the form of peer counselling. In fact, both these methods of training may be used within the same course. Skills practice, whether role played or authentic, has many advantages for students in training. An outstanding advantage is that you can develop counselling skills without harming clients, and when these skills are developed, you can then integrate them into your personal and professional life. One disadvantage is that some trainees may be so lacking in confidence and basic skills to start with, that they are unable to conduct these exercises without causing distress to others. However, teachers and trainers are aware of the difficulties which can arise in these practice sessions, and are usually vigilant in the way they monitor and observe students work. The following descriptions highlight the advantages and disadvantages of both role play and experiential counselling in skills training.

Role play

Role play, as a method of practice in counselling, is used on some course, and has the advantage of being a relatively safe way for students to learn basic kills. This is an approach which requires participants to simulate a counselling situation, and to assume the roles of client and counsellor. Working through role play means that you are unlikely to 'hurt' a colleague who is playing the part of client, and it has the added advantage of allowing you to explore emotions and feelings in a non-threatening context. Trainers often provide their students with specific scenarios or problems, which are then used in the role play situation. The following is an example of a role play brief.

> **ROLEPLAY**
>
> A middle-aged woman has been referred by her doctor for counselling. Her two grown-up children have left home, and she feels lonely and isolated since their departure. She would like to be more socially involved, but lacks the confidence to initiate any real contacts.

There is, of course, a very wide variety of possible problem situations which can be used for role play purposes. Besides the advantages already mentioned, role play also allows you to stop at any stage throughout the session in order to discuss your progress, and the skills being used. On the other hand, role play makes it difficult for participants to become involved on a personal level, and it is also surprisingly difficult to be 'real' when problems discussed are hypothetical. The core condition of empathy (described in Chapter 5) is almost impossible to develop when two people are engaged in a simulated exchange. In contrast, there are substantial advantages to being a real client during skills training.

Using your own problems

When you use your own problems in skills sessions, you will experience exactly what it is like to be a client in counselling. You will also gain valuable insights into your own attitudes, feelings and areas of personal vulnerability. The learning which takes place at this level is probably more important than anything you can read in books, and highlights the experiential aspect of counsellor training which we noted earlier in this chapter. In addition to gaining insight and identifying areas of vulnerability, being a real client during skills training also allows you to develop trust and sharing among your colleagues, and this is certainly important in any training group. However, time is usually limited in practice sessions, and this can cause problems for trainees who are inexperienced as counsellors. Some trainee counsellors may not possess, or have had time to develop, sufficient competence to conduct the sessions within safe limits. There is sometimes a tendency to push the 'client' too far so that what looked like a simple problem on the surface leads to deeper issues which neither student is able to deal with. Students who are working as clients may also be tempted to use training sessions as a means of dealing with outstanding or unresolved personal problems. This is, of course, unfair to colleagues who are, after all, in a learning situation too. Once again, your trainer will be aware of potential problems, and will endeavour to ensure that training programmes are conducted in the safest possible way.

Personal therapy

Many training programmes stipulate that students should have personal therapy as a requirement for the course. Dryden and Thorne (1991) highlight the point that some trainers, especially those with a psychodynamic orientation, place a great deal of emphasis on personal therapy and regard it as an essential element of the course. Some programmes are prescriptive about the number of counselling sessions which students should have, while others may be less specific about this and other aspects of personal counselling generally. However, you are probably aware of these details in relation to your own course. Personal therapy has some advantages, the most important of which is that it enables you to identify and deal with your own problems. It also forms a link between the theory which is learned on the course, and the actual practice of counselling. These two elements (practice and theory) are brought together in what Aveline (1990) refers to as a personal experience which makes sense of the two. Not everyone involved in counsellor training is enthusiastic about personal therapy for trainees, however, and Aveline (1990) also refers to studies which indicate a fairly high level of negative effects on students who received such therapy as part of their courses.

SUMMARY

In this chapter we looked at some of the basic questions which are often asked in relation to counselling. These include questions concerning the nature and function of counselling, and the ways in which this form of helping differs from several others, including for example, nursing and social work. Some definitions of counselling were suggested, and the European Association for Counselling definition (1996) was also quoted. We also looked at a range of occupations which often describe themselves as 'counselling', even though they have little in common with 'therapeutic' counselling. A distinction was made between skills and theory, and we discussed the ways in which counselling skills are used by people who work as health professionals.

The subject of advice and information giving was addressed in the context of the ways in which health professionals and others help their patients and clients. We saw that advice is not normally given in therapeutic counselling, though we considered some emergency situations in which advice and information may become almost synonymous. Aspects of counsellor training were outlined in this chapter: these included time keeping, the use of journals, establishing a training contract, skills training, practice and supervision, personal therapy and role play. The problems which bring people to counselling were highlighted, as were the specific contexts in which counselling is used. One of these, group counselling, will be dealt with in more detail in Chapter 9. In Chapter 2 we shall also consider the individual skills which are used in counselling. An overview of the main historical and theoretical approaches to therapy and counselling will also be outlined.

REFERENCES

Amada, G. (1995)   *A Guide to Psychotherapy.* New York: Ballantine Books.

Aveline, M. (1990)   'The training and supervision of individual therapists', in Dryden, W. (ed) *Individual Therapy – A Handbook.* Milton Keynes: Open University Press.

Burnard, P. (1994)   *Counselling Skills for Professional People.* London: Chapman Hall.

Dryden, W. & Thorne, B. (1991)   'Key issues in the training of counsellors', in Dryden, W. & Thorne, B. (eds). *Training and Supervision for Counselling in Action.* London, Sage Publications.

European Association for Counselling (1996)   European Association for Counselling Newsletter, London.

Orbach, S. (1994)   'Hunger strike' in Orbach, S. *What's Really Going on Here?* London: Virago Press.

Storr, A. (1997)   Sigmund Freud in Storr, A. *Feet of Clay – A Study of Gurus.* London: Harper Collins.

FURTHER READING

Dryden, W. & Feltham, C. (1995)   *Counselling and Psychotherapy – A Consumer's Guide.* London: Sheldon Press.

Feltham, C. (1995)   *What Is Counselling? The Promise and Problems of the Talking Therapies.* London: Sage Publications.

Knight, L. (1995)   *Talking To A Stranger.* London: Hodder & Stoughton.

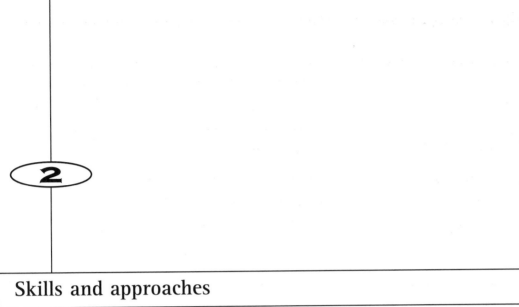

Skills and approaches

INTRODUCTION

This chapter is about interpersonal/communication skills, and their use within a structure or framework designed to help clients in counselling. Skills are the abilities which helpers need to have in order to work effectively with people. They are also central to the theoretical approaches to counselling which will be described in subsequent chapters of this book. Different approaches to counselling place differing emphasis on the use of individual skills – but all, including the three main schools which we shall outline in this chapter, highlight such basic skills as listening as part of their repertoire.

◆ Counselling skills, which are essentially good interpersonal or communication skills, can be divided into several components, verbal and non verbal.

In addition to the verbal and non-verbal skills, however, there are other aspects of communication which have special significance when applied to counselling. These are skills which relate to the actual organisation of sessions with clients and include, among other things, opening and closing interviews, pacing and timing, establishing confidentiality, making contracts, setting targets and referring clients when necessary. Some of these skills will be addressed in this chapter. The subjects of confidentiality, making contracts and referring clients will be considered in more detail in Chapter 10.

THE STRUCTURE OF COUNSELLING

Counselling is a process which requires a coherent framework or structure. This framework is necessary as a guide for both counsellor and client, and although it is not always rigidly followed, it serves as a map or reference point in the practice of counselling. Egan (1994) offers a structural model of counselling which divides the process into three main components as follows:

Stage One	Review of the present situation
Stage Two	Development of a new or preferred scenario
Stage Three	Moving into action
(*Egan, 1994*)	

Within each of these stages, Egan describes a number of skills which are commonly used. These are the skills which we shall consider throughout this chapter. Before doing so, however, it is useful to look more closely at Egan's stages in order to identify the processes which occur in each. Stage One of the model refers to the initial phase of counselling, when clients are encouraged to explore their problems so that they may develop a deeper understanding of them. Stage Two refers to the process of helping clients identify what it is they want and need in order to deal more effectively with problems. Stage Three is the phase of action, during which clients devise ways of actually dealing with problems. This stage may encompass a range of practical activities geared towards achieving results.

Egan divides his three stages into a series of sub-sections, all of which are discussed in his book *The Skilled Helper* (1994). However, other models of the counselling relationship have been described, and Burnard (1994) refers to an eight-stage model which details the various phases through which the counselling relationship evolves. These stages start with meeting the client and they end with disengagement, by the client, from the therapeutic relationship. Another model of the stages of counselling might usefully look at what happens before clients even meet counsellors. The following example illustrates such a model:

Stage One	Pre-contemplation – the client thinks about getting help
Stage Two	Establishment of contact – the client either contacts a counsellor or is referred to one
Stage Three	Imagining the relationship – the client forms a picture of the counsellor and of the relationship which will be formed
Stage Four	Client and counsellor meet – a range of pressing issues is discussed where emotions surface and catharsis may occur
Stage Five	Clarity and focus – problem situations become clearer to the client, who experiences a diminution of tension and a feeling of being understood

Stage Six	Other issues – related problems from the past may surface and need to be addressed
Stage Seven	Management and change – ways of addressing problems are discussed and considered
Stage Eight	Apprehension about change – fears are expressed about the effect of change; these are discussed between client and counsellor
Stage Nine	Achievement – the client moves into action and achieves some changes
Stage Ten	Ending – the relationship between counsellor and client comes to an end; the client is more autonomous and is able to cope alone

It is possible to add yet another stage to those already listed, because many clients remember the counselling process long after it is over. This remembering then serves as a guide or template for future reference, so that similar problems, when they occur, may seem less daunting and are approached more confidently by clients. The relationship which a client forms with a counsellor is also significant in this respect, and even if further meetings never take place, the client is aware that she is capable of sustaining similar bonds.

Although not all client experiences are identical in counselling, it is important to recognise that certain stages of development are likely to occur. Most clients experience a beginning phase where they seek to make sense of their problems, a middle phase during which they consider what to do, and a later stage where they start to act. On the other hand, some clients come into counselling only briefly, and leave once they have been given the opportunity to explore their problems in the presence of someone who really listens. Such clients frequently identify ways of coping with problems early on, and when they have made this kind of identification, feel able to formulate and implement courses of action fairly quickly. However, the following case study is an example of one client who progressed through a number of different stages in the process of counselling.

CASE STUDY — Bethan

Bethan, who suffered from anxiety and panic attacks, was referred to counselling by her GP. She was in her mid-thirties, and worked as a manager in a factory outlet. This was a responsible job which demanded a high level of commitment. Bethan, who described herself as a 'perfectionist', found herself increasingly anxious about meeting customers and dealing with junior staff. Bethan asked her GP about the possibility of counselling, so she had obviously contemplated this course of action for some time. However, before her first appointment she was tempted to cancel it, because her imagined view of the counselling relationship had gradually become a negative one. She believed the counsellor might be 'bossy' and tell her what to do, and this idea increased her anxiety considerably. Bethan had experienced problems with her mother in early life, and she later realised that there might be a connection between this fact and her concerns about control by a counsellor. When she actually met the counsellor, however, Bethan talked at length about her vague feelings of anxiety, and the panic attacks she had been having recently. While she talked, Bethan also expressed a great deal of emotion and afterwards felt relieved that she had been unable to unburden herself in this way. In later sessions she was concerned to identify the causes of her anxiety and feelings of panic. She was also able to make important connections between some aspects of her childhood experience, and her current situation as a manager at work. Bethan's family had been poor, and she was often sent out to collect money from neighbours who had bought items from her mother's catalogue. These neighbours were frequently offensive or verbally abusive towards her, and when she returned home without the money, her mother also became angry and rejected any explanations she gave. At work, customers were sometimes hostile too, especially when they owed money to the firm and were unable to pay it. Any confrontation with customers, or even the thought of such confrontations, was the basis of intense anxiety and sometimes panic for Bethan. Once she had established these connections between past and present, however, she felt more in control of her feelings generally. With the help of the counsellor, Bethan was able to devise ways of adjusting her thinking in relation to customers, and though she was fearful of changing her approach, she did, in fact, manage to do so. Bethan withdrew from counselling once she felt sufficiently confident to deal with her problems.

Many of the stages highlighted in the model described earlier are apparent in this case study. Bethan did, in fact, experience a pre-contemplation phase, and her fantasy about the nature of counselling almost prevented her from attending the first session. She experienced both emotional relief and greater clarity as a result of talking through her problems. Afterwards, she was able to identify important links between past and present, and these served to increase understanding, diminish tension and offer some possibilities for management and change. Bethan's view of her work with customers was changed as a result of counselling, and she felt more in control of her responses generally. Both Bethan and the counsellor had worked through a contract of six sessions and when these were over, Bethan withdrew from counselling, sufficiently confident that she could manage her problems alone.

THEORETICAL APPROACHES IN COUNSELLING

Later on in this book, we shall consider some of the theoretical approaches to counselling which are especially helpful for clients who, like Bethan, experience emotional problems when communicating with other people. At this stage, however, it is useful to look at the three main approaches from which all the others have evolved. These are as follows:

◆ the psychodynamic approach
◆ the behavioural approach
◆ the humanistic approach

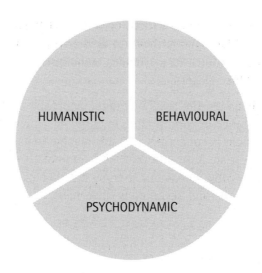

Figure 2.1   *The three main approaches to counselling*

The psychodynamic approach

The psychodynamic approach to counselling stems from the work of Sigmund Freud (1856–1939). Freud's theories will be discussed in much more detail in Chapter 3. In the meantime, it is important to highlight the fact that almost all contemporary approaches to therapy owe at least something to Freud's pioneering work. Ideas which are central to psychodynamic theory include those of unconscious motivation, psychosexual stages of development, innate sexual and aggressive drives, links between childhood and present behaviour, and the nature of defence mechanisms and their use. All contemporary theoretical approaches acknowledge the influence of the past on the present, and all are aware of the various ways in which people seek to defend themselves against unpleasant experience. In addition, all contemporary approaches are concerned to help clients identify the often hidden (or unconscious) factors which can influence behaviour. Relationship difficulties are also highlighted in diverse current theories, and links between childhood and present experience are explored when, and if, clients request such a focus. The degree to which these factors are considered important varies within each school, as we shall see in the following chapters.

The behavioural approach

This approach to counselling is based on the work of a group of behavioural psychologists who were interested in the nature of human learning. It is concerned with the observation of human behaviour, and with the way in which behaviour is perpetuated throughout life by the process of 'reinforcement'. Important behavioural psychologists include Pavlov (1849–1946), Watson (1878–1958) and Skinner (1904–1990). The behavioural approach views human personality as a collection of learned behaviours. This means in effect that when we are rewarded for certain types of behaviour, we tend to repeat them. When we are not rewarded, however, the behaviour tends to diminish. Maladaptive behaviour can be perpetuated through reinforcement, so a focus of behaviour therapy (or behaviour modification as it is sometimes called) is identification of the ways in which problem behaviour is maintained. When this identification is made, techniques can be used to change the problematic stimulus-response pattern.

There is some similarity between the psychodynamic approach and the behavioural, since both emphasise the importance of conditioning in early life. However, behaviourism, unlike the psychodynamic approach, is concerned with observable behaviour. Techniques used in behaviour modification are also quite different, and some of these have been adapted for use within other approaches too. Behaviour therapy has, like psychodynamic theory, been influential in the way its skills and techniques have been taken up by other theoretical schools.

The humanistic approach

In many ways the humanistic approach is diametrically opposed (in terms of ideology) to both the psychodynamic and behavioural traditions. This is because the humanistic view emphasises the innate potential every person is believed to possess. It also highlights what is known as the drive towards self-actualisation (Maslow, 1970; Rogers, 1991). Personality is seen as unique to the individual, and problems are set in the context of each person's unique experience. Important names in the humanistic tradition include Carl Rogers (1902–1987), Abraham Maslow (1908–1970) and Fritz Perls (1893–1970). The influences of these theorists will be discussed in greater detail in subsequent chapters.

Gerald Egan, whose structural model we have referred to in this chapter, was also influenced by the philosophy of humanism, and more specifically by the work of Rogers. Some of Roger's ideas have been incorporated into Egan's systematic approach which is described in *The Skilled Helper* (1994). Rogers and Maslow believed that human behaviour is determined by conscious, as opposed to unconscious processes, a view which is vastly different from the Freudian position. The behavioural is also different, since it focuses on learned behaviours which operate in a fairly mechanistic way. In addition, the behavioural approach indicates that human behaviour is best understood when it is viewed objectively, from a purely external point of view. This belief is at odds with the philosophy of humanism, where the central focus for understanding human behaviour is on subjective and individual experience. The humanistic movement in therapy has exerted significant influence in other areas, including education and the helping professions.

EXERCISE — Theoretical differences

Working individually, consider the three main theories which have been outlined. What, in your view, are their strengths and weaknesses in their assessments of human behaviour and potential? Discuss your ideas with other members of the training group, and indicate ways in which all of these theories might contribute towards our understanding of clients.

COUNSELLING SKILLS

Having considered the three main branches of counselling theory, we can now look at the skills and counselling abilities which are common to all of them. We have already seen that counselling skills can be divided into the two principal components of verbal and non-verbal communication. In this first section on skills, we shall discuss the significance of non-verbal aspects of communication in counselling, with special reference to the substantial influence which non-verbal behaviour exerts in the therapeutic environment.

Listening

Active listening is a term which is commonly used in relation to counselling. Egan (1994) lists several things which are necessary for complete listening, and these include the observation of clients' non-verbal behaviour, as well as understanding of verbal content and meaning. It goes without saying that the 'way' something is said is just as important as the actual words spoken. This last point is especially relevant in the counselling context, for clients often have difficulty in finding exactly the right words to express the way they feel. In these circumstances, accompanying non-verbal cues sometimes speak much more eloquently than words. Culley (1991) describes listening and attending as 'interrelated' skills. This is because it is not possible to give clients full attention without actively listening to them. Attending to clients incorporates many of the non-verbal skills which we listed at the beginning of this chapter. It is not just client non-verbal behaviour which we need to consider therefore. The counsellor also communicates to the client, and much of this communication is conveyed without words. Active listening is probably the most effective form of communication which a counsellor uses, but it is also frequently underestimated by many people. Listening is commonly regarded as a passive rather than an active skill, and you will probably be surprised to discover just how much effort is required to develop it. The following is an outline of some of the distracting factors which impede active listening.

◆ Obvious external factors like noise, interruption and physical discomfort.

◆ Response rehearsal. This happens when we become preoccupied with what we would like to say in reply.

◆ Fact finding. This refers to the practice of searching for details and facts, instead of listening to the overall message which the client wishes to convey.

◆ Being judgmental. Some listeners are concerned to make mental judgements about the speaker's behaviour. As Egan (1994) points out, counsellors can also fall into this trap.

◆ Problem solving. You may find that when you first practise listening skills, you are tempted to solve the client's problem in your own head. This is something which precludes real listening.

◆ Imposing a personal view. This happens when the listener fails to hear the central feeling a client is seeking to express.

A middle-aged woman called Christine wanted to talk about some of the problems she had experienced just before her mother's death. At first she talked to her sister, and later to a minister of religion who was also trained in counselling skills. In the following exchange with her sister, she broaches the subject of her mother's apparent rejection of her.

CHRISTINE: I know I seem to go over this again and again, but I simply can't come to terms with the fact that she told me not to kiss her when she was dying. It is something I can never forget.

SISTER: Well you know she was never a tactile person. She was not one for showing physical affection.

The next exchange took place between Christine and a minister of the church she had attended.

CHRISTINE: I think about it again and again. Just at the end she turned away from me and rejected the affection I wanted to show her.

PRIEST: Causing you real distress and sorrow ...

CHRISTINE: Yes.

In the first example, the response given ignored the central feeling of distress the client was trying to convey. In addition to ignoring the feelings expressed, the listener also imposed her own view or interpretation of events, and in doing so seemed to discount what her sister was saying. The second example, however, shows how the client's feeling were immediately picked up and acknowledged, much to her relief. It should be added that the first example highlights the fact that relatives seldom make good counsellors. This is because they are also often emotionally involved in the problem, and they may not have any training either. Acknowledgement of strong feelings requires active listening and relatives, who may also be suffering themselves, are seldom in a position to extend this skill when it is needed.

Other factors which inhibit listening

There are many other factors which work against active listening, including over-identification with the client or the client's problems. Once again this highlights the importance of self-awareness for counsellors, since it is only through awareness of our own areas of vulnerability and prejudice that we can hope to avoid this kind of over-identification (which often includes sympathy). The essential differences between sympathy and empathy will be highlighted in Chapter 5, dealing with Roger's person-centred approach to counselling, but it should be noted here that sympathy is not appropriate in therapeutic counselling. This is because it is an attitude which tends to be superficial, requiring very little effort to demonstrate. It is also fairly easy to simulate, and is often extended in an unthinking or perfunctory way when people are distressed.

Listening is by far the most important skill in counselling. It is never easy and requires enormous discipline, self-control and an attitude of heightened receptivity. Active listening assures clients they are heard, and that what they say matters a great deal. When we don't listen to people we fail to make any real emotional connection with them. Many clients who seek counselling have never really been listened to. Their parents may have failed them in this respect, and later on at school, or in the work situation, they may not have been heard either. It is sometimes the case that people hide a painful secret for many years which, as Weinberg (1996) says, 'may seem commonplace to us' but is monumental to the owner. Such people are given the courage to reappraise the problem providing someone gives time, attention and the skill of active listening to help them do so.

EXERCISE — Blocks to Listening

Working individually, look at the following list of factors which might affect counsellors and consider their possible effects on their ability to listen.

◆ Tiredness and stress

◆ Personal problems

◆ Minor illness or pain

◆ Similar experiences to those described by the client

◆ Total dissimilarity of experience to that described by the client

◆ Cultural, religious or social difference

Non-verbal communication as an aid to listening

Egan (1994) describes what he refers to as 'microskills' which helpers can use when working with clients. These skills are summarised by Egan in the acronym SOLER. This acronym should help you remember the aspects of non-verbal behaviour which encourage active listening, and it is used in the following way:

S   Sit facing the client **Squarely**. This assures the client that s/he has your attention.

O   Be **Open** in your posture. Do not close yourself off by rigidly crossing arms and legs.

L   **Lean** slightly towards the client in an attitude of interest.

E   **Establish Eye** contact with the client, but avoid staring.

R   **Relax** and don't fidget. Try to adopt a natural posture in relation to the client.

(*Egan, 1994*)

It is obviously difficult to be totally relaxed and un-selfconscious, especially at the beginning of skills training. In addition, what you regard as a relaxed and comfortable position may not be exactly the same as that described above. Some people feel more comfortable when sitting slightly to the client's side. This kind of seating arrangement has the advantage of conveying strong subliminal messages of support to the client. In other words, it is one way of saying 'I am on your side'. However, it may be more difficult to maintain eye contact in this position. The important thing to remember is that your attention should remain with the client, and whatever seating arrangement facilitates this is the right one to use. Obvious barriers like desks and tables should not intrude between client and counsellor, and the overall atmosphere of the setting in which counselling takes places should be comfortable, uninterrupted, and private.

Gestures and touch

You will probably feel quite self-conscious when you first start to practise counselling skills. When video practice is used as an aid to training, students are often disconcerted when they see the extent to which they use nervous gestures or movements while listening to each other. Although it is not very pleasant to see this at first, it is nevertheless helpful in the long-term, since it serves to identify faulty communication styles which can be remedied. Excessive use of gestures can create uneasiness between client and counsellor, so counsellors need to minimise these as much as possible. Clients themselves may be anxious and restless initially, but when counsellors 'model' attitudes of calm and stillness, clients often become more relaxed as a result.

The issue of touch is problematic in relation to therapeutic counselling, and in most instances touch is considered inappropriate for a variety of reasons. There are, for example, clients who have experienced physical or sexual abuse in the past, and they may as a consequence be fearful of this kind of contact. Student counsellors who already work with clients or patients in other settings, like nursing for example, may use touch routinely in their work. However, in these contexts, touch is used impersonally and is unlikely to be misconstrued by the people they help. In contrast, clients in therapeutic counselling may misinterpret any touching which takes place, precisely because it is not, strictly speaking, an essential or integral component of that relationship. This is not to say that some tactile expressions of support are never extended by counsellors. Individual counsellors vary a great deal in the way they use touch, and in the ease with which they do so. Cultural differences are important here too, since what might feel comfortable for one group of people may be less so for another. All these differences highlight the earlier point that tactile communication needs to be carefully considered before it is used, and when any element of doubt exists it is best avoided altogether.

Silence

In order to listen effectively it is, of course, necessary to be silent. Just being silent is not enough, though, since the client needs to know that the counsellor is interested and paying attention to him when he speaks. This means that you need to show by your demeanour that you are, in fact, 'with' the client in everything he says. Silence is another aspect of communication which you might feel self-conscious about at first, and when you are uncomfortable in this way there is always a temptation to fill in the spaces, either through asking questions or finishing the client's sentences for him. However, you should remember that clients often need periods of silence in order to collect their thoughts, or as a way of experiencing a very strong feeling or emotion. If they are not allowed to do this, they will almost certainly regard any intervention as intrusive and insensitive. Clients communicate a great deal through silence, both to themselves and to counsellors. As well as this, clients frequently refer to silence afterwards, and in doing so effectively clarify aspects of their problems which may have been obscured in the past.

The counsellor's dress and appearance

Counsellors, like their clients, reveal much more about themselves than they think. Personal values, and even mood, are often discernible in a person's dress and appearance, and someone who appears scruffy and unkempt is unlikely to retain the confidence of clients. On the other hand, an excessively glamorous or suave appearance might inhibit some clients, especially those who experience problems in relation to body image or personal looks. However, no style of clothing or dress has the same meaning for everyone, which suggests that counsellors should probably dress in whatever way is most comfortable for them personally. There are, moreover, certain areas of counselling in which casual dress seems most appropriate. Counsellors who work with underprivileged groups of people, or with those who have problems in relation to substance abuse, often feel most at ease with their clients when dressed informally. Probably the only hard and fast rule pertaining to counsellor dress and appearance is respect for clients. Counsellors have to be true to themselves, but they also need to dress in ways which inspire some confidence in their ability and competence.

EXERCISE — Designing a room

Working individually, draw a plan of the kind of room which, in your view, would be suitable as a counselling base. Pay attention to such aspects as the arrangement of furniture, position of a clock, lighting and window position, and colours. Afterwards, compare your plan with those drawn by other members of the training group, and discuss why you included or excluded certain items or furnishings in the room. Would it be appropriate to display family photographs, for example? If not, why?

Verbal communication

◆ Reflection

The word reflection refers to the skill of communicating back to the client that her words and feelings have been heard. Carl Rogers (1991) emphasised this particular skill initially, although counsellors and therapists of almost every theoretical school now place a high value on its use. Reporting back to the client what she has said, is one way of indicating that we are listening carefully to her. In a sense, the skill of reflection is like holding a mirror in front of the client so that she can see herself more clearly. Reflection, if it is to be effective, should be done unobtrusively so that the client is hardly aware that it is happening. The concept of empathy is closely linked to reflection, because effective reflective responses are those which stay within the client's 'internal frame of reference' (Rogers, 1991). Staying within the client's internal frame of reference means listening to, and understanding, the problem or problems from her point of view or experience. The following is an example:

LIZ: My mother told me that I was adopted when I was thirteen years old. After that I went wild for a while ... running around with a bad crowd ... I didn't know who I was any more ... my world fell apart.

COUNSELLOR: You were lost and confused.

LIZ: Yes ... and it took me ages to get it all on an even keel again. Actually, I haven't ... got it on an even keel I mean. I feel dislocated ... I still feel lost in some ways.

COUNSELLOR: There is still a sense of things not being right for you ... of missed connections.

LIZ: Parts of the story are missing ... large parts. I want to meet my natural parents, yet I'm terrified too ... terrified that they might not want to know me.

COUNSELLOR: The fear of the unknown ... and of possible rejection ... these are the things which cause you the most anxiety.

LIZ: Yes, and this fear keeps me from doing anything.

The counsellor's responses to this client were framed in a way which kept the focus of attention on the *emotional* content of what the client was saying. This meant that the client felt free to express her deepest fears and anxieties, since she was aware that the counsellor respected and validated these. In her responses, the counsellor also focused on 'feeling' words, including 'confused', 'fear', 'rejection' and 'anxiety'. Clients are sometimes afraid to acknowledge strong feelings, in case the listener becomes distressed on hearing them, or in case they themselves become overwhelmed by them. When strong or negative feelings are validated in counselling, clients often experience great relief. Such relief is frequently the first step towards clarification and management of the problem.

◆ Paraphrasing

The word paraphrasing refers to the rewording of the content of what clients say. Reflection and paraphrasing are very similar, the difference between them being that the former is generally used to describe a rewording of the emotional content, while the latter is mainly concerned with the factual. However, it is certainly not always easy (or necessary) to separate these two things. Some distinction is necessary though, because the two words are often used interchangeably in counselling literature, and this can occasionally prove confusing for students. When responding to clients, it is obviously best to do so in a way which does not simply repeat verbatim what has just been said. It is helpful to practise the skill of paraphrasing by concentrating on the content first, and later on incorporating the emotional content as well. The following are two examples:

Example One

STUDENT: I didn't get the work done because my mother fell ill last week. Then she was taken into hospital for tests and I had to look after the two younger ones. I don't feel so well myself either, especially after all the stress and the extra work.

TEACHER: Other things happened at home and you were too busy to write the assignment. As well as that you've been ill yourself.

In the example just given, the teacher picked up the factual content of what the student said. There is no obvious acknowledgement of the emotional content, however. To reflect back both factual and emotional content, the teacher might have worded her response in the following way:

TEACHER: Things has been hectic and stressful at home for you, and there was no way you could think about writing an assignment. And feeling ill, of course, made it worse for you.

In this second example, the teacher picks up the stress and anxiety which the student expresses, and reflects this back in her response. It is likely that such a response will assure the student that her explanation for not doing the work is respected and understood. On the other hand, it should be remembered that the first response might well have had the same effect, depending on the teacher's tone of voice and general demeanour when she delivered it.

Example Two

PATIENT: I've never been in hospital before. What happens next? When will I know about going home? There was a doctor here a short while ago and he took my case notes away.

NURSE: You've not had this experience before and you want to know all the details.

In this example, the nurse concentrates on the factual aspects of the patient's communication. In the next example, she reflects back both content and feeling.

NURSE: You're obviously anxious about everything that's happening, and that's understandable. I'll talk to you about all the details in just a moment.

This last response acknowledges the patient's fears and her general anxiety about being in hospital.

EXERCISE — Paraphrasing

Read the following passages and paraphrase them, concentrating on the factual content only.

1 Since the car accident, I've been nervous driving. I keep thinking someone will drive into the back of me again ... I'm on the look out all the time, and wondering what will happen next.
2 Yesterday we went to London for a conference. I didn't want to go ... What's the point anyway if I'm going to be made redundant? The others were really enjoying themselves, but I couldn't get into the mood of it.
3 When my illness was diagnosed I didn't believe it. I felt the specialist had made a mistake, and I even argued with him about it.
4 My two children are quite different. The younger one never gave a problem, but the elder one was trouble from the very beginning. I have tried not to compare them, but I've got to the stage where I just have to admit that Harry is different.
5 I don't know how to tell my parents that I am gay ... I just don't know how they will react. They were both quite old when I was born, and they don't talk very openly about intimate issues anyway.

When you have completed the first part of this exercise, read the passages again and reword them, this time reflecting both the factual content and feeling content.

Summarising

The skill of summarising is used when a helper wishes to respond to a series of statements or, in the case of counselling, to a whole session. As with reflecting and paraphrasing, accurate summarising requires empathy and the ability to stay within the client's internal frame of reference. Clients often talk at random, and they are frequently side-tracked into other related (and sometimes unrelated) issues. This can make it difficult to monitor everything they say, and formulating an accurate summary also requires active listening and an ability to draw all the random threads together into a more coherent framework. Egan (1994) refers to summarising as a 'bridging response' which can be used to provide links between counselling sessions and the stages of the three-stage model which he describes. The following is an example of summarising at the end of a counselling session.

A client called Alice talked about her experiences like this:

> The area I live in was flooded about two years ago and we lost almost everything. The insurance did cover a lot of things, but there are some things you can't replace. Then, just about that time, I found out about my husband's affair, something that nearly everyone else seemed to know about. It was devastating and I don't think I'll ever recover from it. Everything seems to happen at once because my youngest child developed eczema at about that time, although I suspect myself that it was linked to all the stress going on in the family. I kept going through it all, but then six months ago I became

very depressed ... I couldn't stop thinking about all that had happened and it just came flooding back to me.

The counsellor gave the following summary of what Alice had said:

You had all those stressful experiences two years back ... being flooded, losing important possessions, your husband's affair and your child's illness. It was terrible for you but you coped. But now you feel the depression linked to it all.

In this summary, the counsellor identified the factual elements of the story. She also highlighted the stressful feelings associated with it, and she used the word 'terrible' to describe the client's experiences. This confirmed for the client that what she had said was understood and validated by the counsellor. Later on, the counsellor also drew attention to the fact that the client had used the word 'flooding' when describing her delayed reaction to the events of the past which had, in fact, started with a flood. Through the skill of summarising the counsellor identified important themes in the client's story. She also clarified the client's experiences and thoughts, and she used the summary as a way of checking her own understanding of what had been said. The client was therefore given an opportunity to add any other details which may have been missed, or to emphasise any aspects of the story which the counsellor may have failed to highlight.

Accurate summarising should:

◆ show understanding of what the client has said
◆ reflect the client's internal frame of reference
◆ show accurate selection of important issues and themes
◆ avoid critical or judgmental statements
◆ be accurately timed: clients should not be interrupted
◆ be tentative: clients need to feel free to add to or correct what has been said
◆ reflect the order of events, so that clients can look again at the story as it unfolds

EXERCISE — Summarising

Working in pairs, take turns to talk about a recent experience you have had. If you are just starting skills training, try to select experiences which were not too problematic or distressing for either of you. While one person talks for about three minutes, the other should listen, concentrating on the factual elements of the story, the order of events and any feelings expressed. Afterwards, summarise what has been said. When you have both completed the exercise, discuss any difficulties you may have experienced in relation to it.

Asking questions

One of the difficulties you may find in listening to others is that your curiosity is aroused, and you are tempted to ask questions in order to get the detail clear in your own head.

Most of us probably ask too many questions in our communications with other people, and active listening is often diminished as a result. Questions can be especially problematic in counselling because they tend to be prompted by an *external* rather than an *internal* frame of reference. In other words, counsellors sometimes ask questions in order to get the facts straight for themselves, rather than from a desire to understand the client's subjective experience of things. Consider the following example:

HUW: My daughter and I have frequent arguments. They seem to become more frequent as she gets older. This gives me the feeling that we are somehow losing touch.

COUNSELLOR: What age is she?

HUW: Fifteen … almost sixteen.

COUNSELLOR: And how often do you argue?

This example may seem like an extreme case of stark questioning, but it does serve to highlight several important points. In the first place, the questions do nothing to help the client examine his relationship with his daughter even though this is clearly a major concern of his. In the second place, it is difficult to see how such questions could possibly aid the counsellor in her understanding of the client, or the problem he is trying to describe. These questions, therefore, work against the client's best interests, and they also place a barrier in the relationship between client and counsellor. How should the counsellor have responded? The following is one way of responding to the client's first statement:

COUNSELLOR: There are more differences now, and greater distance between you.

CLIENT: Yes … I feel very saddened by it.

In this second example the counsellor responded, not with a question but with a reflection of the client's experience and feeling. This response encouraged him to talk in depth about his relationship with his daughter. However, questions do have their place in counselling, though they should be kept to a minimum. When tempted to ask a question it is useful to consider why you need to do so. It is to satisfy your own curiosity, or will it facilitate the client in some way? When questions have to be asked they should always be as *open* as possible, and it is certainly best to avoid questions which begin with *why*. Why questions tend to sound interrogative, and clients frequently respond to them in defensive or resistant ways. Also clients usually don't really *know* why things are the way they are, and it is often a desire to find out which prompts them to seek counselling in the first place.

Open questions

Open questions encourage clients to explore their problems in greater depth. In contrast to 'closed' questions, they require much more than a simple yes or no answer. They also encourage the expression of feelings and help clients to explore issues which concern them in much more specific ways. The following example should illustrate the points just made:

ETHNE: My sister was sent to a really good school. We lost touch for a long time, and the school I went to was local and had a poor record. My parents always gave the impression that I was sent there because I had no real ability.

COUNSELLOR: The separation from your sister ... the second rate school ... how did you feel about all this?

Ethne: Well, for a long time I really resented her ... my sister I mean. Later on, I realised, of course, that it wasn't her fault. When we were in our late teens we started to become closer.

COUNSELLOR: So the resentment was less in your teens ... what was it at that stage which helped you?

ETHNE: We had similar problems then ... with my parents I mean. We both realised that we had more in common than we thought. Also I was able to talk to her about my feelings of being stupid. She really helped me then and was very supportive. Now I don't have that old resentment towards her.

In addition to closed questions, there are others which are problematic in the counselling context. These include:

◆ **Multiple Questions**

Here, several questions are asked at once and the client doesn't know which to reply to. This is especially confusing when people are emotionally upset. For example:

CLIENT: I think I might be pregnant and I'm really scared.

HELPER: Have you spoken to your parents? Maybe you don't want to? What about your doctor?

◆ **Leading Questions**

These are questions which lead the client in a certain direction, usually in the direction of the counsellor's viewpoint. Value judgments are also usually implicit in leading questions, and this is never helpful for clients who often find themselves under pressure to agree with what has been said. For example:

CLIENT: I feel tired all the time. Sometimes I just want to stay in the house and never go out.

HELPER: Doesn't staying in the house tend to make people feel even more apathetic and tired?

◆ **Rhetorical Questions**

These are questions which do not require any answer. They tend to express the questioner's viewpoint, and if they are used in counselling clients may feel obliged to accept what the counsellor has said. For example:

COUNSELLOR: How is it that things always seem to happen at once?

CLIENT: Well yes, I suppose they do.

Greeting clients

Many clients find it difficult to get started unless they are asked at least one opening question. It is important to establish contact with clients as soon as possible, and one way of doing this is by asking a brief question. The following are some examples:

◆ Please sit down. How would you like to start?

◆ Is there anything in particular you would like to begin with?

◆ My name is (name). Can you tell me about the issues which concern you at the moment?

◆ How do you see your situation at present?

◆ Dr (name) referred you to me for ... is this how you see the situation?

◆ How have things been with you since you last saw the doctor?

Once contact has been established and the client starts to talk, the counsellor can then use a range of continuation skills to encourage further exploration. For example:

◆ Yes, I see

◆ And after that ...

◆ You say you were afraid ...

◆ Please go on ...

◆ Then ...

◆ Tell me more about ...

◆ So you feel ...

◆ And that felt ...

You will probably find that once you lose your initial nervousness, your own range of responses will develop naturally. In the meantime, it is a good idea to practise opening questions, along with follow-up responses similar to the continuation phrases given above.

◆ Probing Questions

Probing questions are meant to encourage clients to enlarge or expand on their initial response. The following are examples:

◆ Can you say more about that?

◆ And what happened then?

◆ Could you explain that?

◆ Focusing Questions

Focusing questions encourage clients to look more closely at specific aspects of a problem. Clients are often vague about their problems, and focusing questions are effective in encouraging them to define issues more clearly. For example:

CLIENT: Everybody bullies me ... I am always bullied.

COUNSELLOR: Could we look at an example of the way you are bullied?

Timing of questions

We have already seen that too many questions can be threatening for clients, and may also have the adverse effect of inhibiting communication generally. Timing of questions is also important in counselling. Clients should never be interrupted, no matter how much they seem to talk initially. It is worth remembering that many clients have waited a long time to be heard, and they may have a great deal of information they want to convey. In view of this, counsellors need to keep questions in abeyance until the time is right to ask them. Clients do pause to pick up responses from counsellors, and a counsellor who is truly listening will be in tune with unspoken invitations to speak. Another important point to remember is that clients should not be questioned when they are emotionally overwhelmed, or when they are clearly too upset to answer. Use of excessively probing questions can also cause a great deal of anxiety, especially when these are poorly timed. Asking too many, or badly timed, questions of clients is one way of avoiding real contact with them. Active listening, on the other hand, is a sure way of establishing real contact and understanding.

EXERCISE — Encouraging clients to be more specific

Working individually, look at the following list of client statements. Spend about twenty minutes formulating appropriate questions in response to these, concentrating on the skill of focusing. When you have finished, compare your list with those completed by other members of the group.

- ◆ I have had a terrible time with both my partners
- ◆ No matter what I do I can never get it right
- ◆ People are always picking on me
- ◆ Everything is so stressful at work
- ◆ I get panic attacks all the time
- ◆ Nobody ever listens to me at home
- ◆ I feel much better about life now
- ◆ The illness was what caused me to feel useless
- ◆ My children are so badly behaved
- ◆ I feel totally lacking in confidence

Challenging skills

At the beginning of this chapter we referred briefly to Egan's three-stage model of counselling, and to the skills which are integral to it. So far we have considered the basic skills of *listening, paraphrasing* and *reflecting, summarising, asking questions, using silence* and *helping clients to focus* on more specific aspects of their stories. These skills are used in the first stage of the model, and indeed throughout the whole counselling process. However, the Second Stage of the model requires the use of other skills which will help clients to develop new perspectives about themselves and the problems they experience. During this stage of counselling, which Egan (1994) refers to as the 'preferred scenario', clients are encouraged to identify what they need to do in order to change the situation causing difficulties for them. The skills used in this phase include the following:

◆ Challenging
◆ Immediacy
◆ Counsellor self-disclosure
◆ Identifying patterns and themes
◆ Giving information to clients

Used in the counselling context, the word 'challenge' refers to the skill of encouraging clients to confront their own behaviour, attitudes or beliefs. It should always be done with sensitivity and should certainly never be rushed. Immediacy, counsellor self-disclosure, information giving and the identification of patterns and themes, are all forms of challenge in counselling.

◆ Immediacy

The term 'immediacy' is one which Egan (1994) uses to describe the process of discussing what is actually taking place *right now* in the counselling situation. The following is an example:

CLIENT: I have been to several helpers now, and I don't feel any more hopeful than before.

COUNSELLOR: Perhaps that's something we should talk about now ... is it that you don't have confidence that I can help you either?

In the example just given, immediacy was used by the counsellor in order to draw attention to the client's feelings about him. This is challenging for the client, because it serves to focus attention on his belief that he is impossible to help.

◆ Counsellor self-disclosure

There are specialised areas of counselling in which counsellor self-disclosure is used quite extensively. These include counselling for substance abuse or addiction, and in these contexts self-disclosure is very beneficial for clients since it serves to encourage them to persevere in overcoming problems. However, self-disclosure is by no means always appropriate. It can worry clients if it is done frequently, and it can have the very unfortunate effect of making the client feel responsible for the counsellor. On the other hand, self-disclosure is very effective as a form of challenge, as long as it is correctly timed and carried out with the client's best interest firmly in focus. Another point to remember is that it is important to show interest in clients without in fact being interesting. In the next example, a client called Gillian was worried that she would never get over her panic attacks:

GILLIAN: Sometimes I feel that I might as well just stay in the house and at least feel safe there ...

COUNSELLOR: Yes, I know that feeling ... but when I pushed myself to get out of the house, things started improving from there.

Through self-disclosure the counsellor in this example challenged the client's temptation to give up on her problem and just stay in the house.

◆ Giving information to clients

Information giving can also prove challenging for clients, especially when their expectations are clearly unrealistic in some way. In the following example a client called David wanted to leave his present relationship in order to establish a new life with his new girlfriend:

DAVID: I want to leave everything behind ... I know I can do it, and I can just about afford it.

COUNSELLOR: Taking into consideration maintenance for the two children?

DAVID: My wife is financially OK ... that's one thing, she has never quibbled about money ...

COUNSELLOR: On the other hand, there is probably a certain amount you will need to provide from a legal point of view ...

DAVID: Yes, I suppose you're right.

In this example the counsellor directed the client's attention to the financial details he wanted to minimise. She did this by challenging him with the information that there were certain requirements which, in all likelihood, he would need to observe.

◆ Identifying patterns and themes

Sometimes there are recurrent themes or patterns which are discernible in the problems which clients recount. Once a relationship of trust has been established between counsellor and client, it is possible to identify and highlight these patterns so that clients are challenged to consider them more seriously. A client called Rene talked at length about her problems at work:

RENE: I do seem to get on the wrong side of people ... the rent people, the Social Services. Why me? Would you believe it ... but I was even singled out in my last job, and I'm sure that it was because of my personality ... the fact that I say what I mean.

COUNSELLOR: I know you've mentioned this several times ... that you say what you mean. Maybe we should look at that, to see how much it might be contributing to the problems you describe.

In this example, the counsellor focused attention on the client's insistence that she only said what she felt. This identification of a pattern or theme enabled the client to look more honestly at the way she communicated with other people, and the problems this seemed to generate. If at all possible, it is always best to encourage clients to confront themselves and, in this case, this is exactly what happened. Since the client had already identified her problem in relation to others, the counsellor's task was simplified as a result. Clients also tend to respond best when they are challenged to identify their own strengths and coping resources. For example:

COUNSELLOR: You've said how shy you are, and you lack confidence that people will like you ... On the other hand, you've been chosen twice to represent your colleagues at conferences.

EXERCISE — Self-challenge

Working individually, consider some of the areas of your own life which might benefit from challenge. Are there any patterns of behaviour, for example, which cause some problems for you? In what ways, if any, do you contribute to these problems? The following examples might help to identify some personal problem areas for you.

◆ Keeping others waiting
◆ Refusing to accept compliments
◆ Agreeing to do things you don't want to do
◆ Going into action without first thinking about it
◆ Being defensive when others disagree with you
◆ Not listening when you don't agree with what is being said
◆ Procrastinating about work which should be done
◆ Looking to others to make decisions for you

When you have completed the individual exercise, share your ideas with a partner and discuss any difficulties you experienced in challenging yourself.

The action phase

In the Third Stage of the model which Egan (1994) describes, clients are encouraged to act, aided by the new understanding and knowledge which they have acquired in the previous two stages. Along with the counsellor, the client explores a variety of ways of achieving goals. A plan of action is discussed and formulated, and throughout this process the counsellor supports the client and helps him monitor and evaluate any changes proposed. All the skills of Stage One and Two are used here, along with a new set of skills including the following:

◆ Goal setting
◆ Choosing programmes
◆ Creative thinking

◆ Giving encouragement

◆ Evaluating

◆ Goal setting and choosing programmes

Change is difficult for most people, and clients in counselling tend to find it especially difficult. This is because many of them have endured unsatisfactory work, relationship or other problem situations, over long periods of time. No matter how unsatisfactory their lives have been, however, they are at least familiar with the current situation, and any prospect of change is daunting since change always represents a leap into the unknown. Setting realistic goals in the Third Stage of counselling is one way of helping clients to plan the changes they need to make. Sometimes clients know, as a result of the work they have done in Stage One and Two, the action they need to take. More often than not, however, they need support and encouragement in order to set and achieve goals. Clients also tend to respond much more positively to goals and programmes they themselves have chosen, so it is worth remembering that the counsellor's role is a helping one, which does not include offering solutions to problems. On the other hand, counsellors need to help clients consider a range of options and a number of different ways of achieving goals. Clients may also need to be encouraged to look at their own resources or those within their environment. Realistic goals are dependent on these internal and external resources, and when there is a clear discrepancy between goals and resources, adjustments need to be made. The following questions can usefully be asked in relation to any goals which are formulated:

◆ Are they clear?

◆ Are they specific?

◆ How long will they take to achieve?

◆ How realistic are they?

◆ Are they measurable?

◆ Is the client comfortable with them?

Clients can be encouraged to write down their goals in clear and specific terms. This can be done using the following headings:

◆ What is it I want?

◆ How can I achieve this?

◆ Why should I do this?

◆ Creative thinking

Creative thinking may be difficult for clients, and this is especially true when they are emotionally upset or under great stress. This is why it is important that they should be given sufficient time to talk about and explore their problems before moving into action. When clients are ready to act, however, there are strategies for encouraging creative thinking which often help them to look at new ways of tackling their problems. The following are some examples:

Idea storming

This is a strategy which encourages the generation of as many ideas as possible. Quantity is encouraged and all options are considered. No idea is rejected, no matter how unlikely it might seem. Afterwards, the client should be supported in appraising the list so that real possibilities are highlighted and totally unrealistic ideas abandoned. The following is a list of ideas drawn up by a student who wanted to look at ways of improving communication with her parents.

◆ Tell them I want to talk
◆ Ask for a time
◆ Take assertiveness lessons
◆ Talk to other students about how they communicate with parents
◆ Decide on a date to start talking
◆ Write them a letter
◆ Leave a message on the answering machine
◆ Bang the table at dinner time
◆ Jump up and down to attract their attention
◆ Speak to my mother first
◆ Ask my sister to speak to them first
◆ Leave home and phone them

The student eventually selected three ideas, which she considered to be realistic and workable from her original list. These were:

◆ Tell them I want to talk
◆ Ask for a time
◆ Take assertiveness lessons to improve my communication skills generally

Visualisation and imagery

One of the most obvious ways to formulate an idea is to visualise it. It is through the practice of visualisation and imagery that many athletes achieve high performance in sport. Clients can also be encouraged to use this method to help them look at ways which will lead to success in whatever they choose to do. A client whose ambition was to feel more confident socially was, for example, encouraged to visualise a number of settings in which he wished to feel more at ease. Then the counsellor asked him to imagine how he would think, feel and act in each of these situations. He was also encouraged to visualise himself handling each situation exactly how he would like to. Sometimes clients achieve better results in this exercise when they have been given some time and help to relax beforehand. In Chapter 8, dealing with cognitive and behavioural approaches to counselling, we shall consider various relaxation techniques which clients can be taught to use.

Giving encouragement

Clients need encouragement when they are deciding on change and setting goals. This is essential if they are to sustain their efforts and reach their chosen goals. The idea of giving up is often attractive to clients, especially when impediments or barriers are encountered. Counsellors need to direct attention to any personal resources and achievement which clients have. Attitudes of defeat or perfectionism can be discussed, and clients can also be encouraged to accept any mistakes they may make without seeing themselves as failures. Encouragement is not just appropriate in the last stage of counselling, however. On the contrary, giving encouragement to clients is important throughout every stage of counselling. Clients need to feel valued, and to have their efforts acknowledged. Encouragement also expresses trust and confidence in the client's ability, judgment and capacity for self-development.

Evaluation

An ongoing system of evaluation is necessary if clients are to achieve the results they want. Occasionally the goals which were set originally prove to be unrealistic, unworkable or just too ambitious, and when this is the case changes need to be made. The appropriateness of any goal or action should be monitored and reviewed through discussion in counselling, and when this is done clients tend to feel more confident about their progress overall.

Ending sessions

It is important for counsellors to develop the skill of ending individual sessions. Ending sessions is often more difficult than it sounds, especially when clients talk at great length and it seems impossible to stop them without appearing intrusive or insensitive to their needs. One way of dealing with this issue is to address it at the beginning of counselling, so that clients are aware of time boundaries from the outset. Another useful idea is to state the time ten minutes before the session is due to end. This can be done in the following way:

> We have just ten minutes left. Maybe we could look at what you've said so far, and highlight any points which you would like to talk about further in your next session. Then we can make arrangements for another appointment next week.

In order to end sessions well, closing sentences should be clear. It is important to avoid introducing new subjects at this stage, and if the client introduces a different topic, schedule this for discussion in the next session. A summary of what the client has said in the present session is also helpful, and serves as both a natural ending and a review of topics to be discussed at a later date. It is also worth remembering that although counselling sessions usually last fifty minutes, there are times when the client's conversation comes to an end before this. In these instances there is nothing to be gained by drawing the session out to a full fifty minutes.

> **EXERCISE** — Setting goals
>
> Working in groups of three to four, discuss any goals which individual members of the group have set themselves in the past. What were the factors which helped you to achieve your goals? Identify any factors, either personal or environmental, which hindered you in any way.

SUMMARY

In this chapter we looked at a range of interpersonal or communication skills, both verbal and non-verbal, and identified the ways in which these are used in a structural framework of counselling. Egan's three-stage model of counselling was described, and this was recommended as a paradigm for structuring the counselling process. A case study was included at the beginning of the chapter which illustrated the various stages of counselling. The three main theoretical approaches – psychodynamic, behavioural and humanistic – were outlined and these were linked to the more specific theoretical models which will be described in later chapters, with the counselling skills appropriae to them.

REFERENCES

Burnard, P. (1994)   *Counselling Skills for Health Professionals* (2nd ed). London: Chapman and Hall.

Culley, S. (1991)   *Integrative Counselling Skills in Action.* London: Sage Publications.

Egan, G. (1994)   *The Skilled Helper* (5th ed). California: Brookes/Cole.

Maslow, A. (1970)   *Motivation and Personality* (3rd ed). New York: Harper Collins.

Rogers, C. (1991)   *Client Centred Therapy.* London: Constable.

Weinberg, G. (1996)   *The Heart of Psychotherapy.* New York: St Martins/Griffin.

FURTHER READING

Argyle, M. (1981)   *Social Skills And Health.* London: Methuen.

Hargie, O., Saunders, C. & Dickson, D. (1994)   *Social Skills In Interpersonal Communication.* London: Routledge.

Nelson–Jones, R. (1991)   *Human Relationship Skills* (2nd edn). London: Cassell.

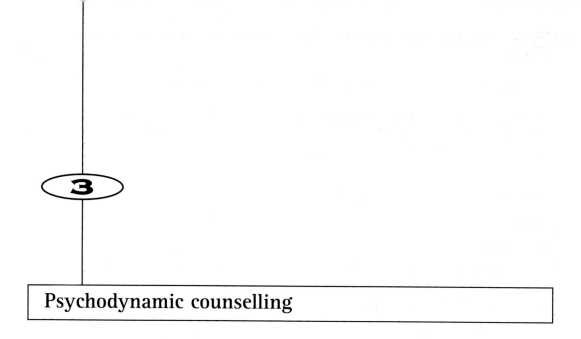

Psychodynamic counselling

INTRODUCTION

In Chapter 2 we considered the main approaches to counselling theory and looked at some of the models which derive from these. However, it is probably true to say that all contemporary models of therapy and counselling are indebted – in some degree at least – to the ideas and techniques first described by Freud. In this chapter and the next, we shall concentrate on those approaches which have retained many of the characteristic features of the psychoanalytic tradition. In order to understand and appreciate those distinguishing features, it is important to look more closely at Freud's early background and history, and to consider the ways in which his ideas were shaped, as well as the ways in which these ideas and techniques have evolved. The counselling skills which are central to the psychodynamic model will also be considered, along with an appraisal of their usefulness, as well as their limitations in relation to some of the problems clients might bring to therapy.

Freud and his background

Psychodynamic counselling is derived from the classical psychoanalytic tradition which has its origins in the work of Sigmund Freud, who was born in Austria in 1856. Freud studied medicine at the University of Vienna where he received his degree. Later, he took up a research post in neurophysiology and afterwards switched to clinical practice. Through his work and association with two colleagues, Charcot and Breuer, Freud became interested in the psychological processes responsible for producing certain physical symptoms. Both Charcot and Breuer had used hypnosis in order to help patients with 'hysterical' symptoms, and Freud used it briefly as well. Over a period of time, however, he came to believe that

talking was as effective as hypnosis in helping patients to locate the cause of their problems, and this belief in the value of the 'talking cure' was, and still is, central to psychoanalysis and to all theoretical models which derive from it.

PSYCHODYNAMIC COUNSELLING: KEY CONCEPTS

The word 'psychoanalysis' refers to the form of treatment invented by Freud. It is also used
to describe his theory of human psychological development, and his hypothesis about the
structure of the human mind. The word psychodynamic, however, is now commonly used to
describe those models of therapy which have evolved from classical psychoanalysis. These
models have retained many of the skills and techniques which Freud pioneered as well as
most of the concepts which derive from his original work. The 'talking cure' is just one
aspect of Freud's original work; there are several other important ideas, including the following:

◆ The role of the unconscious

◆ The structure of personality

◆ The psychosexual stages of development

◆ The importance of the past and childhood experience

◆ The use of ego defence mechanisms

◆ Transference and the nature of the therapeutic relationship

◆ The significance of dreams

◆ Free association or the 'talking cure'

◆ Interpretation

The role of the unconscious

The role of the unconscious is a fundamental concept of psychodynamic theory. As a result
of his clinical experience with patients in hypnosis, Freud came to see that many of their
problems were the result of mental processes which were hidden to them. The idea that
problems could be located in an unknown region of the human mind was a novel and challenging one. Long before Freud expressed these views, it was generally accepted that conscious experience was the motivating factor in all human endeavour. Freud was concerned
to show that the mind is not, in fact, always clear to itself, and that there are many in-
accessible memories, wishes and impulses which are often unacceptable to a person's consciousness. Freud's first description of the human mind is sometimes referred to as a
'topographical model', and includes three dimensions: the unconscious, the pre-conscious
and the conscious. The pre-conscious is that area containing thoughts and ideas which are
available to recall, so in this respect it is quite different from the unconscious where
thoughts, feelings and ideas are repressed and therefore unavailable to recall in the ordi-

nary sense. In the 1920s Freud changed from his topographical to a structural model of personality, in which he renamed the unconscious the ID, and the conscious the EGO. A new and important addition appeared in this new model, an addition which Freud referred to as the SUPEREGO.

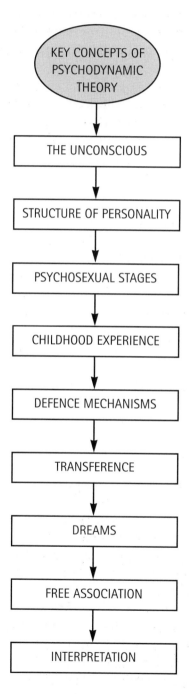

Figure 3.1 *Key concepts of psychodynamic theory*

<> **CASE STUDY** >— Unconscious meaning

A fifty-five year-old man was very upset by what he described as 'sloppiness in dress or appearance'. He became especially irritated when he saw someone wearing a jacket or coat casually over the shoulders. In his view, coats should be worn properly with the arms inserted in the sleeves. Like many personal eccentric views, his opinion did not constitute a major problem for him or his relatives. On one occasion, however, he upbraided his wife for wearing her coat in this fashion. In response to this, she suggested that he should try to remember when he first started to think in this way since, after all, the problem was clearly his and not hers. Several days later he mentioned to her in surprise that he remembered an old man who lived in the neighbourhood where he grew up. This man was a frightening local character who had lost an arm in the war, and frequently shouted at children in the street. Because of his injury, he always wore his coat draped over his shoulders. Once this association had been made by the client, his preoccupation with appearance diminished.

It can be seen from this account that the client, Mr Cater, was unaware at first of the origin of his strong feelings about dress and appearance. His response to his wife's style of dress was irrational, as he himself readily admitted. Many phobias are similar to this, and clients are seldom able to identify the factors which triggered them. With help and encouragement, however, it is possible for clients to locate the original (usually traumatic) event which prompted the fearful response. Mr Cater's wife was interested enough to encourage him to look for the cause of his irritation. The cause was, in fact, repressed and buried in his unconscious mind. Through effort, application and interest, he was successful in recalling this childhood event of the old man in the street who frightened him. Material which is repressed in this way is often of a frightening or disturbing nature, and this is exactly why it is repressed in the first place. However, as Mr Cater's example illustrates, the fact that experiences are consigned to the unconscious does not mean that they will cease to cause problems.

< **EXERCISE** >— Unconscious processes

In groups of two or three, discuss the following short case studies and consider the unconscious processes which may be at work in each.

◆ Bill is often invited next door for dinner. He likes his neighbours and enjoys these visits. However, on each occasion he spills wine on the tablecloth, even though he is normally well co-ordinated and certainly does not drink too much. His neighbours are very gracious about this and always invite him back. They are well off and enjoy Bill's company.

◆ Phyllis is thirty-six, and has to stay overnight in hospital for a minor procedure. The night before she goes into hospital, she packs a small overnight case which includes a soap bag containing a wash cloth and some cosmetics. As she does this, she is suddenly overcome with feelings of sadness and loss. The smell of the soap reminds her of an earlier stay in hospital when she was a child of five. She always felt she had coped very well with this at the time, and her parents had commented on her bravery and stoicism.

◆ Sarah has recently applied for promotion. She wants to get ahead, but is not totally convinced that management is the job for her. The night before her interview she dreams that she is in the driver seat of a large lorry. She is trying desperately to operate the gears, but is unable to do so. After a while she gets out and goes over to a small car. She gets into this and drives away quite happily.

The structure of personality

Freud came to believe that human personality is made up of three connecting systems: the Id, the Ego and the Superego. These three areas of personality constantly interact with one another as a means of regulating an individual's behaviour.

The **Id**, which is the most primitive part of the system, is present from birth, and as indicated earlier in this chapter is derived from Freud's concept of the *unconscious*. The Id can be seen, therefore, as the repository for everything which is fixed, instinctual and inherited in a person's make up. The Id is also, according to Freud, the repository of all our impulses, especially those relating to sex and aggression. These impulses are constantly demanding attention and expression, but because of the constraints placed on us by society and the need for civilised behaviour, immediate gratification of instinctual urges is not always possible or desirable. The Id, which is governed by the Pleasure Principle, needs, therefore, to be modified or regulated, and this function is fulfilled by the Ego, the second part of Freud's system.

The **Ego** is sometimes described as the arbiter, the manger or the executive, of the total personality system, since its function is to deal with the demands of the Id in a realistic way. The Ego is governed by the Reality Principle – which means that it must devise ways of satisfying the demands of the Id, while simultaneously deciding what behaviour and actions are appropriate at any given time. At about the age of one to two, children begin to learn that they must wait for certain things, and that very often it is a good idea to ask. This second part of personality is rational, logical and incorporates problem solving abilities, memory and perception too. Skills like talking, planning, negotiating and explaining are important dimensions of the conscious Ego, and whereas the Id is concerned with subjective needs and internal reality, the Ego is concerned with things as they exist in the real world.

The **Superego**, or Morality Principle, is the third psychological process which Freud included in his model of human personality. This develops at around the age of three and is composed of internalised values, ideals and moral precepts, all of which derive from parental and other authority figures. The Superego is that part of personality which is concerned with right and wrong, and is capable of generating guilt when people transgress their own, or society's moral code. When children develop this aspect of personality they become effective, over a period of time, in regulating their own behaviour. Before this mature stage is reached, however, parents and teachers socialise the child through a system of rewards and punishments. Once society's standards have been incorporated, any infringement of them is likely to produce anxiety or guilt. For some people, the Superego can develop as excessively punishing so that attitudes of perfectionism are fostered which can, in turn, lead to depression and other psychological problems. The task for the Ego is to maintain a balance or equilibrium between the demands of the Id on the one hand, and the strictures of the Superego on the other. Integrated behaviour is dependent on this balance, and on an accurate perception of external reality.

THE PSYCHOSEXUAL STAGES OF DEVELOPMENT

Along with his theories of the unconscious and the structure of personality, Freud's three essays on the theory of sexuality (Freud, 1924) make it quite clear what he considered to be the most significant aspects of mental life. It is difficult for us today to realise just how revolutionary his ideas must have seemed at the end of the nineteenth century and the beginning of the twentieth. Although Freud was living and working in Vienna, his was nevertheless a Victorian and sexually repressive era. One of his most outstanding achievements was to focus on childhood experience, and in doing so to consider the ways in which children develop to sexual maturity and the stages through which they pass in order to achieve this. The subject of sexuality in children had been neglected and even absent before Freud, so his descriptions of infantile sensations and experience were startling and certainly controversial. Freud himself pointed out that previous opinion had inclined to the view that sexual instinct only awakens at puberty (Freud, 1924). He was concerned to show that events take place much earlier than this, and that sexuality evolves through a series of stages which are commonly referred to as the 'psychosexual stages of development'. The following is an outline of the theoretical framework Freud proposed.

The Oral Stage: Birth – 1 year approximately

This is the first phase of a child's life – from birth until about eighteen months – when pleasure is concentrated on the mouth with the experiences of feeding and sucking. In fact, it is probably true to say that the mouth is the *centre* of existence at this stage, since survival is dependent on taking in nourishment. The word Libido, which Freud uses to describe this energy, is a broad term. It does not refer to sexual feelings in a narrow sense; instead, it denotes a comprehensive force or vitality which is found up with feelings of pleasure, comfort and the need to survive.

There are two phases during this stage of development: the first is the sucking phase when only fluids are taken, and the second is the biting phase which is linked to weaning and eating. Weaning can be traumatic for babies, especially if it is introduced abruptly or without sensitivity to emotional needs, and problems associated with either the earlier or later oral stages can be carried over into later life. Food and love are closely linked in infancy, and when early feeding experiences are negative, this link between food, love and security may persist into adult life and become manifest through eating disorders, alcohol or drug addition and smoking. Sarcasm and gossip, which stem from aggressive impulses, are also sometimes associated with problems arising at the weaning oral stage. If weaning is delayed, difficult or emotionally traumatic for example, the natural activities of chewing and biting may not be given adequate expression, and may then seek expression in destructive ways later on. Adult problem behaviours, linked to either of the stages of weaning, tend to become more pronounced at times of stress or unhappiness.

The Anal Stage: Age 1–3 approximately

This is the second important stage of a child's development, and during this time the young child is beginning to understand what is expected by parents and society generally. The Ego is beginning to emerge, and the Reality Principle is replacing the Id or Pleasure Principle. At this time also, a toddler is subjected to a major socialising process in the form of toilet training.

Conflict can and does arise between the wishes of parents and the impulses of the child. These areas of conflict concern issues of power and control'. On the one hand the child derives pleasure from both withholding and expelling faeces, while on the other hand there is the desire to please parents and to establish the kind of routine they demand. The issue of hygiene is an important one too, so several major learning experiences are undertaken in a short space of time. Parents often reward small children for using the toilet at specific times. This teaches children about the need to defer gratification. Parents may also seem disapproving when mistakes are made, and these parental attitudes are linked to the emergence of the Superego in the child.

Attitudes to cleanliness and order are fostered at this stage, and if these are punishing problems can develop in adult life leading to habits of compulsive cleanliness and order. On the other hand, there are those people who tend to spread disorder and mess wherever they go, habits which may have begun at the anal stage when toilet training was not rigorous enough. In psychodynamic literature, faeces and money are often associated. This means that faeces is regarded as a young child's first possession, and in later life this unconscious association remains with the adult (Freud, 1908). Attitudes to money can, according to Freudian theory, shed some light on an individual's toilet training experiences. As we shall see in the next chapter, however, contemporary psychodynamic theory offers some interesting and quite different views about human characteristics generally.

The Phallic Stage: Age 3–6 years approximately

During the Phallic stage, a child's interest becomes focused on the genital area; in psychodynamic theory this applies to both sexes. The Oedipus Complex – which is integral to this phase of development – is also applicable to both boys and girls, and represents a family drama in which individual roles within the group become clearer to the child. In formulating his theory, Freud was influenced by the Greek tragedy *Oedipus Rex* in which Oedipus kills his father and marries his mother.

According to classical Freudian theory, boys at the Oedipal stage become very interested in their mothers and envious of their fathers. Father is, after all, the person who is closest to mother, and to a small boy this represents an impediment to his own – often explicitly stated – ambition to own or 'marry' mother. Since these aspirations cause anxiety to the child – Father might become angry and punish him – the situation is resolved through a process of identification. The identification occurs when the child begins to emulate and adopt his father's mannerisms, style, goals, interests and ambitions. Such a response solves the Oedipal problem and serves a dual purpose: on the one hand the child has established a male role model for himself, while on the other hand he is beginning to learn about the structure of society in general, and his own place within it. The family, as a microcosm of society, is the setting in which this important learning experience takes place. The onset of genital sexual feelings at the Phallic stage also prompts an interest in sex roles as well as an interest in reproduction and birth.

The Oedipal drama is one aspect of psychodynamic theory which students frequently misinterpret. Often it is taken to mean sexual interest in the opposite sex parent only. In fact, it is a much broader concept than this, and incorporates those personal and sociological elements already mentioned. Girls are considered to experience a similar constellation of impulses, except of course that in their case the mother is seen as the rival, and the father as the object of desire. The concept of 'penis envy' is linked to this stage of development in girls, for according to Freudian theory small girls blame their mothers for the fact that they are anatomically different from boys. The punishment which a boy fears from his father (castration) cannot happen to a girl; what she fears therefore, is that it has already taken place. The situation is resolved for her through eventual identification with her mother. Needless to say, this is a much disputed theory, and in the next chapter we shall look at some post-Freudian theories, and consider the very different ways in which they interpret female development and the role of girls within the family.

The Latency Stage: Age 6–12 years approximately

During latency all available energy is directed towards the development of social and intellectual skills. Friendships, especially those with members of the same sex, become very important, and recreational activities including hobbies and sport, are a central focus of this stage. The sexual feelings which are repressed during latency will, however, return at the next (genital) stage of development.

The Genital Stage: Age 12 years – adulthood

The hormonal changes which take place at this stage encourage a resumption of sexual interest generally. This interest is, however, much less auto-erotic than it was in the Oedipal stage, and has the added purpose of establishing romantic, loving and intimate bonds with other people. The main focus of concern, according to Freud, is with forming heterosexual relationships with a view to lasting commitment and marriage. From a strictly Freudian viewpoint, therefore, mature adult sexuality with a member of the opposite sex is the outcome of successful progression through all the earlier stages. Homosexual members of any student group are frequently concerned to question this theory, and to discuss the ways in which it may have contributed to present homophobic attitudes. This is a topic worth discussing (and unfortunately often avoided) but it should be pointed out that Freud's views on homosexuality are complex and thoughtful, and he certainly did not believe that therapy should seek to change a person's sexual orientation. It is a fact, however, that in the history of psychoanalysis, the idea that everyone is constitutionally heterosexual has been a dominant theme.

For those students who would like to do some further reading on this subject, Freud's *Three Essays on the Theory of Sexuality* (1924) is a useful starting point. It is also important to consider contemporary psychodynamic views on the matter, and to look at the ways in which ideas concerning the nature of sexuality have been revised and updated as a result of research and changing attitudes. An overall survey of these latter ideas is contained in *Freud and Beyond* (Mitchell and Black, 1995).

The importance of the past and childhood experience

One of the most important contributions to the psychodynamic approach is its focus on childhood experience, and the way this experience can influence adult life. In the latter part of the nineteenth century Freud decided that many adult problems originated from early childhood abuse. His theory provoked disbelief and hostility, and in fact this reaction was so pronounced that Freud felt obliged to abandon his original idea. Later on he suggested that his patients may have been mistaken in the memories they recounted. Perhaps what they thought were memories were, in fact, really unconscious fantasies and wishes? This second idea led to Freud's theory of the Oedipus Complex (Freud, 1900), and to his conviction that many of the experiences people discuss in therapy are indicative of unconscious conflicts and wishes. Freud was effective, therefore, in drawing attention to the significance of early experience, even though he did seem to abandon his early, and we now know, probably correct, conclusion. It is clear that many children do indeed suffer sexual and other forms of abuse in childhood. Freud's original discovery proved to be prophetic in a sense, and by focusing on childhood experience he succeeded in bringing the subject to public awareness in a way never achieved before. It is probably true to say that Freud started something, although he certainly did not finish it. Ideas about child development and experience continue to evolve. In the next chapter we shall consider some of the contemporary ideas relating to childhood experience. It would be a mistake, however, to assume that it is only sexual trauma, or other child abuse, which is significant in psychodynamic theory. Children encounter numerous problems while growing up, and many of these can also cause difficulties in adult life.

The use of ego defence mechanisms

We have already seen that human personality (from a Freudian viewpoint) is made up of three components – the Id, the Ego and the Superego. The Ego, which is governed by the Reality Principle, has the task of coping with the demands of the Id, while constantly appraising external reality and making decisions about the kind of behaviour which is appropriate at any given time. The threat of punishment from the Superego is another factor to be considered, and the combined pressure from these forces (Id and Superego) has the effect of generating anxiety for the individual. The conflict which occurs between a person's wishes and external reality is dealt with by the use of *defence mechanisms*. These are psychological processes which people use in order to protect themselves against extreme discomfort and tension. They are also effective in maintaining mental composure and self-esteem in a variety of what might otherwise be very painful situations. Defence mechanisms operate at an unconscious level, and all of us use them occasionally. However, prolonged and persistent use of them is counter-productive, because such defences serve to distort reality and falsify experience. They also require a great deal of energy and vigilance which, if liberated, could be used in much more creative ways. The following is a summary of the main defences.

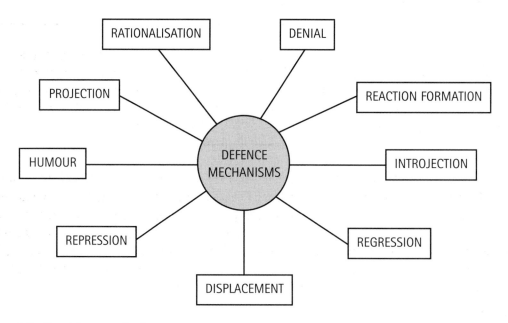

Figure 3.2 *Ego defence mechanisms*

◆ Repression

Repression is a process whereby traumatic or painful experiences are forgotten or pushed out of consciousness. This is the most fundamental of all the defence mechanisms and, like the others, is operated unconsciously. A child might, for example, repress a truly threatening experience like abandonment or loss, since this may be the child's only method of coping at the time. Repressed material does not go away, however, but continues to exist in the unconscious (Freud, 1909). Occasionally disguised signals break through into consciousness, and these may take the form of physical symptoms. Repressed material may also surface in dreams or at times of stress or illness. Certain major life events may prompt the re-emergence of repressed material. The following short case study illustrates this last point.

CASE STUDY — Repression

An eighteen year-old student left home to attend university. During this time she became involved with a boyfriend and fell in love with him. This was her first serious involvement, and it brought into consciousness a painful memory from early childhood. The memory concerned an occasion when she had seen her father being physically abusive towards her mother. The student had forgotten the traumatic incident, but details of it began to surface once she found herself getting close to her boyfriend. She then realised that she had been very reluctant (in her early teenage years) to become involved with boys. This inhibition with the opposite sex stemmed from her fear of involvement, and from her wish to avoid her mother's experience. Her first serious encounter served as a catalyst to release the repressed and painful memories from childhood. During a subsequent period of counselling she was helped to uncover the memory more fully and to understand is effect on her.

A great deal of mental energy is needed in order to ensure that repressed material does not surface into consciousness. However, the force which prevents unconscious material from becoming conscious is particularly strong, and is known as *resistance*. Resistance, like repression, in unconsciously motivated and is used as a means of avoiding the anxiety which awareness of repressed material would entail (Freud, 1909).

◆ Denial

Denial is used as a defence mechanism when reality is unpleasant or disturbing in some way. A person with a serious illness might, for example, deny the condition. This denial may serve a useful purpose initially, since it helps to protect the person against anxiety and high levels of stress. In the long term, though, its use will distort reality and prevent the adjustment and acceptance which are important at such a time. Denial is also used frequently by people who have been bereaved. In this context, it also works effectively in the short term but can lead to complicated grief reactions in the long term.

◆ Rationalisation

Rationalisation is a face-saving defence which people often use to explain away personal failures, vices or inadequacies. Instead of accepting that failure has taken place, 'rational' explanations are given, and these explanations are sometimes partly true. A parent might, for example, say that a particular child is 'difficult' and this label may then be used to excuse parental aggression towards that child.

◆ Projection

The defence mechanism of projection ensures that internal anxiety or discomfort is directed outwards towards other people. It is a way of attributing our own faults to others. A person with a tendency to be hypocritical might, for example, suspect or even accuse other people of hypocrisy. In a similar way, someone who is aggressive or domineering, may see these characteristics in others, but fail to recognise and own them personally.

◆ Displacement

Unacceptable impulses and desires are often aimed at the wrong person. This is most likely to happen when the real target is seen as too threatening to confront. Thus, a man who has had problems with his boss at work might be tempted to take it out on someone else – his wife or children for example. Strong feelings are also sometimes displaced towards authority figures in public life. A person who has had a difficult relationship with a parent may develop hostile attitudes towards the police, judges or even the Pope.

◆ Reaction formation

Reaction formation is a defence in which the conscious feeling or thought is exactly opposite to the unconscious one. An example of this is the person who expresses strong views against liberal sex attitudes, while at the same time fighting to control personal sexual impulses. Reaction formation is evident in many areas, and may be implicit in a variety of attitudes. People who claim to dislike lateness may have a tendency in that direction, while those who deplore bad manners may well lack social confidence themselves. It is probably true to say that when strongly held views are evident, there is some likelihood that the opposite impulse is present. The degree of emotional investment in the view expressed is a fairly reliable indicator of this particular defence.

◆ Introjection

This describes the process of taking in the views and attitudes expressed by other people. This can work in either a positive or a negative way. One example of positive use is the process whereby children incorporate the values and standards of parents and teachers. Introjection is problematic when less healthy experiences are taken in and held as part of the self. An extreme example of this is the person who has been kidnapped and who, in order to survive mentally, identifies with the captors and their cause. A less dramatic, though equally problematic, use of the defence is evident when abused children absorb their experiences and then pass them on to the next generation. With regard to the last point, however, it is important to remember that not all abused children become abusing adults in this way.

Making assumptions about people, and attaching labels to them is a trap which people who work in a caring capacity are liable to make. Counsellors are no exception in this respect, and this is why regular supervision is an essential component of their work.

◆ Regression

People often retreat to an earlier stage of development in the face of threat or failure. Regression is a defence hospital nurses are familiar with: patients often revert to less adult forms of behaviour once they find themselves in hospital. This defence works well for people in many situations, since it ensures that care and attention are elicited from others.

It works well for victims of trauma who certainly need the added care and attention. Regression is a problem when it is used habitually as a way of being noticed.

◆ Humour

Some people use humour as a shield or barrier against painful experience and trauma. It is interesting that many comedians have suffered from depression, which would seem to indicate a close link between humour and sadness. Humour is, of course, not always used as a defence mechanism, it is quite possible to be funny without any underlying agenda. Freud refers to the 'high yield of pleasure' which people derive from humour (Freud, 1907). However, clients sometimes use humour as a way of avoiding serious and reflective consideration of their problems. Humour may have become an habitual defence with them, and one which is difficult to relinquish.

◆ The concept of anxiety

Anxiety is an important concept in psychodynamic theory, and in Freudian terms is seen as the catalyst which signals impending danger to the Ego. Defence mechanisms are used in order to reduce anxiety. Danger situations include fear of losing another person's love, the fear of punishment (by others or by the Superego) and the fear of abandonment (Freud, 1932).

◁ EXERCISE ▷ —— Looking at defences ————

Working individually, identify any defences which you have used in the past at times of anxiety or stress. How did the defences help or hinder you at the time?

Transference and the nature of the therapeutic relationship

Transference is a term which – in psychodynamic literature – refers to the client's emotional response to the counsellor. Clients' emotional responses are, of course, highlighted in all the theoretical approaches, but the concept of transference is especially significant in the psychodynamic model. Freud was the first person to identify the phenomenon; while working with his colleague Breuer he witnessed it at first hand and later described it both in lectures and in his writing (Freud, 1909).

Clients may 'transfer' to counsellors feelings which are either positive or negative. These feelings stem from childhood emotional responses to parents, and are therefore not based on any real relation between counsellor and client. Transference feelings operate at an unconscious level, so the client is unaware that responses to the counsellor may be inappropriate or out of date. Evidence of the client's early emotional life is, therefore, often clearly seen in the counselling relationship. This has obvious advantages for the client, since (with help) he will be able to identify the cause of some of his current difficulties. The following case study illustrates this last point.

A twenty-six year-old client became angry because his counsellor had gone into hospital for a minor operation. The client (Colin) had been told in advance that the counsellor would be away for a week, but this notice did little to reassure him. During a subsequent counselling session he discussed his reaction with the counsellor. At first he was puzzled by the strength of his own reaction, but he later identified some earlier experiences which had some bearing on his heightened emotional response to the counsellor's absence. Colin's parents had divorced when he was five years old, and shortly afterwards his father had been ill with allergy problems. No one had taken time to talk to the small child, nor had he been taken to visit his father in hospital. One consequence of this was that, for many years, Colin blamed himself for his father's illness and departure. Once he was able to explore all these issues, Colin understood why he became angry and frustrated when the counsellor left to go into hospital. The feelings which he had transferred to the counsellor were really feelings stemming from the past and his relationship with his parents. In exploring them, however, he was able to look more realistically at his childhood experience of loss and at the burden of blame he had carried for so many years.

It is important to make clear that transference is not a mysterious occurrence only seen in counselling and therapy. People may experience strong emotional responses in a variety of 'helping' situations. These situations include patient/doctor and nurse/patient relationships, and indeed any other context where one person is depending on another for assistance or support. Nurses, doctors, social workers and ministers of religion are aware that the people they help often respond in inappropriate emotional ways. Problems often arise because helpers do not understand the reasons for such feelings, and may indeed be flattered to receive them. This is especially true when the feelings transferred are loving, idealising, admiring or erotic. Abuse of clients can arise in these circumstances, so the underlying dynamic of transference needs to be understood and the central role of supervision for counsellors recognised.

Countertransference

The word countertransference refers to the counsellor's emotional response to the client. Counsellors are also capable of displacing feelings from the past into the present situation with the client. If Colin's counsellor (see the case study above) had taken his attitude personally such a response would have been inappropriate in the therapeutic context and would not have helped the client in any way. The counsellor needed to understand that the client was not angry with her personally. His reactions – which were unrealistic in the present context – were used by the counsellor in order to help him achieve deeper understanding of his problems.

However, counsellors, since they are human, may never be wholly objective in their response to clients. Counsellors have life histories which can colour or affect their reactions, and it is these areas of personal bias which are defined as countertransference. Once again, this highlights the importance of supervision for counsellors, since it is only through supervision that they can identify and deal with their countertransference reactions.

There are some forms of countertransference which are more common than others. Seeing clients as helpless, or as victims, is one form. When this attitude is pronounced, over-protection or even advice may be offered by the counsellor. This kind of over-protectiveness says a great deal about the counsellor's need to be in control, and it will certainly inhibit the client's self development and autonomy. Countertransference responses may also appear in the counsellor's inability to confront or disagree with a client. This may stem from a fear of being disliked, or of being seen as incompetent. Counsellors may also feel themselves to be in competition with particular clients, or to feel envious of them. These responses may be related to childhood problems with siblings and parents. Whatever the reason, it is essential that counsellors monitor their countertransference feelings and discuss them in supervision. Issues concerning supervision will be dealt with in Chapter 10.

On the subject of countertransference however, it is important to remember that every imaginable human prejudice or bias may present itself in this form and when such bias is left unexamined it will ultimately distort the therapeutic relationship and work against clients. It is also possible for counsellors to have biased feelings towards certain people or groups of people. One example of this is the kind of partiality which may be extended to specific groups such as women, minority groups or people seen as disadvantaged in some way. The crucial point to make here is that individual clients are entitled to be treated as individuals, and not as stereotypes.

◁ EXERCISE ▷ — Student self-assessment

Working in pairs, identify some of the countertransference feelings which you have experienced in relation to the people you help. How did you deal with these feelings, and what, if anything, did they tell you about yourself? Take turns to discuss your individual experiences.

The significance of dreams

Freud regarded dreams as 'the royal road to a knowledge of the unconscious activities of the mind' (Freud, 1900). It follows therefore that in classical psychoanalysis dream interpretation is a central component of therapy. Dream interpretation is important in all other psychodynamic models of therapy and counselling too. The difference here is that whereas in the past psychoanalysts might devote long periods of time in the analysis of just one dream, psychodynamic counsellors and therapist focus on them only when clients request or understand such a focus. The point to be made here is that not all clients are regularly in touch with their unconscious and dream life, although it's probably true to say that any client who requests psychodynamic counselling is aware of the importance given to dreams and to dream interpretation. Such interpretation is, of course, entirely subjective; only the client can say what the dream means for her personally, though counsellors who work from a psychodynamic perspective can help clients to examine the symbolism contained in dreams and to discuss what they mean. It is important to add here that dream interpretation through the use of standardised symbols found in popular self-help texts is not useful for clients. This is because dreams are unique to the individual dreamer. Later in this chapter we shall look at some of the skills which can be used to help clients interpret their dreams.

Free association or 'the talking cure'

All theoretical models of counselling are based on the premise that clients need to talk through their problems in order to make sense of them. The term 'free association' was first used by Freud to describe the process of encouraging his patients to say whatever they liked on the grounds that whatever occurred to them would be relevant and revealing (Freud, 1909).

In psychodynamic counselling clients are encouraged to talk at their own pace and to express their feelings and thoughts, no matter how insignificant these may appear to be. What clients wish to say is obviously important to them in any case, and it is never the counsellor's task to decide what should be voiced by clients during sessions. What is important is that counsellors listen carefully to clients, and respond appropriately and at the right time.

Free association also forms the basis of dream interpretation. When clients use this technique in relation to their own dreams, significant links are often made so that apparently disconnected symbols come together and form a more coherent picture.

SKILLS USED IN PSYCHODYNAMIC COUNSELLING

All the basis skills described in previous chapters are applicable to the psychodynamic approach. In addition to these skills a number of others are also used, which have evolved from the original Freudian psychoanalytic model. Psychodynamic counselling is obviously very different from psychoanalysis, however, so the techniques, methods and skills of psychoanalysis have been adapted to suit the approach and to facilitate the client's needs. The following is a list of skills which are central to the psychodynamic approach.

◆ Making contracts
◆ Listening
◆ Observing
◆ Clarifying
◆ Linking
◆ Interpreting
◆ Attending to transference

◆ Looking at dreams

◆ Giving reflective responses

◆ Drawing attention to parallels between past and present

The importance of structure: Contracts

We have already seen that counselling takes place in sessions which last for fifty minutes. Clients need to know the basic details of counsellor/client contracts well in advance of sessions if possible, so that structure and stability are an integral part of the relationship. It is essential to establish clear boundaries with clients, a practice which is not, of course, exclusive to the psychodynamic approach. However, the difference is that in psycho-dynamic counselling the client's response to such a contract has special significance. A client who misses sessions, for example, or who arrives late, is clearly expressing something which is not being said in words. Clients can, of course, arrive later for sessions or miss them occasionally because of transport or other problems. But when poor time-keeping is habitual, there is always the possibility that some for of *resistance* is operating within the client. Such resistance is usually unconscious or outside the client's awareness

In a situation like this, the counsellor's task is to encourage the client to look closely at the underlying meaning of the behaviour, and to place it in the context of any other problems or difficulties which the client is experiencing. It may be that the client is avoiding some painful subject, or it may be that she feels unable to disagree with the counsellor or to express negative or angry feelings. Even though clients come into counselling with the intention of sorting out and understanding their problems, the exploration this involves is often so difficult for them that the temptation to resist further self-scrutiny is often hard to overcome. The following case study is an example of this last point.

◁ **CASE STUDY** ▷─ Lydia ─────────────────────

Lydia, who was thirty, wanted to talk to a counsellor about her relationship with her grandmother who had died. She attended three counselling sessions and seemed to be keen to understand why she continued to feel depressed, even though two years had passed since her grandmother's death. In the third session Lydia referred to the fact that she had gone to live with her grandparents after her parents split up. This was a diffi-cult subject for her to talk about and it gradually became apparent to the counsellor that Lydia wanted to avoid it altogether. In addition to the fact that she obviously wanted to avoid the subject, she also decided to leave early, and on the next occasion arrived late for her session. The counsellor offered a tentative interpretation of Lydia's behaviour in the following way:

COUNSELLOR: You talked a little about living with your gran and grandad last time we met. Then I sensed that it was difficult for you, that you wanted to leave it.

CLIENT: It's not difficult really ... [pause] ... I usually don't mind talking about it. I loved staying with them, although I was sad about my parents.

COUNSELLOR: The sadness about your parents, tell me about that.

CLIENT: [long pause] I suppose I never really allowed myself to think about it. I felt I had to be strong for Gareth [her brother].

COUNSELLOR: Not thinking about it and being strong for Gareth, all that meant that you could never get a chance to grieve for the upheaval in your life.

CLIENT: I think in a way my depression is linked to that ...

COUNSELLOR: To your parents splitting up ...

CLIENT: Yes. for ages I thought it was to do with my gran's death. Maybe it has more to do with other things.

COUNSELLOR: Things you thought you had best avoid.

CLIENT: Yes. But then the depression doesn't go away ...

COUNSELLOR: The depression stays with you as long as you don't let yourself remember how it felt when the break-up happened.

It can be seen from Lydia's exchange with the counsellor, and her actions and behaviour before this, that she wanted to avoid the anxiety which awareness of repressed material would entail. The counsellor used the *skills* of *listening, observing, clarifying, linking, interpreting, giving reflective responses* and *drawing attention to past events and present behaviour*, in order to help the client become conscious of experiences she had previously avoided. In making these responses the counsellor was precise though respectful in the way she framed them. If the client had not sensed the counsellor's respect for her defence against deep feelings of anxiety, it is unlikely that she would have been willing to continue in counselling. The client, Lydia, was sufficiently reflective, thoughtful and courageous to benefit from psychodynamic counselling. She was also capable of insight and self-awareness, so the interpretations and links which the counsellor made were carefully considered by her before she either accepted or rejected the. Clients are free to accept or reject interpretations, because what is said must make sense to the client and should, moreover, 'feel' right and appropriate if they are to be helpful.

Students often ask about the similarities between *confrontation* and *interpretation*. On the surface it may seem that they are very alike, and in some ways they are. Successful interpretation does contain some degree of challenge and confrontation. Moreover, it is quite possible to use the skill of interpretation in a challenging way with clients. A client who is indirectly expressing suicidal thoughts, for example, might benefit from this kind of interpretative approach. The following is an example.

CASE STUDY —— Confrontation and interpretation ————————

A middle-aged man was referred for counselling because he suffered from panic attacks following his redundancy. He had some ongoing problems in his marriage as well, and six months earlier financial difficulties had also featured prominently in his life. During counselling sessions he often referred to the fact that many young people were out of work, so why should he, a middle-aged man, feel entitled to a job? He spoke of his life as if it was already over, and though he denied feeling depressed the counsellor sensed that he was masking some deep presentiments of despair.

COUNSELLOR: You mentioned several times that other people are more entitled to things than you are, that maybe you are not entitled to hope for much now?

CLIENT: I do feel like that sometimes, yes.

COUNSELLOR: Is that something you feel about your own life ... that you are not entitled to it either?

CLIENT: [slowly] I had not thought about it in those words. I suppose I have been that despairing.

The counsellor's interpretation here was effective in making the client aware of something which had previously been outside his awareness. He had not consciously thought about suicide but it was, nevertheless, a recurrent though disguised motif in his communication. This client also received medical help for his depression and continued to see the counsellor on a weekly basis. It is important to mention here that counselling is limited in its application and usefulness. Many clients require other forms of help, and one of the counsellor's essential skills is the ability to identify these areas which need extra attention and support.

In Chapter 1 we looked at the people who use counselling skills and saw that many of these are professionals qualified in other areas. This makes a great deal of difference as far as counselling is concerned, because a sound professional foundation also means that a fairly comprehensive knowledge base is already in place. This knowledge base should ensure that potentially serious medical conditions can be identified, and further help is enlisted for the client when needed. If a counsellor is also a qualified nurse, occupational therapist or social worker, for example, then it is reasonable to assume that sufficient knowledge will have been acquired in the course of training to ensure this kind of competence. On the other hand, it would be wrong to suppose that people without this kind of training are never in a position to function effectively when extra help is required. What is important is a willingness to pursue further and specialised training, as and when necessary, and to remain aware of personal and professional limitations at all times. Supervision helps in this respect and is an essential component of counsellor training and practice, a fact which cannot be stated often enough.

EXERCISE — Identifying skills

Read the following passage and identify the counselling skills you could use to help the client. Identify the basic skills (for example listening, asking questions) as well as the psychodynamic skills which might be applicable in this instance. Discuss your ideas with a partner, highlighting any helpful techniques you think a psychodynamic counsellor could use.

◆ Lynda, who is thirty, has a history of relationship problems. Her first boyfriend was addicted to drugs and was emotionally abusive towards her. A later boyfriend left her when he met someone else, and shortly afterwards she joined a dating agency in the hope that she would meet someone more reliable. Although she met several interesting people through the agency, Lynda was unable to form a lasting commitment with anyone. In counselling she talked about her childhood, and about her father who was distant and emotionally uninvolved with her. She is confused about her present situation, since she feels that she is 'full of affection' and has a lot to offer in a relationship.

Attending to transference

Attention to transference is an important aspect of psychodynamic counselling, since transference is the mirror in which the client's past is reflected in the present. Clients bring all their early experiences with them into counselling, and these experiences are frequently manifest in the relationship the client forms with the counsellor. Because they know very little about the private lives of the counsellors who help them, clients use imagination to fill in the gaps, and the imagined figure who emerges from this process may bear little resemblance to the real person. In order to form a picture of the counsellor, the client will draw on past experience, especially on past experience of relationships with important figures like parents. This process is carried on at an unconscious level, so clients are unaware that the information they are using is unrealistic and outdated. From a psychodynamic viewpoint, counsellors can help clients to use this information in a way which will help them understand some of the problems they may have. A client may treat the counsellor as a mother or father, for example and, depending on the nature of the relationship which the client had with the parent, respond to the counsellor in either a positive or a negative way. The following is an example.

CASE STUDY — Attending to transference

A middle-aged woman, who was completing a course at college, attended counselling sessions because of problems she was having with her elderly parents. Her parents were controlling and demanding, and the client (Sylvia) felt that they constantly criticised her. In particular, they accused her of being 'dependent' and lacking in initiative. Sylvia did, in fact, live with her parents, and she was financially dependent on them. In her relationship with the counsellor, who was a woman, she was timid and sometimes ingratiating.

It was clear that she desperately wanted to please and be a 'good' client. The counsellor drew attention to this attitude of wanting to please, but she did this only after she had established a trusting relationship with the client.

COUNSELLOR: You mentioned yesterday that it was sometimes difficult to know if you were getting it right, that you were worried about getting it right with me.

CLIENT: Yes I do worry about it. It's hard to say why but I feel I would like to be more myself.

COUNSELLOR: You would like to be more yourself with me and not feel concerned with pleasing me in the way you try to please your parents?

CLIENT: I'm always trying to please them and I suppose that's what I'm doing with you. Yes, I probably do it with everyone, come to think of it.

There are many factors which can cause transference reactions to occur in counselling. These include the counsellor's physical or behavioural characteristics, voice sound and accent, similarity in dress, and indeed any characteristic which acts as an unconscious reminder of significant people in the client's past. Once the transference reaction is brought into the open, it serves as an important vehicle for learning, and clients can identify from it faulty patterns within their own behaviour in relation to others. Counsellors are not always automatically aware of transference reactions from clients, and occasionally it is experienced or 'felt' by the counsellor before it comes into consciousness. The counsellor's own countertransference response acts as an indicator of its presence, and once the counsellor is fully aware of the transference it is possible to use this knowledge for the client's benefit.

Looking at dreams

We have already considered the importance of dreams in the psychodynamic approach to counselling, and the point has been made that only clients themselves can interpret their dreams accurately. However, counsellors can encourage clients to become more interested in the contents of their dreams, and to record them as an aid to self-knowledge and greater awareness. Some clients are more keen than others to do this, and there is no doubt that certain clients have an intuitive or innate knowledge of symbolism and the language of the unconscious. The following is an example:

CASE STUDY — Dreams

◆ A forty year-old woman recounted two dreams she had before she came for counselling. Both dreams convinced her that she needed to talk to someone. The counsellor encouraged her to recount these dreams in the present tense, a technique which gives immediacy and vividness to the experiences of the dream.

I am going on a journey, on a train or a bus. It is a double-decker vehicle. An old woman directs me on to the lower section. I have a small child with me and I feel very responsible for her. We travel along and eventually get out at a large area of wasteland. There are bars all around this area, like a prison.

In the next dream I am due to see a therapist who is a well-known person or celebrity. She lives in London, and I find myself there. I have a child with me in a pram. I climb the steps to the therapist's house, taking the pram with me. The therapist is sitting in a room which is too big. It is uncomfortable, too open and there are too many people around. The therapist is not really interested; she gets up, then comes back with a book. Meanwhile, the child has gone.

During the counselling this client was able to identify several important key elements in both dreams.

COUNSELLOR: And the old woman and child in the dreams?

CLIENT: I think they are two aspects of me; one is the old worn out me, the other is the new beginning which would like to develop.

COUNSELLOR: The journey ... what you have just come through, your mother's death and the changes you have had to make.

CLIENT: Yes. And those I still have to make.

COUNSELLOR: So the challenge is between staying with the old (and with the wasteland) or getting onto the top deck, which might be harder to get to but where you can see more?

These two dreams are very rich in symbolism and meaning, and the client was able to learn a great deal from them. Before she came for counselling there were many futile attempts to enlist help from others, but none were successful. The client could see clearly that the therapist in the dream, for example, represented her hopes and her frustration at not getting help.

◁ **EXERCISE** ▷ — Looking at dreams

Think about any dream you have had recently. Try to recall as much detail as possible, then write it out in the present tense. Then complete the following:

◆ Give the dream a name
◆ Describe, in one word, the emotional atmosphere of the dream
◆ Describe, in one world, the location of the dream
◆ Describe, in one word, any aspect of time in the dream, for example time of day, time of year, time of life
◆ List the various elements of the dream
◆ Start with the most recognisable element and free associate to it, for example say whatever comes into your head in relation to it

◆ Put yourself in the position of each element in the dream and say what you are doing in the dream. If a door features in your dream for example, pretend to be the door, describe yourself and explain your presence.

◆ Consider the ways in which the dream has any relevance to current issues or problems in your life

◆ Circle any key words in the dream

◆ Circle any key people in the dream.

When you have completed this exercise you should have some idea of what the dream means to you. This is an individual exercise which you don't have to share with anyone else, unless you wish to. Dreams are, by their nature, private, and it is often the case that dream interpretation reveals intimate information about ourselves. If you are interested in your own dreams you should keep a record of them. Working with dreams takes time and dedication, but unless we are aware of our own inner lives it is presumptuous to expect clients to be familiar with theirs. Finally, this is not an exercise designed for use with clients: it is meant as a *student* exercise.

Clients who benefit from this approach

Though we may not agree with all of it, Freudian theory has taught us a great deal about human personality and motivation. We know, for example, that influences from the past are frequently implicated in current problems. Knowledge of Freudian concepts is very important, therefore, in our understanding of people, and in this respect all clients should benefit – if only indirectly – from this approach. The concept of transference/countertransference is central to Freudian theory, and this is another area of knowledge which is essential for every counsellor – regardless of the theoretical approach used.

There are many other examples of Freudian theory which have contributed a great deal towards our understanding of clients. The use of defence mechanisms is a case in point, and the significance of the past and childhood experience are further examples. Psychodynamic counselling is certainly appropriate for many clients, but it is especially useful for those who have suffered trauma in the past, for people who are depressed and unable to locate the cause, and for others who feel compelled to repeat destructive patterns of behaviour or relationships. People who are interested in personal growth and increased self-awareness are also likely to benefit.

Some limitations

The psychodynamic approach is adaptable for use with many clients providing, of course, that counsellors who use it are adequately trained in terms of both theory and practice. Short and long-term therapy is available in some – mainly city – urban areas, and there are

many other counsellors who incorporate aspects of psychodynamic theory in other theoretical approaches. An exclusively psychodynamic approach may not be useful for clients in
crisis (crisis intervention) or for those who are very recently bereaved. People in this last
category will probably benefit more from bereavement counselling, or from participation in
a support group with others who share their experience. Clients who are addicted to alcohol or drugs are also unlikely to benefit from a purely psychodynamic approach. This is
because they may be extremely anxious, disorientated or simply not committed to the personal and emotional involvement needed. People who suffer from problems of addiction
may also need extra support and back-up services. Cost is another consideration because
therapy can be long term, although counsellors and therapists are often flexible about this.
Although some clients with severe mental illness might benefit from this approach, they
are only likely to do so within the security of a hospital where there is back-up support.
This is especially true for those who are receiving medication.

SUMMARY

In this chapter we considered the basic principles of psychodynamic theory. These have
evolved from the work of Sigmund Freud and from classical psychoanalysis. Freudian theory
is based on the assumption that much of what we think, feel and do is determined by
unconscious motivation. There is an emphasis on sexual and aggressive drives, and on key
stages of development from childhood until adolescence. The Freudian structure of personality (Id, Ego and Superego) was discussed, along with the defences which people use to
guard against anxiety. The importance of childhood experience was highlighted, and this
was linked to the ways in which people transfer emotional experience from the past into
the present. Client's experiences in counselling were described, along with the key concepts
of transference and countertransference. We looked at dreams and considered their significance in psychodynamic theory. Psychodynamic counselling skills were also described,
and examples of these were given. The usefulness of these approaches was also discussed,
along with consideration of some of its limitations. In the next chapter we shall look at the
way in which psychodynamic theory has evolved over time, and we shall discuss the effectiveness of these approaches for different client groups.

REFERENCES

Freud, S. (1924)   'Three Essays on the Theory of Sexuality', in Gay, P. (ed.) (1989)
                    The Freud Reader. London: Penguin Books, 1991.

Freud, S. (1908)   'Character and Anal Eroticism', in Gay, P. (ed.) (1989) *The Freud
                    Reader*. London: Penguin Books, 1991.

Freud, S. (1900)   *The Interpretation of Dreams*. London: Penguin Books, 1991.

Freud, S. (1909)   *Five Lectures on Psychoanalysis*. London: Penguin Books, 1995.

Freud, S. (1907)   'Creative Writers and Daydreaming', in Gay, P. (ed.) (1989) *The Freud Reader*. London: Penguin Books, 1991.

Freud, S. (1932)   'Anxiety and Instinctual Life', in Gay, P. (ed.) (1989) *The Freud Reader*. London: Penguin Books, 1991.

Mitchell, S. A. &   *Freud and Beyond: A History of Modern Psychoanalytic Thought*.
Black, M. J. (1995)   New York: Basic Books.

FURTHER READING

Bateman, A. & Holmes, J. (1995)   *Introduction To Psychoanalysis*. London: Routledge.

Roycroft, C. (1992)   *A Critical Dictionary Of Psychoanalysis*. London: Penguin.

Stafford-Clark, D. (1992)   *What Freud Really Said*. London: Penguin Books.

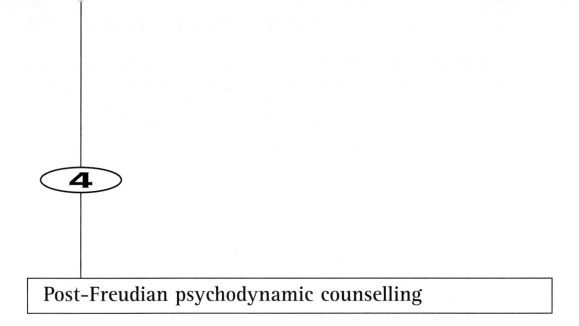

Post-Freudian psychodynamic counselling

EVOLUTION OF THEORY

Freud attracted a number of talented people who were interested in psychoanalysis, and who wished to be associated with the work he was doing. However, not all of them agreed with him on every aspect of psychoanalytic theory. Two of the earliest revisionists were Adler and Jung, both of whom disagreed with Freud's emphasis on the central role of sexual instincts in human behaviour. The Oedipus complex was another key concept which caused disagreement among some of Freud's early and later colleagues. Many of these followers developed theoretical frameworks which differed in many respects from Freudian theory. Therefore, Freudian theory began to evolve and expand at a very early stage, and it continues to develop and expand today. This chapter is concerned with these revised ideas, and with the theoretical concepts which have developed from the work of Freud.

ALFRED ADLER (1870–1937)

Individual psychology

Alfred Adler was a qualified doctor who practiced for a time in ophthalmology. Later he qualified as a psychiatrist, and in 1902 joined Freud's circle of admirers and friends.By 1911, however, Adler's theoretical views were becoming more divergent, and he criticised many aspects of Freudian orthodoxy. These differences of opinion forced Adler to resign as President of the Vienna Psychoanalytic Society and in 1912 he formed the Society for Individual Psychology.

Adler disagreed with Freud's emphasis on the sexual instincts, and on biological determinism as the basis for human behaviour. In contrast to this, he believed in social determinism, and in the influence of family and environmental factors in shaping the individual's behaviour. The following is a summary of the main areas in which Adler has made significant contributions:

◆ the development of personality and family position
◆ the inferiority complex
◆ style of life
◆ social interest

The development of personality and family position

An important departure from traditional Freudian theory concerned Adler's emphasis on the relationship between children and parents, and his focus on sibling relationships, and ordinal position within the family. Freud did address the parent/child relationship, but only in so far as it affected the development of sexuality and the resolution (or otherwise) of the Oedipus complex. Adler's focus was much more comprehensive than this, and encompassed other variables, including family size and the way in which parents relate to individual children. Adler's interpretation of what he termed the 'so-called Oedipus complex' is that it occurs when the family is too insular and lacking in healthy relationships outside the home (Adler, 1931). In other words, victims of the Oedipus complex are, in Adler's view, people who have been constrained by the family in a way which inhibits the development of maturity and social skills. The Oedipus complex is, therefore, adapted by Adler to explain certain kinds of anti-social and selfish behaviour, and it is this shift away from the original, and much more specifically sexual definition, which marks the different between Freud's views and the ideas expressed by Adler. Certain experiences within the family, and the position of each member within the group, could produce, according to Adler, unique problems for the individual. Distorted goals and life styles can also result from the influence of these factors. Adler described several formative childhood influences which he believed were important in determining later adult behaviour, including illness and physical disadvantage, neglect, lack of affection and spoiling.

EXERCISE — Family Position

In groups of three to four, discuss your individual family positions and say how you think these positions have affected you. Are there any differences, for example, between those who are first, second or only children?

CASE STUDY — Tony

Tony, by his own admission, had never wanted for anything in his life. Then, at fifty-three years of age, he found himself widowed, alone and unable to cope. He was the only child of older parents who had never believed they would actually have a child, and he had received a great deal of attention throughout his childhood, much of it pleasant but some of it oppressive too. When his wife died, Tony felt that he would not be able to manage. and he became resentful that other people were unwilling to help him more. Tony's wife had continued where his parents left off, so his home life had been comfortable, even indulged. It took some time, and a great deal of support, before he was able to function in an autonomous way. Tony's experiences in childhood had not prepared him for certain aspects of adult responsibility. He received bereavement counselling, and over a period of time was able to see that he would, in fact, be capable of coping, once the acute trauma of his bereavement had diminished. This realisation was not achieved without a great deal of effort on Tony's part. One of the factors which helped him was an interest in his own past experience, and an ability to look critically at outdated assumptions and beliefs. It should be added that the Adlerian approach is one which may not be suitable for all bereaved clients, a factor which is discussed at the end of this chapter.

The Inferiority Complex

In Adlerian terms, sexual impulses are not accorded the central position which they hold in Freudian theory. As far as Adler was concerned, sexual problems represent another aspect of what he called the 'inferiority complex' (Adler, 1931). People who confine themselves to the family, with little or no outside contact, are bound to lack healthy sexual and relationship interests. A sense of inferiority follows, therefore, and in adult life such people tend to strive for superiority through attachment to others they can dominate. Adler described many other factors in family life which can produce feelings of inferiority for the individual. A belief that one is not intellectually inclined could, for example, lead to feelings of inferiority, and a person whose home environment is impoverished in any way, is liable to feel inferior as well. Indeed Adler believed that inferiority feelings are inevitable in childhood, since children are small, weak and subject to adults and their whims. It was the ways in which people deal with feelings of inferiority which interested Adler. *Compensation* is the term which he used to describe the mechanism whereby people strive for recognition or superiority (Adler, 1927). The desire to compensate is seen as a healthy one, since it motivates people to achieve their potential. When people are unable to develop successful compensation, an inferiority complex follows. Adler believed that all of us strive for superiority in some area of our lives, and it is this striving which moves us towards achievement and perfection.

Style of life

Adler believed that each person develops a strategy for living, and that this *life style* as he called it, is firmly established by about the age of five years (Adler, 1931). The strategy which each person adopts is designed to cope with feelings of inferiority, and may take the form of artistic or intellectual achievement, for example. Other, less positive, strategies are also sometimes used however. One example is the kind of superiority which some people achieve through bullying or domination of others. Others may seek superiority through illness, an approach which serves two purposes – on the one hand, the child who is ill receives a great deal of attention, while on the other hand the illness can be used as a weapon to control others. The idea of life styles is one which features in other theoretical approaches to counselling – Transactional Analysis, which we shall consider in Chapter 7, is one example.

> ### ⬭ **EXERCISE** ⬎ — Lifestyle
>
> Working individually, try to remember when you first decided what it was you were good at and wanted to do. What were the factors which prompted you to choose a particular life style in the Adlerian sense? Then discuss your recollections with other group members.

Social interest

The concept of *social interest* is an important one in Adlerian theory. The foundation for social interest in nurtured within the family, and encompasses an interest in and a feeling for others. Again we see the contrast with Freudian theory, which pays little attention to this human predisposition and need. Altruism is another way of describing this specific Adlerian concept, and it indicates a radical shift in perspective from the orthodox psychoanalytic position. People are, according to Adler, much more than a mass of conflicting biological needs. There are people, however, who because of early experiences do not develop social interests, and the price they pay for their isolation is unhappiness and neurosis. Adler's view about social interest and involvment is, in fact, a very pertinent one today. We are increasingly aware of the problems which isolated people have, and social workers, nurses and care workers generally are constantly in touch with many of these people. The elderly population is a good example of one section of society which is acutely affected by this problem. Many of the people who seek counselling are also frequently isolated and lonely.

The position of women

We have seen that Adler did not give sexual impulses a central role in his theory of human development. The experiences of men and women were, however, of great interest to him, and he used the term *masculine protest* to describe an attitude which he felt was manifest in many aspects of male and female behaviour. This attitude takes the form of chauvinism and macho behaviour in men, while it may be seen in aggressive and resentful behaviour in women. Adler did not subscribe to the notion that men are in any way inherently superior, and he was concerned to point out that most relationship problems were, in fact, caused by this very attitude. To Adler, male dominance was not a 'natural thing' (Adler, 1927). In this respect his work antipated many later psychodynamic theories.

Counselling skills

All the basic skills which have been described in earlier chapters are used in Adlerian counselling. These include the skills of listening, attending, reflecting content and meaning, asking questions and helping clients to set goals. The following is a summary of other skills and attitudes which are highlighted in the Adlerian approach:

◆ the counsellor/client relationship is a collaborative one in which both people work towards agreed objectives and goals;

◆ the major goal of therapy – for the client – is the achievement of insight. (the major goal for Freud was also client, or patient, insight);

◆ the counsellor is concerned to understand the client's individual experience or *subjective* reality;

◆ the counsellor's role is a teaching one. There is an emphasis on helping clients identify self-defeating behaviour;

◆ there is a corresponding emphasis on helping clients re-educate themselves for positive change;

◆ the Adlerian approach encourages clients to become more socially involved – relationship problems are identified, and clients are encouraged to relate more effectively to others;

◆ interpretation is used in the approach, and is specifically meant to help clients identify faulty attitudes and motivation;

◆ confrontation and encouragement are used in the approach: these are set within the framework of an empathic relationship;

◆ clients are encouraged to pay attention to dreams, to record them and use them as a means of gaining further insight;

◆ transference, while acknowledged, is not regarded as a problem in Adlerian counselling because the relationship between counsellor and client is seen as one based on equality.

Clients who benefit from the approach

There is a wide spectrum of clients who would probably benefit from this approach. These include people with relationship difficulties, those with problems of addiction or substance abuse, and clients who specifically need marriage and family counselling. It can also be used to help older people who – like the client Tony mentioned earlier – have reached a stage in life where change is imperative. Adlerian counselling is applicable to groupwork: in fact Adler and his colleagues used groupwork extensively, especially when he worked in the field of child guidance. Groupwork is the ideal medium for this approach, since the educative or learning aspects of it are reinforced in a groupwork setting. When there are a number of people present to give feedback and encouragement – two important elements in the Adlerian approach – participants are more likely to gain positive results from the experience.

Some limitations

Adlerian counselling may not be suitable for some clients. A person who is in the middle of a crisis situation, for example, will want immediate help and may be unwilling to engage in the process of looking at the past and the influence of family position and relationships. Another potential limitation is concerned with cultural expectations. People from different cultural backgrounds will have different views about family relationships, and may indeed not wish to discuss them as a part of counselling. Although the Adlerian approach is *phenomenological* in the way that the person-centred approach is, the former is nevertheless more directly educative in a way which may not suit everyone. Clients who are in deep distress, or those who are grief stricken, will probably not benefit (initially at least) from this approach. This is not to say that they might not benefit later on, because in many instances they could well do so.

CARL JUNG (1875–1961)

Analytical psychology

Jung was another admirer and one-time associate of Freud. He too became disenchanted with several aspects of Freudian psychoanalysis and broke away from the original school in 1913. The main point of difference between the two men was Freud's definition of sexuality and libido. Although Jung conceded the importance of the sexual instinct, he considered Freud's view of it to be imbalanced. He pointed out, for example, that there are societies and cultures in which the instinct for food and survival must take precedence over sexual interest (Jung, 1957). In addition to this, Jung's theory of libido is more wide-ranging than Freud's and is invested with spiritual, mystical and, above all, creative meaning. His theory of personality has a much wider base, and in this sense his approach to psychoanalysis is quite different from the orthodox position. Another important difference between Freud and Jung is the kind of clinical experience they both had. Freud had worked with patients who suffered from neuroses, whereas Jung's experience was largely with schizophrenics. Jung may have developed his interest in symbolism as a result of his work in this area, although he probably drew on other sources including archaeology, religion, astrology and Eastern philosophy. Like Adler, Jung was a qualified doctor and psychiatrist. His branch of psychoanalysis is called analytical psychology. The following is a summary of his most important contributions:

◆ Personality structure
◆ Archetypes
◆ Ego orientations or personality types
◆ Symbolism and dreams

Personality structure

Jung formulated his own version of personality structure and divided it into three basic components. These components are the *ego*, the *personal unconscious* and the *collective unconscious*. The ego is the conscious part of the self, and is made up of thoughts and feelings, perceptions and memories. In this sense, the ego is the centre of awareness and is similar to Freud's Ego. In contrast to this, the personal unconscious is that area of personality which contains forgotten and repressed material which can, however, be made conscious without great difficulty. It is the third part of Jung's personality structure, the idea of collective unconscious, which is the most radical and innovative in terms of theory and which sets Jung apart from any other thinker in the field. In Jung's view the collective unconscious is common to all of us and is the foundation of what people in ancient times referred to as the 'sympathy of all things' (Jung, 1961). By this Jung appeared to mean that each person has an area of mental functioning which is shared by all of humankind. The collective unconscious is, therefore, impersonal in a sense, and contains universal elements which are of significance to all of us. Every society has, according to Jung, collective convictions and problems which affect each person in the group (Jung, 1957). The cumulative experience of our ancestors is contained within the collective unconscious and dates back millions of years in time. This knowledge acts as a guide and is essential for our survival.

Archetypes

Archetypes are primordial images which form the structural elements of the collective unconscious. These images present themselves in symbolic form, and though there are many of them Jung described just four in detail. They are as follows: the *persona*, the *anima* and *animus*, the *shadow* and the *self*. The word persona describes that part of ourselves which we present outwards to society. This is an image of how we think we should appear, and it is based on convention and defined largely by the way other people expect us to be. There are certain accepted images of individuals, or groups of people, which are almost universally familiar. In many ways this is similar to stereotyping, but it does serve a purpose in that it gives us a blueprint or formula for viewing people and interpreting their behaviour. Problems arise when we identify too closely with our persona. When we do this, we hide behind the mask and fail to acknowledge the existence of our true selves.

The anima describes the collective image of woman in the male psyche, while the animus describes the image of man in the female. These images have arisen over millions of years, and are derived from contact with and observation of the opposite sex. A symbolic anima image might, for example, take the form of goddess, witch, prostitute or seductress, while the animus might take the form of hero, adventurer or villain.

The shadow is the base, evil or sadistic side of our personality, and accounts for the cruelties which people have inflicted on each other since the beginning of time. In religious terms, the shadow is symbolised by Satan, and in fiction the shadow is seen in many guises. Faust, who made a pact with the devil, is one example, while Dr Jeckyll, who is turned into the evil Mr Hyde, is another (Fontana, 1993).

The self is that image of perfection which prompts us to search for meaning, unity, wholeness and harmony in our lives. According to Jung, religion is one aspect of this search for integration, although there are others (Jung, 1978). Full integration is impossible to achieve before middle age, however, but when it is achieved the individual becomes more balanced, more *whole* and more in tune with all aspects of the personality.

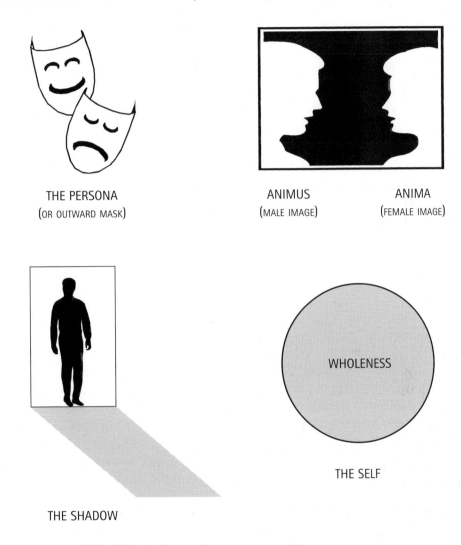

THE PERSONA
(OR OUTWARD MASK)

ANIMUS
(MALE IMAGE)

ANIMA
(FEMALE IMAGE)

WHOLENESS

THE SELF

THE SHADOW

Figure 4.1   *Archetypes of the Collective Unconscious*

CASE STUDY — Carol

Carol was a middle-aged woman whose children had grown up and left home. She was going through the menopause and had suffered several physical and psychological symptoms as a result of it. In addition to her health problems, Carol felt strongly that she lacked a sense of purpose and self-fulfilment. Once her menopausal symptoms were under control, she decided to ask for careers guidance at her local college. As a result of this she was able to go into full-time education and train for the kind of work she wanted to do. During this time she had a series of dreams in which she was swimming strongly, although in reality she couldn't swim at all. Carol was able to interpret her dreams without too much difficulty, and could see that they reflected, in symbolic form, the success and harmony she felt she was currently achieving in her life.

Ego orientations and personality types

The terms *introversion* and *extraversion* refer to personality types, and are used by Jung to describe the way people relate to others and their surroundings. The word introversion is meant to denote a subjective orientation, while the word extraversion denotes an interest in external reality or the outer world. Introverted people are more inclined to be reserved and interested in ideas. The extravert person is likely to be sociable and more involved with others generally. These orientations are not static, however, and may change with life experience. It is also possible that a natural introvert may, for example, live life as an extravert in order to fit in with the expectations of others. The same is true of course for extraverts. One reason personality types are of interest to counsellors is that they highlight the importance of clients' subjective experience and the way other people and reality are perceived by them. It is also important that counsellors know as much as possible about themselves, including the ways in which they relate to others and to the external environment.

< EXERCISE >— Personality types

In groups of two to three, discuss the two ego orientations just described. Say whether you think they help us in our understanding of clients, and whether they also help us in our understanding of ourselves. Then consider your own individual preferences and share these ideas with the group. Are you interested in thoughts, feelings, ideas and imagination, or are you more concerned with your surroundings and with other people? Remember when you do this exercise, that imagination is just as real and valid as external reality. Jung himself pointed out that much of what exists in the outside world existed in someone's imagination first (Jung, 1957).

Symbols and dreams

Jung was interested in symbols, and he believed that they represent complex ideas which cannot be described in any other way since these ideas defy reason (Jung, 1957). Symbols are the language of dreams and often give us clues about important issues in our lives. The following dream illustrates this last point.

< CASE STUDY >— Mrs Edwards

An elderly woman, called Mrs Edwards, was very ill in hospital and recounted this dream to one of the nurses.

In the dream I am near the sea, and I suddenly realise that the water is coming over the sand beneath my feet. I am not worried about this, just mildly excited. At the same time I am filling my old car at a petrol pump which is just there on the sand. There is something about the amount of petrol: I don't seem to need as much as I thought.

The nurse who took care of Mrs Edwards was a student on a counselling skills course. She was interested in the patient's dream and discussed it with her. Mrs Edwards was aware that she was dying, and could therefore make sense of the symbolism in her dream. She could see that the car represented her now almost complete journey through life, while the sea represented the next stage of experience. It should be emphasised that the nurse listened carefully to the patient's account of her dream, and did not at any stage try to impose her own interpretation on it. As a result of her dream, Mrs Edwards was less frightened about the prospect of dying.

EXERCISE — Symbols

Working individually, take a large sheet of paper and divide it into six squares. Draw a symbol in each square to represent the following: Life, Love, Food, Rebirth, Mother, Loss. When you have finished, discuss your images with other members of the group. Are there any which are common to all of you? Where do you think these images came from?

It has often been pointed out that Jung's theories are not 'scientific' and cannot be tested or proven in any way. In spite of this, however, his ideas have had a substantial impact on various theoretical approaches to therapy, including the person-centred approach and the work of Abraham Maslow. Jung was also interested in the whole of a person's life span, and in this sense he differs from Freud. This is not to say that Freud was actively disinterested, but he certainly did not focus extensively on the middle or later years of life. Jung's emphasis on the spiritual dimension is also important, and his description of the process of *individuation* is significant in this respect. This concept is roughly equivalent to Rogers' actualising tendency (to be discussed in the next chapter) and to Maslow's description of self-actualisation needs. In Jungian terms, individuation is a process of psychic development which culminates in the achievement of wholeness or selfhood. He likens it to an evolutionary process, similar to that which takes place biologically in the body (Jung, 1957).

Skills used in Jungian therapy

Although there are Jungian therapists who train exclusively in this approach, it is a model which tends to influence rather than dominate the work of some counsellors. All the basic skills of counselling are used in this approach, along with others listed as follows:

◆ assessment and the establishment of a contract
◆ free Association; the client speaks at his/her own pace

◆ interpretation, including interpretation of dreams and of transference

◆ interpretation, by the therapist, of personal counter-transference feelings: this is seen as an invaluable aid to understanding the client

Jungian therapeutic techniques do vary, but the general aim of therapy is to help clients/patients to become more reflective, self aware and more in harmony with their internal world without losing touch with the realities of the external world. The relationship between client and therapist is a co-operative one. A central goal of therapy is the integration of all aspects of the personality, including the shadow and the anima or animus. Spiritual awareness and problems of later life are also a focus. Clients may be asked to fulfil certain tasks, including reading books, doing homework or drawing to illustrate dreams ('active imagination'). The issue of transference is discussed when it arises. In Jungian therapy, the concept of transference has special meaning, since it is understood that clients project on to the therapist archetypal images, as well as images derived from important early figures like parents.

Clients who benefit from this approach

Clients who are sufficiently interested in a Jungian approach would certainly benefit from it. In its purest form, analytical psychology is time-consuming and requires some dedication and commitment. Some therapists see clients once or twice a week, others may see them as many as five times. Time and cost are important considerations, therefore, for clients. In Jungian terms, therapy is a spiritual quest with the aim of achieving individuation for the client. People who feel alienated or psychologically 'stuck' will probably benefit from the approach. Those who have reached a certain stage of maturity, the middle years for example, may also find it helpful, and problems related to meaninglessness or *disease* in life are addressed in Jungian therapy. Because of its emphasis on creativity as a medium for healing, Jungian therapy tends to attract people who are involved in the arts.

Some limitations

Although trained counsellors often use ideas borrowed from Jungian therapy, there are some limitations in terms of the way it can be used with certain clients. In common with Freudian psychodynamic counselling, it is not suitable for clients in acute crisis situations with presenting and pressing problems which need to be addressed fairly quickly. The approach may also be too intellectual for some clients, and its use in groupwork is limited though this situation may be changing (see Chapter 9). Commitment is essential, and some clients may not be able to give this. Length of time is another consideration, and although some shorter forms of therapy are available, clients may need to travel some distance for this.

EGO PSYCHOLOGY AND OBJECT RELATIONS THEORY

Ego psychology and object relations theory represent two important extensions of Freudian psychology. To some degree, both Adler and Jung had focused attention on certain aspects of both these schools. Adler had, for example, looked at the central role of relationships in shaping personality, and human relationships, especially those which are formed in infancy and childhood, are a fundamental consideration in object relations theory. Although Jung gave special emphasis to the collective unconscious, he is also noted for his descriptions of personality types or ego orientations. In this sense it could be said that he gave a greater role to the ego, a role which is extended and highlighted in the work of the ego psychologists.

EGO PSYCHOLOGY

Heinz Hartmann (1894–1970)

Heinz Hartmann, an American doctor and psychiatrist, is generally considered to be the father of ego psychology. Hartmann did not believe that the ego is simply a mediator in conflicts among id and superego. On the contrary, he took the view that the ego is responsible for many important functions, including perception, language development, attention, planning and learning (Hartmann, 1958). To Hartmann, therefore, the ego is capable of interaction with the external world, and is much more autonomous than Freud's definition of it. Hartmann was influenced by the work of Darwin (as was Freud) and he believed that humans, like animals, are designed to fit into their environment. This ability to fit into the environment is reflected in each person's physical *and* psychological make up. An important point of difference between Hartmann and Freud is that the latter was preoccupied with the physiology and biology of human nature – what Guntrip refers to as the *machinery* of personal life (Guntrip, 1977). Hartmann, on the other hand, shifts attention to the essential quality of the ego and identifies it as the core of human selfhood.

Anna Freud (1895–1982)

In Britain, Anna Freud was the leading proponent of ego psychology. She continued the work of her father, Sigmund Freud, and became a pioneer of child analysis. Her most important work was, however, devoted to the subject of ego defence mechanisms, and in 1936 she wrote *The Ego and the Mechanisms of Defence*. Like Hartmann, Anna Freud attached more importance to the ego or conscious mind. What interested her most was the way in which the ego seeks to defend itself against external as well as internal forces, and she was especially concerned with the ways in which children deal with threats from the external environment. She also stresses the role of environmental conditions and their critical influence on human development. Her work is important because of its focus on the ego rather than on the id. This represents a significant shift of emphasis, as well as a departure from her father's insistence on the supremacy of the id. Although Anna Freud did not abandon interest in the unconscious, and in human sexuality, she did, nevertheless, give a greater role to the ego and in doing so paved the way for further developments in ego psychology and object relations theory.

EXERCISE —— Environmental factors ————

Working in groups of three to four, identify any environmental factors which could have adverse effects on growing children. What are the coping strategies children might use in adverse circumstances? How do children deal with loss, pain, abandonment or threats, for example? Which defence mechanisms are they likely to use?

Implications for counselling

Most ego psychologists subscribe to the belief that the ego is present from birth, and is capable of developing independently of the id. In their view the ego is able to deal with the demands of the environment and is concerned to make sense of experience. Cognitive processes are emphasised in this approach; these include learning, perception, thinking and memory. The importance of the id, and of biological drives, have not been totally rejected by ego psychologists, but the balance has been redressed in favour of a more comprehensive and less mechanistic view of human development and motivation. People are seen as independent and autonomous in a way which conflicts with the orthodox Freudian model. This has implications for counsellors – and for people who work in a helping capacity with others generally – since it emphasises cognitive and thinking processes as well as *emotional* experience. If each person has an autonomous ego which is concerned to make sense of experience, then each person is also capable of change, adjustment and control of the environment when necessary. In simple terms this means that people have the resources to deal with problems, even if they need some help initially in order to identify these resources.

Another important contribution of the ego psychologists – especially in the work of Hartmann – is the idea that pleasure does not depend solely on the satisfaction of instinctual impulses but is, to some extent, dependent on the quality of a person's external environment and the amount of pleasurable experience it provides.

In common with orthodox Freudian theorists, ego psychologists have concentrated their interest on childhood experience, with particular reference to the anxieties of early childhood and the development of psychopathology. The ego is also regarded as a representation of the 'self' and in this respect ego psychology has some affinity with object relations theory, which we shall now consider.

OBJECT RELATIONS THEORY

Object relations theory is concerned with human relationships and the way these are imagined and represented mentally by each individual. This is quite different from a theory of interpersonal relationships where, for example, the focus is on the dynamics of an external relationship rather than on each person's experience of it. In classical Freudian theory, the word *object* refers to a person or thing, towards which an individual's emotional or libidinal drive is directed.

In object relations theory the objects referred to are mental representations of significant people in an individual's life. The word *subject* is frequently used to describe the individual whose mental representations we are concerned to discuss. Object relations theory may also involve consideration of the way in which parts of other people are represented mentally by the subject. Objects (or part objects as they are called) include anatomical divisions of others, such as hands, voices, breasts, hair and so on. Human relationships theory is another, and more straightforward, way of describing this particular psychodynamic approach, although it should be added that the term object relations is probably more precise since it does not denote *interpersonal* relationships in the way that the former tends to. However, the point to be emphasised here is that object relations theory *does* highlight the importance of relationships in human development and motivation. In this respect it differs quite significantly from the Freudian approach with its stress on the gratification of sexual and aggressive drives as the prime motivating forces of all human endeavour. Object relations theory is associated with several important names in psychodynamic theory, including the following:

◆ Melanie Klein
◆ Donald Winnicott
◆ W. R. D. Fairbairn
◆ Harry Guntrip
◆ John Bowlby

Melanie Klein (1882–1960)

Melanie Klein, born in Vienna and the youngest of four children, is generally regarded as the most significant figure in the context of object relations theory. She was a contemporary of Freud, and trained as a psychoanalyst after which she developed a special interest in working with children. During the 1920s and 1930s many prominent analysts, including Freud, left Germany and settled in either England or America. Melanie Klein moved to London where she became acquainted with Anna Freud and other members of the British Psychoanalytical Society. Many in the society came to regard Klein's work as heresy, although Klein herself claimed that she was fundamentally orthodox in the Freudian sense.

In spite of her claim, however, there are certain important points of difference in her work. Perhaps the most striking of her contributions is the emphasis on early infancy, and the primitive phantasies, or unconscious mental images, which a small baby experiences in relation to the mother. Although Freud had certainly been interested in family relationships – especially in the context of the Oedipal drama – he had not focused attention on the mother-infant bond to the extent that Klein eventually did. While continuing to use Freudian terminology and many of his concepts (for example, the structural scheme of id, ego and superego) Klein succeeded in opening up the realm of psychodynamic thinking so that her work has become an evolution as well as a departure from Freudian theory. It is worth mentioning here that Freud never worked directly with children, whereas Klein did.

His experience of children was limited, in the main, to adult recollections, including his own, of early childhood. Klein also pioneered a method of analysing children using play therapy as the basis of her work, which enabled her to communicate directly with them. The most significant contributions of Kleinian theory include the following:

◆ The belief that an infant has, even before birth, some innate, unconscious knowledge of the mother. As Cashdan points out, this is similar to Jung's concept of the collective unconscious (Cashdan, 1988).

◆ The belief in a destructive inner force or death instinct. Klein suggested that the infant is caught up in a struggle between the forces of life and death. Another way of saying this is that human beings are, from the very beginning, striving to deal with feelings of goodness and badness.

◆ The concept of positions, as opposed to developmental stages, in the early life of the infant. Klein agreed with Freud's emphasis on oral, anal and genital preoccupation in early childhood, but she suggested that movement from one to the other is not rigid or definite. The positions which Klein describes are the *paranoid-schizoid position* and the *depressive position.*

◆ The paranoid-schizoid position

The *paranoid-schizoid position* spans the first three or four months of life. After the trauma of birth and the loss of security in the womb, the baby feels persecuted and distressed. The word paranoid is appropriate in this respect, since the idea of attack or imminent attack is very real. During this time the baby encounters its first 'object', which is the mother's breast. According to Klein, this presents an opportunity to vent the strong aggressive feelings which she believes the child to have. Aggression, then, is directed towards the mother's breast which is also the source of sustenance and comfort. Positive feelings are also experienced in relation to the breast, but these are less powerful than those which are disturbing, frightening and destructive.

One way of dealing with the intense and conflicting sensations, and also of making them more manageable, is to 'split' or separate the images one from the other. The baby's inner world is thus divided into good and bad experiences which are kept rigidly apart. This 'splitting' is necessary from the infant's point of view, since it serves to identify the nature of 'goodness' and 'badness' – a distinction which is important if parents and others are to be trusted. Later on, these good and bad sensations become, according to Kleinian theory, the very foundation of feelings about oneself. An infant who is subjected to neglect or cruelty for example, is likely to *introject* or 'take in' negative images about 'self', and these will persist into adult life. It would be impossible, however, to eliminate all frustrating experiences in early life, and fortunately most of these experiences do not cause lasting damage. Episodes of frustration are usually balanced by the love and attention which the mother frequently provides. Problems arise when strong feelings of worthlessness are absorbed early on, with no modifying influence to temper these. A client called Alan recounted the following experience.

I can remember several times in my life when I became very depressed when things did not go the way I wanted them to go. The depression was usually out of all proportion to the incident which triggered it, and I can honestly say that I never really understood why my reactions were so marked and so illogical. I remember once when I entered a drawing competition, and failed to make the grade, I became depressed for a very long time and felt that I was 'no good' and a failure. Even when I became successful in art, I still felt hopeless when I thought about that early rejection. Another time I got depressed for a long period, when a girl I really liked wouldn't go out with me. Again, the depression lasted for ages, and even though – on one level – I knew we weren't really suitable for each other, I felt intensely rejected and worthless.

Alan was unaware of the origin of his depression, but he did identify it as illogical though very real. One possible reason for his feelings concerns his early experience (which he could not remember but which he believed may have had a detrimental effect on the way he regarded himself). He had been neglected and abandoned by his mother, though he was adopted by parents who loved him a great deal. It is important to remember that experiences like these are recorded by the child at an early stage, even before language has developed. This explains why it is impossible for some clients to put into words the nature of their experience, or the reasons for the feelings they have in relation to these. In Alan's case he was baffled by the intensity of his depression, though he knew it was out of proportion to his disappointments. It is quite likely that his exaggerated reactions were prompted by feelings about himself which he had absorbed in early infancy. In his view, he was never good enough or likeable enough to make the grade with other people. Fortunately, he was interested enough to seek help in finding out why he should feel like this.

◆ The depressive position

The second position – the *depressive* – begins at around four months, and continues until the end of the first year. During this time the baby begins to perceive the mother as a whole and separate object in whom both good and bad are simultaneously embodied. This dawning realisation that mother is fallible is a significant step in terms of development and maturity. It does, however, present other problems for the baby at this stage. The intense and aggressive feelings which were first experienced in relation to the mother are now a source of guilt, sadness and anxiety. The person for whom both love and hostility were felt, is now identified as mother. This necessitates some form of *reparation* for the imagined damage and hate which have been directed against her (Klein, 1932). The outcome of this crisis is important for later development, and people who suffer depressive problems in adulthood are said to be fixated at this point. Other problems, related to both positions, include difficulties in forming relationships, low self esteem and inability to make commitments or trust others. In addition, small babies do not possess language, so distress is often registered at a physical level which may lead to psychomatic conditions in later life.

Some difficulties

There are several aspects of Kleinian theory which are often the focus of controversy when students discuss the subject. It is often pointed out that not all babies are breastfed, for example, and of course this is true. However, both object relations theory and psychoanalytic theory use symbolic language and metaphor in order to illustrate complex ideas. A bottle-fed baby cannot make the distinction between a bottle as object, and the breast as object. At that early stage both serve the same function. It is important also to remember that the mental activity Klein referred to is taking place at an unconscious level, and the Kleinian concept of *phantasy* is relevant here. Phantasy describes a different, more primitive kind of mental activity, composed of vague, often frightening images and sensations present long before the development of language. This is a term which is used very specifically in object relations theory and differs from the word 'fantasy', which usually refers to conscious mental activity. The word *projection* is also significant in relation to Kleinian theory, and described the way in which the infant disowns everything which he or she experiences as 'bad'. These disowned parts of the 'self' are then attributed to the 'other'. *Introjection* is another term which Klein used more specifically than Freud, and refers to the process of internalising external material – especially external material relating to the mother. Aspects of the mother are monitored and metabolised in this way.

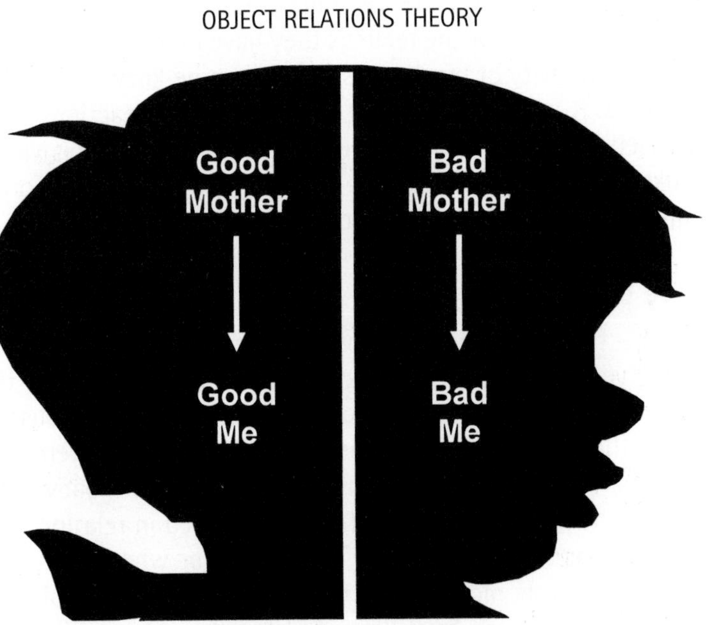

OBJECT RELATIONS THEORY

Figure 4.2 *Transformation of Maternal Images into Images of 'Self'*

Donald Winnicott (1896–1971)

Winnicott was a paediatrician as well as a psychoanalyst. He worked closely with mothers and babies, and was in a very good position to observe infant/mother interaction at first hand. One of Winnicott's most important contributions concerns the concept of *transitional objects* (Winnicott, 1991). These transitional objects include dummies, pieces of cloth, teddy bears, blankets or clothing, all of which are invested with emotional significance by small children. The purpose of these intimate possessions is that they provide comfort and security when a child's mother is absent. Winnicott also highlighted the need for continuity of care in childhood, and stressed the importance of a mother being there when she is needed. He elaborated on this, however, by saying that it was equally important for a mother to give a child space by receding into the background when she is not needed. The position of the father is emphasised too, especially in relation to the necessary and supportive family environment which he needs to help create.

EXERCISE — Transitional objects

Many adults retain their childhood transitional objects, including teddy bears or other toys. Work with a partner and discuss the range of objects which children value in early life. Did you have a transitional object, and if so, what was it? Can you remember what it represented to you and how long you kept it?

CASE STUDY — Loss of a transitional object

A twenty-five year-old client recalled the loss of a blanket which she had valued highly as a small child.

CLIENT: I can't remember what age I was at the time, but I must have been very small. My mother was in hospital and an aunt came to stay. She burned the blanket, she said it was smelly.

COUNSELLOR: She took it from you and burned it?

CLIENT: Yes. She did tell me she was going to do it, but in a way which didn't give me any choice.

COUNSELLOR: So this possession which was valuable to you ... she couldn't see that ...

CLIENT: No, and the thing is that it was smelly. It smelt of my mother. That is why I liked it.

COUNSELLOR: It was a link to your mother who was in hospital, when you couldn't see her.

CLIENT: Not see her, or even know where she was.

COUNSELLOR: And that would have made the blanket very important to you. And it was taken away too when you needed it most.

CLIENT: I've never cried about it until now. In fact, I've never known why it should have been so important. A bit of old blanket, after all. But yes, it was my mother I was trying to hold on to at the time.

EXERCISE — Adult transitional objects

Many adults also have 'substitute' transitional objects which are very important to them. These include the following:

◆ photographs
◆ items of jewellery
◆ special items of clothing
◆ books
◆ cars
◆ furnishings

Can you add anything to this list and say what you think these possessions mean to people? There are other, less healthy transitional objects which people become attached to in adult life. Look at the following list and say what you think these might represent to the people who use, or abuse, them:

◆ cigarettes
◆ alcohol
◆ drugs
◆ food
◆ mobile phones

OTHER VIEWS

Fairbairn (1899–1964)

The other object relationists, including Fairbairn, Guntrip and Bowlby, added their individual ideas to this theoretical approach. Fairbairn, for example, published a series of papers in the 1940s in which he stated that human behaviour is motivated towards the establishment of meaningful human relations. He also emphasised the importance of the mother/child relationship. His special area of interest concerned the nature of dependency, and his description of child development focuses on three phases through which he believed each child would pass. The first stage is *early infantile dependency*, in which the child is psychologically fused with the mother. In the second and last stages, the child becomes gradually more independent, while still remaining (maturely) dependent on the mother. Fairbairn also addresses the subject of ego 'splitting' and divides the infant's inner world into 'good' and 'bad' objects. His system of inner objects is quite complex, and really requires a more detailed study than the scope of this text can provide. However, Fairbairn did believe that abnormal behaviour in later life was the result of extremes of splitting at this vital stage of a child's life.

John Bowlby (1907–1990)

Bowlby also argued that human nature is orientated towards relationships with other people. Like Winnicott and Fairbairn, Bowlby did not subscribe to the Kleinian view that aggression is innate. On the contrary, he believed that human beings only become aggressive when they need to defend themselves against threat. It is on the subject of deprivation, however, that Bowlby has proved to be most controversial. In his view, the infant needs a continuous bond with the mother during the first two years of life. Bowlby believed that the infant/mother bond – or infant/mother substitute bond – is different from all other relationships. Changes from one mother figure to another during the first three or four years would, in his opinion, result in emotional problems for young children (Bowlby, 1990). Even though these views have been disputed by other child care experts, they have, nevertheless, had an influence on child care practice generally. This is especially true in areas like social work where it became usual to keep children at home if possible, rather than have them cared for by numerous other people. Hospitals also developed more flexible attitudes to visiting in mother and baby units, and maternity hospitals stopped separating babies from their mothers. Feminists have not been entirely happy with Bowlby's views, since they place enormous pressure on women to supply the continuous and uninterrupted care which he felt was necessary. There is resentment, too, that women are almost invariably blamed when children do develop emotional problems.

Object relations theory and its influence on therapy and counselling

Object relations theory has had an enormous influence on the therapy movement generally. The emphasis on human relationships and their central importance for everyone, is one aspect of the theory which has changed the way clients and their problems are viewed. This means that transference issues, for example, are highlighted and regarded in a specific way. Countertransference is especially significant here, since the emotional response which the therapist has in relation to the client, will invariably give some clue about the nature of the client's interpersonal problems with others. A client whose mother had been depressed, for example, might very well respond to the counsellor as if she too were depressed. Children of depressed mothers quickly learn that their needs will not be met and that parental requirements are more important than theirs. This attitude will probably be transferred to the counsellor at some stage. The following is an example of this situation.

CASE STUDY — Veronica

Veronica came into counselling because of the eating problems she had suffered for many years. She had difficulty in expressing her feelings, and in many ways could hardly identify what her feelings were. Veronica's mother had been depressed for as long as she could remember. Each time she expressed any negative feeling as a child, Veronica's mother became upset and anxious. When her mother was 'down' however, Veronica had to console her. This pattern meant that the client had difficulty in separating herself from her mother, and indeed she had no clear idea who her 'self' was. The anorexia which had plagued her for so long was an attempt to regain some control of her relationship with her mother. She described it as a form of control herself, and added that it was one way of getting her mother to notice her and show concern. During sessions Veronica seemed concerned to please the counsellor at all costs, and this was something which the counsellor was able to sense and experience at an emotional level. The task for the counsellor was to highlight the client's relationship style, and then help her to establish a firmer sense of who she was. This was done over time, and involved encouraging the client to identify and express her feelings and needs in a supportive and accepting environment.

The therapeutic relationship

While object relationists do accept the concept of the Oedipus complex, they differ from Freudian theorists in that they stress the importance of the overall relationship with parents, rather than the purely sexual dimension. Bowlby took the view that therapy could provide the kind of secure corrective experience which clients may have lacked in childhood. In therapy, clients are given the opportunity to find themselves and to explore other, more healthy, ways of relating to other people. The therapist becomes another, temporary, attachment figure who should prove to be more reliable, more consistent and certainly more accepting than parents may have been in the past. There is a definite switch of focus, in object relations theory, from the father to the mother, and this is both problematic and reassuring from a feminist viewpoint, since it stresses the role of the mother while highlighting the problems which can arise in relation to maternal provision.

Other important contributions: Erik Erikson

There have been many other contributions to psychodynamic theory which come under various headings, including *Self Psychology, Interpersonal Psychology, Neo-Freudians, Freudian Revisionists and Feminist Revisionists* to name just a few. These theories are too numerous and detailed to include in this chapter, but the work of Erik Erikson certainly merits some consideration. He is sometimes referred to as an interpersonal psychologist, while at other times he is called a self psychologist. It may even have been appropriate to include his approach along with the work of the ego psychologists mentioned earlier in this chapter. In any case, Erikson's theory of psychosocial development, which he first described in 1950, is an approach which has certainly directed attention to difficulties which can arise throughout the human lifespan. Erikson had little formal education to begin with, but having met both Freud and his daughter Anna, he became interested in psychoanalysis and completed his training in it. After this he became a full member of the Vienna Psychoanalytic Institute. Erikson, who was Jewish, was forced to emigrate to the United States when Hitler rose to power, and in 1950 he published his book *Childhood and Society*, which laid out his theory of psychosocial development. The following is a summary of these stages:

Erikson's psychosocial stages of development

◆ Trust versus Mistrust: from birth to one year

- ◆ Autonomy versus Shame and Doubt: from one to three years
- ◆ Initiative versus Guilt: from three years to six years
- ◆ Industry versus Inferiority: from six to twelve years
- ◆ Identity versus Role Confusion: from twelve to twenty years
- ◆ Intimacy versus Isolation: from twenty to thirty-five years
- ◆ Generativity versus Stagnation: from thirty-five to sixty-five years
- ◆ Ego Integrity versus Despair: from sixty-five years until death

(adapted from Erikson 1995)

Erikson asserted that Freud's stages of psychological development are paralleled by psychosocial stages. At each of these stages the individual is presented with a crisis and the way in which this is dealt with will determine the person's capacity to cope successfully with the next stage. Although Erikson, like Freud, highlights the concept of stages, there are some vital differences. In the first place, Erikson places more emphasis on the *social* aspects. There is also more focus on problems of adolescence and old age. This has implications for people who work with the elderly, for example, and indeed for counselling, where the concerns of the elderly have not always been adequately addressed. Helpers who work with the elderly, whether in a residential or hospital setting, should be encouraged to read Erikson's work. His theoretical approach will illuminate some of the special difficulties elderly clients have.

Skills which are central to the theoretical approaches outlined in this chapter

The theoretical approaches described here are important because of the way they increase our knowledge of human development, and the problems which can arise at different stages of life. All the basic counselling skills, including listening, reflecting and asking questions, are used by counsellors who are familiar with, and influenced by, any of these theories. However, the relationship between counsellor and client is perhaps more important than anything else, since it is relationships which are generally highlighted by all these theorists. This is referred to in the section entitled 'The Therapeutic Relationship' in this chapter on page 92. A central aim of therapy is to help clients become aware of their inner emotional world, in the hope that their capacity to relate to others will improve as a result. The skills identified in Chapter 4 are also applicable to the approaches described here. Transference and countertransference are of special significance, especially in the context of object relations theory. The skills of *interpretation*, especially in helping clients connect the past to the present, is a central skill of Kleinian therapy, but this should be used very gradually, and with great sensitivity.

Clients who benefit from these approaches

Because of the emphasis on early development (central to all these theories) and the focus on problems which can arise in later life (implicit in psychosocial theory) the approaches are certainly applicable to clients who experience relationship problems. Many people have

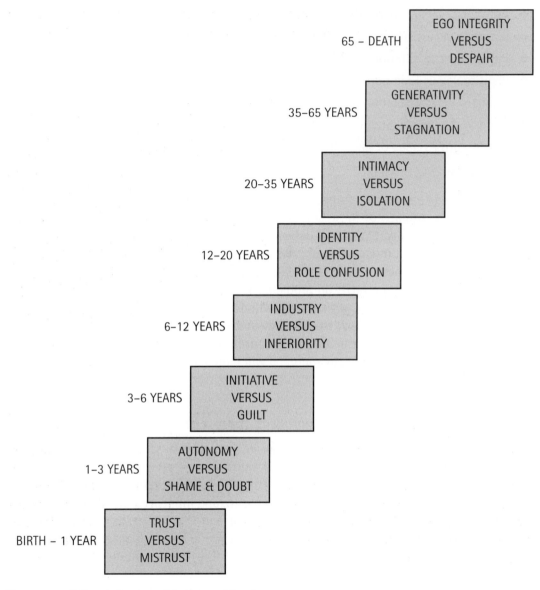

Figure 4.3   *Erikson's Psychosocial Stages of Development*

the experience of repeated difficulty in relating to others, and attempts to resolve these problems alone are often doomed to failure. This is because of the unconscious components which frequently operate in the perpetuation of interpersonal problems. In such instances, outside help may be needed in order to locate the source of current difficulties. Disturbed relationships in childhood are often re-enacted in the present, and clients who become aware of this repetition are likely to benefit from these approaches. Clients who experience crises at different life stages are also likely to be helped by a therapist who is familiar with (among others) Erikson's psychosocial stages of development. People who feel *stuck* and unable to make sense of their lives may also benefit through working from this perspective.

It should be added, however, that it is not enough for a counsellor or therapist – or indeed any other helper – to be well versed in theory. Practical experience of working with people in a caring capacity is essential too.

Some limitations

Clients who are in an *immediate* crisis situation may not wish to examine relationships straight away, at least not until the critical phase of the crisis is over. Clients who are in the acute stages of addiction will hardly benefit either, although they may well come to understand their problems more fully once they have committed themselves to change. Working with problems which stem from the past requires some dedication, as well as a capacity for reflection and self awareness. Clients who are deeply depressed may not have these capabilities, though, once again, they might well re-discover them once the depression is lifted. Any form of long-term psychodynamic therapy can be expensive for clients, and in some parts of the country it may simply not be available. This last point highlights a major limitation in relation to those clients who cannot afford long-term therapies. Many of these people might welcome the chance to have counselling or therapy if such services were offered to them. On the other hand, practical and environmental problems often need to be addressed first if any other kind of help is to be of value.

SUMMARY

In this chapter we considered the psychodynamic theories which have evolved from the Freudian approach. These include the work of Adler, Jung, the ego psychologists, the object relationists and the psychosocial stages described by Erik Erikson. The counselling skills which are central to these approaches were also discussed, with special reference to the importance of the therapeutic relationship in all of them. We considered the influence of different theories on counselling and stressed the need for adequate training – both practical and theoretical – for students who wish to develop their skills in these areas. The usefulness of each theoretical model was discussed, along with consideration of their limitations for certain clients.

REFERENCES

Adler, A. (1931) *What Life Could Mean To You*. Oxford: Oneworld Books (1992).

Adler, A. (1927) *Understanding Human Nature*. Oxford: Oneworld Books (1992).

Bowlby, J. (1990) *Child Care And The Growth Of Love*. London: Penguin.

Cashdan, S. (1988) *Object Relations Therapy – Using the Relationship*. New York: W. W. Norton & Co.

Erikson, E. (1995)　　　　　*Childhood and Society.* London: Vintage.

Fairbairn, W. R. D. (1954)　　*An Object Relations Theory Of Personality.* New York: Basic Books.

Fontana, D. (1993)　　　　　*The Secret Language Of Symbols.* London: Pavillion.

Freud, A. (1936)　　　　　　*The Ego And The Mechanisms Of Defence.* London: Hogarth Press (1937).

Guntrip, H. (1977)　　　　　*Psychoanalytic Theory, Therapy and the Self.* London: Basic Books Inc.

Hartmann, H. (1958)　　　　*Ego Psychology and the Problem of Adaption.* New York: International Universities Press.

Jung, C. G. (1961)　　　　　*Memories, Dreams, Reflections* (ed. Jaffe A.). London: Fontana Press (1995).

Jung, C. G. (1957)　　　　　*C. G. Jung Speaking: Interviews and Encounters* (eds McGuire, W. & Hull, R. F. C.). London: Picador (1980).

Jung, C. G. (1978)　　　　　*Man and his Symbols.* London: Picador.

Klein, M. (1932)　　　　　　*The Psychoanalysis of Children.* London: Hogarth Press.

Singer, J. (1995)　　　　　　*Boundaries of the Soul.* Dorset: Prism Press.

Winnicott, D. W. (1991)　　　*Playing and Reality.* London: Routledge.

FURTHER READING

Fordham, F. (1991)　　　　　　　*An Introduction to Jung's Psychology.* London: Penguin Books.

Hughes, J. M. (1990)　　　　　　*Re-shaping The Psychoanalytic Domain.* California: University of California Press.

Mitchell, S. A. & Black, M. J. (1995)　*Freud And Beyond.* New York: Basic Books.

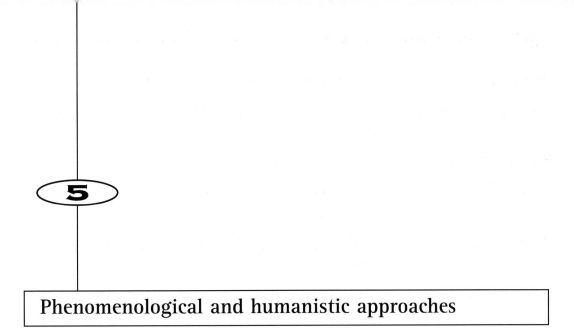

Phenomenological and humanistic approaches

INTRODUCTION

In the last two chapters we looked at a range of psychodynamic theories, all of which are related, either directly or indirectly, to Freudian psychoanalysis. This chapter is concerned with some approaches which differ quite substantially from those already described. These approaches are often defined as *phenomenological* or *humanistic*, two terms which in fact mean slightly different things. The word phenomenology refers to the way in which each person experiences reality, while the word humanism is meant to denote an attitude towards people.

The attitude enshrined in humanism is essentially positive: it identifies and upholds the basic goodness of each individual, while at the same time recognising the adverse circumstances which may obscure these qualities at various stages throughout life. This is in sharp contrast to the theory of personality described by Freud, a description which stresses drives, instincts, impulses and urges as motivating factors in human behaviour. In Freudian terms, people are governed by powerful forces originating in the unconscious, and it is these forces which compel them to act in certain ways.

Both Adler and Jung moved away from this deterministic position, and in doing so highlighted other aspects of experience they felt could explain human development and behaviour. In Jung's paradigm, however, unconscious forces are still very much in evidence, although his overall view of people is more extensive, with a focus on adult dilemmas not found in Freudian theory.

The work of the ego psychologists indicates another, fairly radical, shift of emphasis, with their focus on thinking and other cognitive processes they believed to be present at an early stage of life.

In this and the next chapter we shall discuss those models of counselling which have been directly influenced by phenomenology and humanism, and we shall also consider the concepts and skills integral to each theoretical approach. The following are the theories and counselling models to be dealt with in this chapter:

◆ Rogers and the person-centred approach

◆ Maslow and humanism

◆ The existential approach

THE MEANING OF PHENOMENOLOGY IN RELATION TO CLIENTS

The word phenomenology stems from philosophy, and refers to the way in which individuals perceive and interpret events. Another way of stating this is to say that it is not actual events which cause people to behave in certain ways; instead it is each person's unique perception of these events which determines their responses. The recognition that each individual is influenced by their own phenomenal field is important in the counselling context, since it underlines the need to discover clients' individual perceptions if we are to be effective in helping them. It is not enough for counsellors to simply assume that clients will respond in specific ways to certain situations or events. On the contrary, counsellors need to be aware of the vast spectrum of individual difference which have to be taken into consideration in relation to the experiences which clients describe. The following example gives some idea of the way in which two people, who appear to have exactly the same experience, record entirely different perceptions of it.

CASE STUDY — Recalling an accident

A client called Rosaleen came into counselling because she had been in a car accident, and had suffered post traumatic shock as a result of it. Her sister had also been in the accident, and though neither of them sustained physical injury, both had taken time off work in order to recover. The difference between the two sister's responses lay in the fact that whereas Rosaleen felt immensely traumatised by it, her sister seemed relatively unaffected by events, although she did concede that it had been frightening initially. Rosaleen's sister took some time off work on the advice of her doctor, but she was anxious to get back to the office just as soon as she could. The resilience of her sister caused some difficulty for Rosaleen, because it made her feel guilty about her own response. She discussed her feelings with the counsellor.

CLIENT: I worry that people might think I'm putting it on. Jean [her sister] never seemed to look back. I'm sure people must think it's all in my mind.

COUNSELLOR: That's obviously something that concerns you a great deal ... the idea that people will think badly of you.

CLIENT: Well yes ... Because of the way she is. There is such a contrast in our reactions.

COUNSELLOR: Yet people do react in very different ways ... to a whole lot of situations.

CLIENT: People can't be the same in the way they see things ... I suppose I'm ... maybe weaker in some ways. But its hard to believe we were both in the same car.

COUNSELLOR: With different experience of the accident ...

CLIENT: Yes, and different reactions too.

COUNSELLOR: In the way that people tend to respond quite differently to things.

The counsellor who worked with Rosaleen was concerned to help her explore all the circumstances of the accident. She also wanted to show the client that her individual response to the accident was a perfectly valid one, even though it differed from her sister's response. To do this the counsellor listened carefully to the client's story, and encouraged her to voice all the worries she felt in relation to other people's views. It might have been tempting for the counsellor to *reassure* the client that she was not, in fact, weaker than her sister, but such reassurance would have been misplaced. From a purely person-centred perspective, it is important to remember that client's feelings are real to them, and the counsellor's task is to stay within the client's *internal frame of reference* – a concept which we shall discuss later in this chapter.

However, there are several other points which are significant in relation to this client's experience and the counselling which she received. The first point concerns the two quite different responses to the car accident, a difference which can be explained in various ways. In the first place, no two people are ever entirely the same, even when they are sisters. In the second place, Rosaleen's life experience just prior to the accident was very different from her sister's. It emerged in the course of counselling that the client had recently been ill with glandular fever, a fact which compounded the trauma of the accident. Rosaleen's relationship with her parents was different too. She had never felt as close to them as her sister seemed to be, and just before the car accident she had argued with her father. All these factors combined to influence the client's unique response to the accident, but once she identified them she felt less guilty about any differences in relation to her sister.

ROGERS AND THE PERSON-CENTRED APPROACH

Carl Rogers (1902–1987) is the psychologist whose name is synonymous with the person-centred approach to counselling. Rogers, who was born in Illinois, studied theology, but later switched to psychology and received his Ph.D. in 1931. During this time he worked at a child guidance clinic in New York, and published *Clinical Treatment of the Problem Child* in 1939. After this he was invited to become a member of the Psychology Department at

Ohio State University. However, it was not until 1945 that Rogers' counselling theory and practice began to make an impact. Throughout his academic career he also gained a great deal of experience as a therapist and continued to write books, including *Client-Centred Therapy* (1951) and *On Becoming a Person* (1961). The emphasis in all of Rogers' later writing is on the importance of each person as the architect of individual destiny. Rogers firmly believed that everyone has sufficient innate resources to deal effectively with life, and with the various problems which living entails. These innate resources are, according to the person-centred approach, sometimes obscured, forgotten or even denied, but they are, nevertheless, always present with the potential for development and growth (Rogers, 1951). The impact of Rogers' work is best understood when we contrast it with the world of therapy which had existed before he contributed to it. Freudian theory and practice was in the ascendant, especially in America where many prominent psychoanalysts had been forced to emigrate from Europe. The other major influence which had dominated North American psychology was the behaviourist school (which we shall discuss in a later chapter) with its emphasis on learned behaviour as the basis of human personality development. Against the background of these major influences Rogers' insistence on the uniqueness of the individual, and the individual's innate tendency towards growth and wholeness, certainly seemed to represent a much more optimistic and positive viewpoint.

Rogers' concept of 'self'

Rogers believed that people will, if given the right conditions and opportunities, move towards autonomy and self direction (Rogers, 1961). The concept of *'self'* is important here, and refers to the 'I' or the 'me' part of each person. According to Rogers, personality development can be viewed in terms of *self-concept* development, which in turn depends on the individual's interaction with other people and the environment. Rogers did not describe stages or phases of development in the way that Freud, Klein or Erikson did, for example. Instead, he concentrated on the individual's perception of self, as well as the ways in which these perceptions are coloured by other people's evaluations and expectations. From a very early age children seek to please their parents who are, after all, the most important people in the world to them. Each person's self-concept is acquired in this way, and is continually reinforced throughout life as a result of ongoing interaction with others. The small child sees herself reflected in the attitudes expressed by parents and other important people, and when very little love and a great deal of criticism are received, a negative self-concept is bound to follow.

The real or organismic self

No matter how traumatic or negative the environment, however, there remains within each person a core or inner self which is never entirely obliterated. Each person's innate tendency towards growth is always present, and with the right conditions will emerge and flourish. Clients in counselling often refer to their 'real' selves, and they often do so with regret and sadness, especially when they have never before been given the opportunity to identify and express their authentic needs and feelings. The following client had such an experience.

─ CASE STUDY ─ Identification of needs ──────────────────

A sixty-five year-old woman received counselling while in hospital suffering from cancer. She talked to a nurse who was specially trained to help people in her position, and during their exchanges she referred to her early years as a mother bringing up a large family.

MRS COOPER: I did most of it without too much thought ... I certainly didn't have much time to think about myself!

NURSE: You were just too busy attending to everyone else ...

MRS COOPER: It's a funny thing [pause] ... when I was younger ... As a child, I didn't get time to think of myself either. It probably sounds like self pity, but it's only now that I'm ill ... that I've thought about it seriously.

NURSE: So it feels like self pity because you've never had anyone else ask you or seem interested before.

MRS COOPER: That's it. I even feel guilty talking to you ... that I might be wasting your time.

NURSE: You are not wasting my time. I am interested in what you say, and it's your time too.

MRS COOPER: Well I would ... [hesitates] I would like to start some studies ... if it's not too late.

NURSE: It's not too late to do that. Maybe we could talk about what it is you would like to do?

MRS COOPER: Well when I was in my teens, I loved poetry and literature ... Then I just got away from all that ... and then marriage and the family intervened [laughs]. The thing is, my husband will think I've gone crackers.

NURSE: But you don't think you're crackers.

MRS COOPER: No.

NURSE: So now, you're really sure of what you really want to do, and that's a very important start.

MRS COOPER: It is, I don't think I would be happy at this late stage ... if I didn't try to do something for myself ... for the real me.

───

It is often very difficult for people to identify the real self, and many people go through life convinced that the outer self, or self-concept, is the only reality they have. It sometimes takes a crisis to highlight the 'falseness' of the image which someone presents to the world. At times like these, a person may finally get in touch with the feelings, needs and ambitions which had previously been obscured. The fact that people do frequently alter their lifestyles in the wake of a crisis, illustrates this last point. Clients also come into counselling in the aftermath of a crisis, or indeed even in the middle of one, and it is at these times that they often sense some intimation of disquiet or regret which prompt them to pursue the idea of change. When there is a vast difference between a person's self-concept and the real self, problems of identity will certainly arise at some stage of life.

The actualising tendency

The term 'actualising tendency' is one which Rogers uses to describe the human urge to grow, to develop and to reach maximum potential (Rogers, 1996). It is the actualising tendency which is responsible for every aspect of human endeavour and achievement, and in some ways it resembles the Freudian concept of libido or life force. The actualising tendency is present from birth onwards, and is not just concerned with achievement in a narrow sense. On the contrary, it has a much broader meaning than this, and describes the holistic development of all aspects of the person, including the spiritual, emotional, physical and creative dimensions. The concept of the actualising tendency is important in the counselling context, since it underlines the idea that clients have the necessary resources for dealing effectively with their own problems. If counsellors truly believe this, they are likely to value and respect the people they help. It is sometime the case that a client's actualising tendency is, for whatever reason, temporarily stultified, but when the right conditions are present in counselling there is a strong possibility that the client's inner resources will be located.

The core conditions

Rogers identified certain core conditions which he believed to be necessary if clients are to make progress in counselling (Rogers, 1951). These conditions really describe counsellor qualities and attitudes which, if present, will facilitate change and growth within the client. Among the most important of these attitudes is the counsellor's ability to *understand the client's feelings.* Another is *respect for the client,* while a third is described as *counsellor congruence or genuineness.* In summary then, the Rogerian core conditions are as follows:

◆ empathy
◆ unconditional positive regard
◆ congruence or genuineness

◆ Empathy

The word empathy describes the counsellor's ability to understand the client at a deep level. This is something which is, of course, much easier said than done, since it involves an awareness of what it is that the client is actually experiencing. Earlier in this chapter we discussed the word phenomenology and looked at the different ways in which people experience reality. Rogers refers to the *internal frame of reference* to denote the client's unique experience of personal problems. The task for the counsellor is to get inside the client's frame of reference. If this is not achieved, then no real point of contact is made between counsellor and client.

Rogers uses the term *external frame of reference* to describe this lack of understanding and contact (Rogers, 1951). When a counsellor perceives the client from an external frame of reference, there is little chance that the client's view will be clearly heard. It is important for clients (if they are to benefit from counselling) to sense that their individual experience of 'self' and reality is appreciated by the helper. However, this does not mean that counsellors should experience the emotions a client experiences. In fact, it would be counter-productive for the counsellor to become emotionally involved in this way, and would certainly upset the balance of the relationship between client and counsellor. In order to stay within the client's internal frame of reference, it is necessary for the counsellor to listen carefully to what is being conveyed (both verbally and non-verbally) at every stage of counselling. The counsellor needs to imagine and appreciate what it is like to actually be the client, and this appreciation of the client's experience then needs to be conveyed to him.

<< EXERCISE >> —— Sympathy and empathy ——————————

In groups of three to four, discuss the words sympathy and empathy and say what you think the differences between them are. Are there any circumstances (outside of counselling) when it might be appropriate to use sympathy? What are the skills which are necessary in order to convey empathy to clients?

◆ Unconditional positive regard

The need for positive regard is present in all human beings from infancy onwards. This need is so imperative that small children will do almost anything in order to achieve it. People need love, acceptance, respect and warmth from others, but unfortunately these attitudes and feelings are often only given conditionally. Parents may say, or imply, that their love is given on condition that certain criteria are met, and when this happens it is impossible for children to feel valued for themselves alone. Many people who come into counselling have experienced these parental attitudes, attitudes which are often re-inforced throughout life. Rogers believed that counsellors should convey unconditional positive regard or *warmth* towards clients if they are to feel understood and accepted. This means that clients are valued without any conditions attached, even when they experience themselves as negative, bad, frightened or abnormal (Rogers, 1996).

Acceptance implies a non-judgmental approach by counsellors, and it also means caring in a non-possessive way. Rogers refers to a counsellor attitude of positive regard which clearly acknowledges the client as a separate person, a person entitled to his own feelings and experiences (Rogers, 1996). When attitudes of warmth and acceptance are present in counselling, clients are likely to accept themselves, and become more confident in their own abilities to cope. However, acceptance of clients does not mean that counsellors must like or approve of everything they do. What is important is that counsellors are able to separate their own views from those of clients. The values and views held by clients may differ quite dramatically from those held by individual counsellors, but even in these circumstances clients deserve (and should receive) respect and positive regard from the people in whom they confide.

EXERCISE — Conveying warmth

Working individually, think of a time in your life when you received warmth and positive regard from someone who helped you. How did this person convey these attitudes to you? What were the circumstances in which you needed help? How did these attitudes help you at the time?

◆ Congruence or genuineness

The words genuineness and congruence describe another quality which Rogers believed counsellors should possess. This quality is one of sincerity, authenticity and honesty within the counselling relationship. In order to be congruent with clients, counsellors need to *be themselves*, without any pretence or façade (Rogers, 1996). This means, of course, that counsellors need to *know* themselves first. In the absence of self knowledge, it would be totally impossible to develop attitudes of openness and honesty in relation to clients. Honesty and openness do not imply uninhibited frankness, however, though when empathy and positive respect are also present in the relationship, uninhibited frankness is hardly likely to be a problem. A very important aspect of counsellor genuineness is that it acts as a model for clients who may find it difficult to be open and genuine themselves. Appropriate and genuine responses to clients are always prompted by real concern for them. The following exchange between counsellor and client illustrates this point.

CASE STUDY — Being open

CLIENT: My boyfriend has been really nasty at times ... Sometimes, well last week he did go over the top and lashed out.

COUNSELLOR: He hit you ...

CLIENT: Well maybe I asked for it [smiles] ... we both have tempers. He's OK really.

COUNSELLOR: I'm a bit puzzled by what you've just said ... and the way you said it. You smiled when you mentioned that he hit you.

CLIENT: It's just that I don't want to make too much of it ... or blame him for everything.

COUNSELLOR: But still the situation makes you tense and nervous?

CLIENT: It does. I want to understand it ... him I mean. He wasn't always like that. He used to be so kind to me [starts to cry].

During this exchange with the client, the counsellor identified what she regarded as a discrepancy between what the client said and the way that she said it. The counsellor was confused by this discrepancy, so she referred to it in order to clarify things for herself. However, she was also concerned to encourage the client to look more closely at her own feelings, including those feelings which she had expressed and those which were unexpressed. Being open with the client was the counsellor's way of indicating that she wanted to understand her more fully. This openness also helped the client to understand herself at a deeper level.

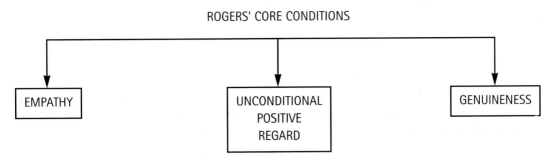

Figure 5.1 *Rogers' core conditions*

The counselling relationship

We have already seen that the person-centred counselling relationship is based on respect for the client, on the establishment of an empathic bond, and on a willingness on the counsellor's part to be open and genuine with the client. In addition to these qualities, however, there is also an emphasis on facilitating each client's growth or self actualisation. Self actualisation can only be achieved when the core conditions described above are present in the relationship. The counselling skills which were discussed at the beginning of this book are used in the person-centred approach, and are necessary for the development of a therapeutic relationship between counsellor and client. These skills include:

◆ active listening
◆ responding to clients through reflection of feeling and content
◆ paraphrasing and summarising
◆ asking open questions
◆ responding appropriately to silence and client non-verbal communication

Helpers who are interested in the person-centred approach must be prepared to encounter clients on a basis of equality and to work with them in a non-directive way. In many respects, the person-centred approach is characterised more by what the counsellor does not do, rather than what he does do. Offering psychodynamic-style interpretation, for example, is avoided and the main focus of therapy is on clarification of the client's feelings so that identification of the 'real' self is facilitated. In conclusion then, the essence of person-centred counselling lies in the attitudes and values of the helper, and this, of course, necessitates proper training and adequate supervision for those counsellors who wish to use it.

Transference

Although the possibility of transference reactions is acknowledged in the person-centred approach, these reactions are certainly never highlighted or encouraged by the counsellor. A basic aim of the model is to help clients achieve independence and autonomy, so the projection of dependent feelings on to the counsellor would be viewed as a hindrance to this. The attitude of the counsellor to the client should indicate acceptance and equality from the outset, and this in turn will lessen the possibility that transference reactions are sustained. It should be added that unconscious motivation is also acknowledged in the person-centred approach, but counsellors do not focus directly on it, nor do they ask clients to work with dreams. However, since the model is person-centred, clients who wish to look at dreams or the unconscious are at liberty to do so.

Clients who benefit from this approach

The person-centred approach has wide application within the helping professions, the voluntary sector, human relations training, groupwork, education and institutional settings where the goals are to foster good interpersonal skills and respect for others. This last group would include, among others, churches, businesses, youth organisations and crisis centres. In the context of therapy and counselling, the person-centred approach is suitable for use with clients in the first stages of crisis. Later on, however, clients in crisis may need a more directive approach to help them cope with the practical and long-term aspects of their problems.

From a feminist viewpoint, person-centred counselling has significant advantages over some of the other models. This is because it encourages clients to consider and identify their own feelings and needs, something which many women (especially those who have spent a lifetime caring for others) may never have been able to do before. Clients who have been bereaved should also benefit from the person-centred approach, since one of the things which bereaved people appear to need most of all is validation of their individual responses to loss. People with relationship difficulties should derive some advantage from working with a counsellor who gives them respect, understanding and openness which they may not have experienced in every day life.

The principles of the person-centred approach have been applied to a variety of therapeutic situations including marriage counselling and family therapy. It is worth mentioning here that many support groups work by extending the core conditions to its members. Alcoholics Anonymous is a case in point, and is a good example of the therapeutic effects of respect, understanding and openness for people who want to change. Telephone counselling is another therapeutic medium through which Rogerian attitudes can be extended to clients, especially to those clients who are in deep distress or crisis.

Perhaps one of the greatest strengths of the person-centred approach is that it is often the training of choice for health professionals and others who are affiliated to hospitals, health centres and other organisations where people work together to help clients and patients. However, other models can be used in these settings too.

Some limitations

Person-centred counselling may not be helpful for clients whose problems are linked to deeply repressed unconscious traumas, memories or conflicts. Such clients are more likely to benefit from a psychodynamic approach, although the core conditions which Rogers described would certainly work effectively if combined with appropriate skills and techniques from the psychodynamic model. People with depression, addiction, phobias or eating disorders are also likely to derive more help from other models, and some of these will be discussed in later chapters. Clients with alcohol problems may need more support than the kind which can be offered through individual counselling. Even when the core conditions are present in a one-to-one therapeutic situation, they may not be enough to sustain change for clients with some addictive problems. Another important factor to remember here, is that deeply distressed and addicted clients (providing they are committed to change) may respond more positively in the presence of others with similar problems. Clients with repetitive thoughts and obsessions will probably gain more from a cognitive behavioural approach to counselling, and there is no doubt that certain clients benefit from a more directive and structured approach generally. Cultural difference can also influence the way clients perceive those who help them, and person-centred counsellors may sometimes be seen as passive or lacking in initiative by people who value advice or other more directive forms of intervention.

EXERCISE — The core conditions

Working in pairs, look at the following relationships. How might Rogers' core conditions facilitate the work of the helper or manager in each case? Discuss a range of issues which might crop up in these relationships.

◆ Nurse / Patient
◆ Doctor / Patient
◆ Lecturer / Student
◆ Social Worker / Client
◆ Priest / Parishioner
◆ Manager / Worker
◆ Mother / Child
◆ Health Visitor / New Mother
◆ Elderly Resident / Care Assistant
◆ Youth Worker / Teenager

MASLOW AND HUMANISM

Implicit in Carl Rogers' person-centred theory is the idea that people have free choice and the ability to exercise control over their destinies. This is essentially an optimistic view of human nature, since the emphasis is on each person's creativity and strengths, rather than on weaknesses or failings. Such ideas are common currency in phenomenology and humanism, and it is this latter concept which has come to be associated with the work of Abraham Maslow.

Maslow (1908–1970) was born in Brooklyn, New York, where, as the only Jewish boy in the neighbourhood, he had a difficult and lonely childhood. His parents were keen that he should become a lawyer, but Maslow studied psychology instead and obtained his Ph.D. in 1934 from the University of Wisconsin. Maslow's first interest was in behavioural psychology, but over a period of time he became dissatisfied with this approach since it did not, in his view, adequately explain what it is that motivates people and gives meaning and purpose to human life.

Although he did acknowledge the existence of evil and destructiveness in the world, Maslow's primary focus of interest was in the more positive aspects of human experience. His views about aggression and hostility in children clearly show him as an advocate of humanism, since he highlights the fact that although children have been represented in a negative way throughout the history of psychoanalysis and psychology, there is a remarkable lack of scientific evidence to support this view (Maslow, 1970). Maslow refers to the selfishness and innate destructiveness of which children have been accused, and proposes instead that other, more positive, qualities are just as evident, especially in those children who are loved and respected by parents. This last point is important, because it stresses the central role of parents in the child's psychological development.

In addition to this, Maslow's focus on the formative influence of parents, and on the need for positive emotional experiences in childhood, links his ideas to those of several other theorists whose work we have already considered. Relationships, and the need to be valued by others, is a central theme of Maslow's work, and in this respect it echoes the approaches described by Adler, the ego psychologists and, of course, the work of the object relationists. Although Maslow did not set up his own specific school of therapy or counselling, his influence on all contemporary approaches is considerable. In addition to this, he was certainly interested in ideas connected with therapy generally, and he was concerned to offer his own views about the helping process and the factors which facilitate or hinder it. The following is an outline of some of the contributions which Maslow has made to our understanding of human motivation, personality and the nature of the helping relationship.

- the hierarchy of needs
- self actualisation
- self actualising people
- psychotherapy and other helping relationships

The hierarchy of needs

Maslow formulated a theory of human motivation and outlined a series of innate needs which, he believed, gave purpose, satisfaction and meaning to life. These are arranged in a hierarchy, and include physiological, safety, relationship , esteem and finally self actualisation needs (see Figure 5.2 below). Obviously those needs which are lowest in the hierarchy (hunger, thirst and so on) must be satisfied before any of the higher needs can be pursued. People living in circumstances of extreme poverty and privation, for example in certain third world countries, are unlikely to be concerned about self actualisation needs when they are preoccupied with basic survival instead. This is not to say that people in these situations do not have the higher order needs which Maslow refers to. Indeed, their self actualisation needs may simply take a different form. To produce healthy children and to live on through one's family is one example of a self actualisation variant which might well be applicable to different cultural groups. Maslow was, however, concerned to describe what he perceived to be the needs of people in America and other western cultures. In any case, the point which he wished to make was that satisfaction of basic needs is generally important if people are to be motivated to achieve those higher up.

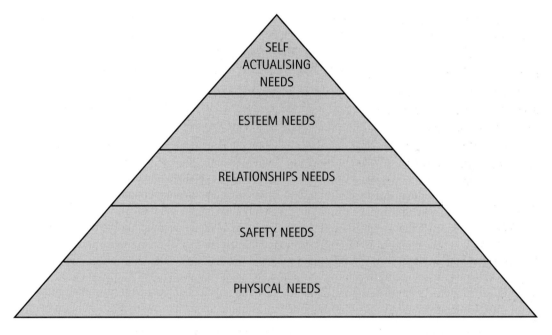

Figure 5.2   *Maslow's Hierarchy of Needs*

> **EXERCISE** — Needs
>
> Working in groups of two or three, discuss Maslow's hierarchy and say how you think a deficit in any of these needs might affect others in the hierarchy. What are the possible effects on those children whose safety and relationship needs are neglected, for example? How do neglected relationship needs affect an individual's chances of achieving full potential, educationally or otherwise?

Self actualisation

A significant point of difference between the work of Maslow and most of the other theorists we have discussed in this book (apart from Rogers), concerns the emphasis which Maslow places on psychological health and well being. Many of the others, including Freud, were preoccupied with illness or pathology. This switch of attention from illness to health is evident in Maslow's concept of self actualisation. A truly healthy person is one who is capable of developing innate talents and achieving maximum potential. In Maslow's opinion it is impossible to understand human motivation if we look at it purely from a psychotherapist's viewpoint (Maslow, 1970). Any motivational theory, he believed, must consider the ultimate potential of healthy people, as well as looking at the problems and neurosis of those who are ill or debilitated. True understanding of human development and motivation is only achieved through a more comprehensive and holistic appraisal of humanity generally.

These ideas, expressed by Maslow, are similar to those articulated by Rogers, and indeed the self actualization concept is common to both of them. This is not surprising since both men worked together, and in 1962 helped to found the Association for Humanistic Psychology along with other colleagues (including Rollo May, whose ideas we shall consider later in this chapter). Maslow's definition of self actualisation is that it is a process whereby each person strives to become what they are actually *intended* to be. People with specific talents like art or music, for example, must develop these abilities in order to be psychologically healthy and at peace with themselves. The need to self actualise may of course take various forms. These include excellence in sport, success in parenting or caring for others, or indeed achievement in any other personal area which has meaning and importance for the individual. One difficulty which clients often express in counselling is that they are unable (for various reasons) to develop the skills and natural talents which they feel they possess. This inability to fulfil potential can cause a great deal of suffering. Some aspects of this problem have been discussed in the section which deals with Rogers' concept of self actualisation.

Self actualising people

Maslow studied a group of healthy people in order to identify their characteristics, and to show how they differed from other, less fulfilled individuals. Maslow described his work as 'a study of psychological health' (Maslow, 1970) and selected his subjects from his personal acquaintances and friends. However, he also included a selection of public and historical figures whom he studied through biography. Among these were the philosopher Spinoza, Aldous Huxley, Eleanor Roosevelt, Abraham Lincoln and Thomas Jefferson. Maslow's study points to several significant characteristics which his selected group of people seemed to share. These include the following:

◆ the ability to perceive reality clearly – this includes the ability to judge people and situations accurately

◆ acceptance of self and of others – this includes acceptance of one's own human nature, without too much concern about personal shortcomings

- ◆ spontaneity in thinking and behaviour, as well as a sense of humour
- ◆ the capacity to be problem-centred rather than ego-centred – this means the ability to look outside oneself to the problems of the wider world
- ◆ a quality of detachment and an ability to be self-contained when alone
- ◆ the ability to resist cultural pressure without being deliberately unconventional
- ◆ the capacity to appreciate the good things of life, including everyday experience
- ◆ the capacity for heightened or transcendent experience
- ◆ interest in social issues and the welfare of other people
- ◆ the ability to form deep and satisfying relationships, although these may not be as numerous as those of other people
- ◆ originality and creativity and a willingness to experiment with new ideas
- ◆ the ability to tolerate uncertainty

The significance of Maslow's work in relation to counselling

Maslow is at pains to point out that the self actualising people he describes, are, in fact, also imperfect in many ways (Maslow, 1970). Many of these people are, he says, sometimes boring, silly, vain, irritating, depressed and quite capable of losing their tempers. These qualifications are helpful, since they indicate that Maslow's self actualising people are, after all, human. Without these qualifications it would be impossible to look at the qualities listed without feeling slightly intimidated by them. However, what Maslow proposes is that there are people who are capable of developing their potential to a very high level, while at the same time remaining essentially human. This, of course, highlights the point that a great many people never achieve this kind of development, and there are others whose innate potential is inhibited for a variety of reasons.

There are many reasons for this kind of inhibition, and clients who come into counselling frequently exhibit some, if not all, of them. If we look at the list again, it becomes clear that the qualities Maslow describes are strikingly absent when people are distressed or emotionally upset, as clients often are. Distressed people find it very difficult to tolerate uncertainty, for example, and they frequently lack spontaneity, creativity and a sense of humour. Perceptions of reality may be very distorted, while acceptance of self and others may be lacking too. Autonomy and self reliance are easily impaired when problems seem insurmountable, and relationships with other people, if not actually the cause of difficulties, may well suffer as a result of them. Appreciation of life experience is often diminished, and there may be no interest whatever in wider social issues. Transcendent or heightened experiences, which are in any case associated with psychological well-being, may be non-existent during a time of crisis or emotional upheaval. However, implicit in the work of both Maslow and Rogers, is the belief that people can be helped to overcome their problems, so that some measure of self actualisation can then be achieved.

One way of helping people to realise their potential is through a truly therapeutic relationship, although this is by no means the only route to self actualisation. In the next section we shall look at some of the experiences and relationships Maslow believed could help people achieve maximum development and fulfillment.

Psychotherapy and other helping relationships

Maslow points out that psychotherapy has always existed in one form or another (Maslow, 1970). These forms of helping include shamanic healing, religion, the physician and the wise man or woman within communities. Common to all these is the ability to help people heal themselves, and Maslow outlines what he believes to be the therapeutic character-istics of such relationships. He also highlights the point that many people are helped by untrained workers who are, nevertheless, often effective in the work they do. These untrained therapists may include nurses, teachers, social workers, psychology graduates and so on. This is not to suggest that counselling and therapy training is superfluous; on the contrary, it should encourage us to look more closely at those skills and natural abilities which effective helpers do possess. We have already considered some of these qualities in Chapter 1, but it is worth reflecting on Maslow's views in this context. In Maslow's opinion, clients appear to make more progress when the following factors are present in the helping relationship:

◆ the helper shows real interest in the client, and a willingness to listen
◆ there is obvious concern for the client
◆ the helper's efforts are clear to the client, which assures the client that he is worthwhile as a person
◆ the client feels safe and protected, and feelings of vulnerability and anxiety are diminished
◆ there is an absence of judgmentalism on the helper's part
◆ the helper is accepting
◆ the helper is frank and encouraging
◆ the helper is kind
◆ the client perceives that the helper is on her side
◆ the client feels the helper's respect

(Maslow 1970)

The helper's attitude

Maslow makes the further point that it is not what is said or done by the helper which seems to make the difference. Rather, it is the presence of certain helper attitudes, uncon-sciously transmitted, which appear to encourage clients in the process of therapy. There is a close similarity between attitudes discussed by Maslow, and those proposed by Carl Rogers in the person-centred approach. If we analyse Maslow's attitudes, we can see that he refers to Rogerian-type conditions which are implicit in terms such as interest, frank-ness, accepting, respect, concern and absence of judgmentalism. Furthermore, the idea that the helper's partiality should be perceived by the client is one which clearly echoes the Rogerian concepts of unconditional positive regard and empathy.

The only skill which is mentioned by Maslow is that of listening. This also ties in with Rogers' view that therapeutic progress results from the relationship between client and counsellor, and may have little to do with any 'verbal interchange' which takes places between them (Rogers, 1951). There are clear implications here for counselling and counsellor training, since it illustrates the importance of self-development and self-awareness as prerequisites for admission to, and progress through, any training programme. Counselling skills can certainly be learned, but personal characteristics are much more difficult to acquire and sustain.

Therapeutic life experience

It is worth pointing out once again, that therapy and counselling are not the only helping activities which facilitate change when people are in crisis or emotional distress. Maslow was at pains to remind us that helpers from diverse backgrounds are also effective in these situations, and some of these have been mentioned in this section. As well as the helping relationships discussed, however, Maslow also points to the fact that certain life experiences are in themselves therapeutic. Among these are the experiences of friendship, good marriage relationships, education, job satisfaction, overcoming difficulties, creative activities and family security (Maslow, 1970). However, Maslow does concede that certain clients, especially those who suffer from long-term and intractable problems, need the kind of help which can only be given by trained therapists or counsellors. Furthermore, he is concerned to point out that it should be possible to extend such training to those untrained professionals who already work effectively with clients. This is, in fact, what is currently happening in many areas like social work, nursing, occupational therapy, teaching and church ministry.

THE EXISTENTIAL APPROACH

The existential approach is one which, more than any other, stresses the individual's capacity for freedom and choice. Earlier in this chapter we noted that psychology had, until the middle of the twentieth century, been dominated by two major ideological traditions. The first tradition was that of scientific behaviourism, while the second was Freudian psychoanalysis. Gradually, however, a new tradition began to emerge whose adherents, including Maslow and Rogers, were convinced of the limitations of behaviourism and psychoanalysis. Behaviourism, with its view that freedom is restricted by social and cultural conditioning was, in their opinion, a limiting one. By the same token, the psychodynamic explanation that unconscious forces also restrict the ability to make free and informed choices, seemed limiting too. Behaviourism and psychoanalysis did not, as far as Rogers and Maslow were concerned, acknowledge important human qualities like creativity, self actualisation, self awareness, love, choice and freedom. By 1950 they had established a new force in psychology which they called *humanistic psychology*, and which later became known as the *third force*. Many of the ideas expressed by Rogers and his colleagues are similar to those enshrined in the existential approach to therapy. These include the qualities already mentioned, as well as an emphasis on the need to value the unique and subjective world of the individual.

Further background information

Existential psychotherapy is influenced by the philosophy of existentialism. This philosophical tradition is, in turn, associated with the work of Kierkegaard, Nietzsche, Heidegger and Sartre. These philosophers were concerned with the meaning of human existence, and with the concepts of free will, subjectivity and the nature of individual experience. It can be seen, therefore, that humanism and existentialism are closely allied.

In the context of psychotherapy, the existential tradition was established first in Europe, and later emerged as a theoretical approach among certain psychologists in America. In both countries, however, existentialism and psychotherapy were seen to have much in common since, as Rollo May says, 'both are concerned with individuals in crisis' (May, 1986). Important figures in the European therapy movement include Luwig Binswanger and Medard Boss, while those within the American tradition include Rollo May, Otto Rank, Karen Horney, Eric Fromm and Irvin Yalom. Within the European therapy framework, the emphasis has always been on the need to face anxiety, uncertainty and the prospect of death. In contrast to this, the humanistic/existential approach in America tended to be more concerned with the development of human potential, self awareness, a holistic view of the person, the importance of meaningful relationships and the possibility of transcendent experience. Irvin Yalom points out that many of the humanistic and anti-intellectual trends in America were effective in causing a split between humanistic psychology and members of the academic community who were interested in existential issues (Yalom, 1980). Although the humanistic and existential approaches in therapy are now identified as separate, they still have much in common, and humanistic psychologists like Rogers and Maslow retain their association with existential concerns.

The British existential psychiatrist R. D. Laing was another significant contributor to this field, although his focus was somewhat different in the sense that his special interest was schizophrenia. Laing's views were controversial and include, among other things, the belief that people who suffer from severe mental illness may have a clearer grasp of reality than those who do not (Laing and Esterson, 1990). Orthodox psychiatry takes the contrasting view that schizophrenia sufferers are at odds with reality.

The existential view of the person

In contrast to Freudian theory which is based on the premise that human behaviour is determined by unconscious forces and past events, the existential approach assumes that people are free and responsible for their own choices and behaviour. According to the theory, human beings cannot, therefore, escape the necessity of dealing with, and making sense of, existence. The unconscious is certainly acknowledged in existential psychotherapy, but it is not viewed as a repository of culturally unacceptable impulses and desires. On the contrary, it is seen as an often neglected area of human potential which, according to Rollo May, is sometimes difficult for people to actualise (May, 1986). From an existential perspective, fear and anxiety result from an individual's awareness, albeit at an unconscious level, that such potential exists, and is being neglected. Anxiety or *angst* is an important concept in existentialism, and refers to feelings of dread which are associated with extreme threat. Perhaps the greatest threat of all is contained in the knowledge that we are indeed free, and if this is true then it follows that we are entirely responsible for how we act and what we do. The first principle of existentialism is, in the words of Jean-Paul Sartre, that 'man is nothing else but that which he makes of himself' (Sartre, 1958; 1973). This may seem like a bleak proposition, but it is a fundamental idea in existentialism.

Application to clients

A central goal of the existential approach to therapy is to help clients become more personally *authentic*. Authenticity is a prominent theme in the approach, and refers to the individual's ability to define who they are and what they feel. The person who is not authentic accepts, without question, that it is others, including family, culture and religion who are responsible for this important definition. Alienation is seen as a direct result of allowing oneself to become separated or detached from personal experience.

The four dimensions of human experience are the physical, the social, the psychological and the spiritual (Avery, 1996). Physical experiences includes our relationship with all our basic needs, and with the world around us. Our social experience encompasses our relationships with other people, while our psychological experience is concerned with the way we feel about ourselves and our personal identity. Finally, experience of spirituality describes the individual's relationship with the transcendent, the mysterious or the unknown.

It can be seen from these descriptions that clients do indeed have frequent problems in relation to them. Many clients recount experiences of alienation in relation to themselves and to others, while others may feel despair and loss of purpose in life. Isolation and meaninglessness are further problems described by some clients, and these are among the themes highlighted in the existential approach to therapy. Certain significant life stages may also precipitate crises which prompt clients to seek help through psychotherapy and counselling. These include adolescence, mid-life and old age. Other experiences, including bereavement, redundancy or divorce may also act as catalysts for change or a search for meaning. The following case study illustrates this last point.

CASE STUDY — Searching for meaning

Mrs Jackson, who was in her early fifties, took early retirement to care for her elderly mother who was dying. Her relationship with her mother had not been good in childhood, and she hoped to redress the balance by forming a more positive bond before her mother died. Mrs Jackson had spent her life caring for other people, and although she was an intelligent woman she had not gained any satisfactory educational qualifications. She lived with her husband who had separate interests, while their three children, who were now adult, had left home. Mrs Jackson found the task of nursing her mother much more difficult than she had expected, and the relationship between them did not improve. After her mother's death, Mrs Jackson moved house with her husband, and six months later their new home was burgled. She described her experiences to the counsellor.

CLIENT: About two days after the break-in I started to cry and couldn't stop. It was just as if I could take no more ... first my mother ... then the move, and now this.

COUNSELLOR: It all seemed like too much ... and in such a short space of time.

CLIENT: Yes that's right. And then ... and then to make it all the more frightening, I found that I didn't believe in anything any more.

COUNSELLOR: You lost your faith.

CLIENT: I always relied on my faith in God's will. But how can God have willed this? [starts to cry].

COUNSELLOR: That is a frightening thought for you ... To have lost so much, and now to feel that you have lost your faith too.

CLIENT: It's terrifying ... I can't tell you what it's like. It's as if the ground has opened up beneath my feet. I don't know where I am any more.

COUNSELLOR: Nothing makes sense to you any more ...

Counselling skills

The counsellor worked with this client in order to help her explore her feelings in relation to her mother's death. Mrs Jackson experienced despair and outrage following the break-in at her new home, and these feelings were also discussed in counselling. After several sessions it became clear that other disturbing issues were causing concern for the client; she was preoccupied with ideas of her own mortality, and with her inability to accept her mother's uncaring attitude towards her when she was a child. She also felt guilty that she had not helped her mother more, and she blamed her husband for his inability to support her emotionally after her mother's death. The counsellor was concerned to understand the client's subjective experience or *internal frame of reference*, and in this respect the existential approach is similar to Rogers' person-centred view of the helper's role in therapy.

In order to achieve these goals, the counsellor used the skills of active listening, clarification of content and meaning, asking relevant and open questions, and encouraging the client to look more closely at all her beliefs, both past and present, so that she could identify her own inner feelings in relation to these. Mrs Jackson had, throughout her whole life, behaved in a way which she thought would please her mother. In fact this had never worked, and now that her mother was dead Mrs Jackson realised that she was free to be herself. This realisation of freedom was, in itself, frightening, and it was this fear which presented her with the greatest challenge for the future. A fundamental task for the counsellor was to encourage the client to listen to *herself*, an exercise which many clients find difficult to undertake. There are no specific techniques in existential therapy, but counsellors who are interested in it need to be skilled in a wide variety of techniques which may be used in other approaches. Existential psychotherapy is often referred to as an intellectual approach, so a knowledge of philosophy, psychology and literature are prerequisites for anyone wishing to undertake training in it. The *person* of the therapist is important as well and in this approach, more than in any other, self knowledge is essential.

EXERCISE —— Ultimate concerns

In existential therapy certain important human concerns are highlighted. Yalom (1980) lists four 'ultimate concerns' which, according to him, underlie all existential conflict. These four major concerns are as follows:

◆ death

◆ freedom

◆ isolation

◆ meaninglessness

(Yalom, 1980)

Working in groups of three to four, discuss these concerns, focusing on the ways in which each of them may cause tension and conflict at different stages of life. How might a helper's inability to confront these issues at a personal level affect the therapeutic relationship?

EXERCISE —— Individual freedom

We tend to think of freedom as a wholly positive concept. However, in the existential sense, freedom has a different meaning, and refers to the absence of external structure or security. Working individually, consider the ways in which freedom of choice can cause problems for clients in counselling. What are the factors which inhibit the individual's ability to choose. Afterwards, discuss your views with members of the class group.

Relationship between counsellor and client

The therapeutic relationship is the most important factor in the existential approach. It is much more significant than skills or techniques, and although this probably applies to any theoretical model it is certainly emphasised by practitioners of existential therapy. Irvin Yalom, for example, refers to the relationship between client and counsellor and observes that a positive encounter is 'positively related to therapy outcome' (Yalom, 1980). From both the client's and counsellor's point of view therefore, the relationship should be *real* and *genuine*, which means that the counsellor should concentrate on the quality of the encounter, rather than on the application of techniques which are designed to help solve specific problems. In order to establish this kind of rapport with the client, the counsellor must first be *interested* in him, and in the story he wishes to communicate. This means being receptive and sensitive to all aspects of the client's communication, both verbal and non-verbal.

Rigid theoretical views tend to work against this kind of receptiveness and interest, since they frequently inhibit real person-to-person contact. The experience of true human contact and understanding is what benefits clients most, and it is this experience which often convinces them that they are indeed valuable and capable of sustaining, not just this relationship, but others as well.

The concept of transference is addressed within the existential approach, but any preoccupation with it, or specific focus on it, is viewed as an impediment to an authentic person-to-person encounter. If transference becomes an issue between client and counsellor, there is little chance that an authentic relationship will develop. Counsellors can easily hide themselves by focusing on transference, and when this happens the therapeutic relationship is demeaned, because it becomes nothing more than a vehicle for interpreting the client's difficulties in relation to other people.

Clients who benefit from this approach

The existential approach to therapy is appropriate for clients who are concerned about meaning, or loss of meaning, in their own lives. Attitudes to personal freedom, and to isolation and loneliness, are also addressed from this theoretical perspective. There are a great many clients who do, in fact, suffer from feelings of isolation and alienation, and some of them would probably benefit from this approach. The experience of isolation and separateness arouses immense anxiety, and such experience may indeed be what Eric Fromm calls the 'source of all anxiety' (Fromm, 1995). If clients are to benefit from the approach, however, they need to be committed to it. The aim of existential therapy is not to change people, but to help them accept themselves and to face, with courage, the major issues which concern them and brought them for help in the first place. Clients who are interested in personal growth and greater self awareness should also benefit from this perspective. Some of the basic concepts of existential therapy can be integrated with other models, and in this way problems relating to developmental crises, for example, may be addressed. These include issues which arise at certain times, or at certain stages of life. Adolescence, mid-life, retirement, redundancy, illness, disability and divorce are examples. Existential therapy is also sometimes applicable in brief therapy, and in certain crisis situations once the initial trauma phase is over. It can be used in either individual or groupwork settings, and is appropriate for use in family therapy too.

Some limitations

Perhaps the most important point to make about existential therapy is that counsellors who use it need to be well trained in the approach. They also need to understand (and be interested in) the philosophical tradition from which it stems. All this takes time, and training may not be available in some areas. A corollary of this is that clients who seek therapy need to be interested in, and committed to, the approach if it is to be of any use to them. The language of existentialism is fairly esoteric, and some clients may not understand it. Existential concepts tend to appeal to people with an intellectual rather than an emotional orientation, and the kinds of insight which it offers may not be useful for clients who are very disturbed or mentally ill. A question arises as to whether the existential perspective is suitable for clients from certain minority groups or for people who are very poor. Some of these clients may not feel that they have the kind of choices which the approach suggests we all do, and certain environmental factors may limit choice even further.

SUMMARY

In this chapter we looked at the concepts of phenomenology and humanism in relation to counselling. The person-centred and existential approaches were discussed in some detail, and the work and influence of Maslow was highlighted. Comparisons were made between these models and the psychodynamic approaches which were dealt with in the previous chapters. The nature and importance of the therapeutic relationship was highlighted within each approach, and the concept of transference and its various interpretations was also considered. The need for adequate training in all aspects of theory and practice was emphasised, and some of the difficulties inherent in the existential perspective were outlined. We looked at the benefits and limitations of each theoretical model, and considered the counselling situation in which each might work effectively for clients.

REFERENCES

Avery, B. (1996)   *Principles of Psychotherapy.* London: Thorsons.

Fromm, E. (1995)   *The Art of Loving.* London: Thorsons.

Laing, R. D. &   *Sanity, Madness and the Family.* London: Penguin Books.
Esterson, A. (1990)

Laing, R. D. (1990)   *The Politics of Experience and The Bird of Paradise.* London: Penguin Books.

Maslow, A. (1970)   *Motivation and Personality,* 3rd edition. New York: Harper Collins.

May, R. (1986)   *The Discovery of Being.* New York: W. W. Norton & Co.

Rogers, C. (1951)   *Client-Centred Therapy.* London: Constable (1991).

Rogers, C. (1961)   *On Becoming a Person.* London: Constable (1993).

Rogers, C. (1996)   *The Carl Rogers Reader* (ed.). Kirschenbaum, H. &
                             Henderson, V. London, Constable (1996).

Sartre, J. P. (1985, 1973)   'Freedom and Bad Faith', in Hanfling, O. (ed.). *Life and
                             Meaning.* London: Blackwell (1987).

Yalom, I. (1980)   *Existential Psychotherapy.* U.S.A.: Basic Books (1980).

FURTHER READING

Mearns, D. (1994)   *Developing Person-Centred Counselling.* London: Sage
                               Publications.

van Deurzen-Smith, E. (1987)   *Existential Counselling In Practice.* London: Sage
                               Publications.

Yalom, I. (1991)   *Love's Executioner And Other Tales Of Psychotherapy,*
                               London: Penguin Books.

6

Gestalt therapy and psychodrama

INTRODUCTION

This chapter is concerned with two models of therapy which are often referred to as *active* and *experiential*. Although quite different in many respects, both Gestalt therapy and psychodrama share the premise that people come to know themselves best through direct experience. There are other similarities between these two approaches, including the fact that both are commonly practised in groupwork settings, with individual clients receiving individual therapy within the group. In addition, Gestalt therapy and psychodrama are sometimes described as *existential* models, and both stem from the *humanistic* tradition which places a great deal of emphasis on the uniqueness and creative potential of each person.

However, the differences between Gestalt therapy and psychodrama are also quite marked. Perhaps the most significant point of difference between the two models concerns the way in which group members participate, for example, in psychodrama, but remain as spectators in Gestalt groupwork. Fritz Perls, one of the founders of Gestalt therapy, highlighted this difference in his book *Gestalt Therapy Verbatim* (1992). Here he referred to the practice of group participation in psychodrama, and made it quite clear that this was a faulty method (Perls, 1992). These and other criticisms will be discussed in this chapter, along with details of the various skills, techniques and underlying philosophies which are peculiar to each model.

GESTALT THERAPY: FRITZ PERLS (1893–1970)

Fritz Perls, a founder of Gestalt therapy, was trained as both psychiatrist and psychoanalyst in pre-war Germany. His wife, Laura, a psychologist, was jointly responsible for developing the work, although Fritz Perls' name is commonly associated with it. Perhaps one of the reasons for this credit imbalance is that Fritz Perls was a charismatic, dynamic and colourful character, who certainly impressed those people who met him. He appears to have cultivated a particular style which blended well with the mood of his time. M. V. Miller, who met him in 1966, describes, in his introduction to *Gestalt Therapy Verbatim*, Perls' style and impact in the way he conducted his seminars (Miller, 1988). From this description, it is quite clear that Perls did not conform to the image of the classical Freudian psychoanalyst which is, in fact, what he actually was. Perls, who was born in Berlin, completed his psychoanalytic training and was influenced by many of the major figures in psychoanalysis, including Freud, Rank and Jung. Like many other Jewish psychoanalysts, he was forced to leave Germany when the Nazis rose to power and in 1933 he went to Johannesburg with his wife Laura. Later, in 1946, he left South Africa and emigrated to New York. From here he made his way to California. Perls was influenced by all the trends of the 1960s, including the peace movement, flower power, drugs, meditation, Zen Buddhism and the cult of the guru. There is no doubt that this was an exciting time for anyone interested in humanistic psychology and therapy, though Perls certainly condemned what he called the mere 'jazzing-up' of therapy (Perls, 1992). He was concerned to point out that the Gestalt approach does not rely on quick fix solutions, but is a serious, though different, form of therapy, designed to promote human growth and potential – processes which require time, dedication and skill.

Other Influences

In developing Gestalt, Perls was also influenced by his association with Dr Kurt Goldstein, whom he had met in the 1920s. During this time Perls worked at the Institute for Brain-Damaged Soldiers in Frankfurt, where Goldstein, a neuropsychiatrist had pioneered a 'holistic' approach to caring for people. Fritz Perls' wife, Laura, a Gestalt psychologist, was another significant influence on his work. Perls was further impressed by the achievements of a group of psychologists, including Max Wertheimer, Kurt Koffka and Wolfgang Kohler. These psychologists formed what came to be known as the Gestalt School of Psychology.

Finally. the work pioneered by J. L. Moreno in the 1920s, and which later came to be known as psychodrama, was in some respects a forerunner of Gestalt therapy. This approach is the subject of the second part of this chapter, but it should be emphasised that Gestalt terminology owes much to Moreno and his revolutionary work. The term 'here and now', for example, is one which has special meaning in Gestalt therapy, though it is certainly derived from Moreno's reference to the 'now and here' (Zinker, 1978).

Origin of the word Gestalt

The word Gestalt is a German one and means *pattern, shape, form* or *configuration.*

Christian Von Ehrenfels (1859–1932), an Austrian psychologist, was the first person to use the term. He described the pattern or shape which is characteristic of a whole structure, and which is absent in any of its constituent parts. Later on, in 1912, Koffka, Kohler and Wertheimer founded the Gestalt School of Berlin, and studied the organisation of mental processes with special reference to the importance of perception in determining each person's view of reality. As a result of their work, Wertheimer and his colleagues formulated a set of theories which considered the manner in which people organise stimuli into patterns and shapes. According to Gestalt theory people are concerned to create meaning in their lives, so the whole pattern of each person's sensory experience is seen as more important than the individual elements of that experience, in deciding meaning. An illustration of this principle of perceptual organisation is the way in which we see a picture or hear music, for example. When we look at a picture we see it as a coherent whole, rather than as a set of random colours and shapes. Our response to music is the same. We do not hear all the individual notes which make up the harmony; instead we perceive the totality of the music, which is in effect the tune. This awareness of structure and form gives meaning to experience, and according to the Gestalt psychologists all our perceptions are similarly organised.

The Gestalt approach was in many ways a reaction against some of the limitations of other schools. Behaviourism, for example, is concerned to break up complex mental processes into simple conditioned reflexes – a view which is certainly the opposite of Gestalt theory. Perls took up the ideas expressed in Gestalt theory and emphasised the point that each person's experience of reality is dependent on how she or he perceives the world (Perls, 1992). This idea is similar to Rogers Person-centred philosophy and has further echoes in the work of Maslow, for example.

Figure and ground

Perls drew upon the principles of perceptual organisation, first described by the Gestalt psychologists, and incorporated these into Gestalt therapy. The Gestalt psychologists were interested in external perceptions, and were especially concerned with the way in which people deal with visual and auditory experience. Perls, on the other hand, was interested in the ways in which people deal with more complex internal experiences, and the issue of how each person becomes aware of individual needs in relation to the environment. The environment in this context refers, of course, to other people as well as to things. According to Perls' theory, it is necessary for people to be fully aware of all aspects of themselves, including their defences. If this awareness is not present, psychological growth is impaired and symptoms will appear.

The word *figure* in Gestalt theory refers to a person's need at any given time. These needs may be relatively simple ones like hunger and thirst, but they also include emotional, relationship and esteem needs. People obviously experience different needs at different times, but when an individual is functioning well in relation to the total environment, each need is clearly seen against the background or *ground* of awareness. Needs continually emerge and become figures against the background of awareness, and the individual's task is to deal with the most important need as it emerges. When needs are dealt with in this way, they are then able to fade into the background and other pressing needs appear. In Gestalt theory this process is referred to as the formation and destruction of Gestalts. Figure and ground form a pattern or whole which is known as a Gestalt. A simple example of the way in which needs emerge and are dealt with is outlined in the following scenario.

CASE STUDY — Figure and ground

Marian got up late and went to work without eating breakfast. She had been stressed the night before, because her five year-old child had a temperature and was clearly unable to attend school. Throughout the morning at work Marian felt hungry and slightly unwell. She found it difficult to cope without food, and although she also worried about her daughter she was constantly aware of the empty and queasy sensation in her stomach. In this situation, Marian's current physical needs controlled her experience, and it wasn't until she managed to eat in the canteen that she was able to address the next most pressing need which was information about her child. Once she had eaten, she phoned her baby sitter and got news of her daughter's condition. After that Marian was in a position to deal with the other pressing needs of the day. If Marian had not bee able to eat when she did, she could not have dealt effectively with other figures or needs which emerged in the course of the day. Her perceptual field would have been cluttered and confusing.

This example explains why it is that people tend to become ineffective when they are caught up in several activities and preoccupations, none of which are ever properly addressed. The same principle applies when needs are more complex, as the second example illustrates.

CASE STUDY — Unfinished business

A patient attending his GP surgery was referred for counselling because he was depressed. The patient (Simon) had been bereaved two years earlier, when his father died of a heart attack. Since that time Simon was unable to shake off the depression, and had been taking medication for sleeplessness and anxiety. During counselling it emerged that his brother had also died ten years previously as a result of suicide. His brother was a student at university at the time, and Simon had never been able to accept his death. In fact, he felt a great deal of guilt and responsibility in connection with it. Because of his unresolved grief about his brother, Simon could not adequately address the issue of his father's death either. In addition to this, there were other factors in Simon's life which had never been properly dealt with. His relationships were problematic, largely because (as he said himself) he was difficult and moody to live with. Simon felt drained of energy, and confused about which issues he should tackle first since his job situation was not good either. It was some time before he came to see that the unfinished business of his brother's death needed to be dealt with if the other factors were to be seen in clearer focus. In Simon's case there was a lack of purpose and clarity, which meant that he was unable to separate the important from the unimportant things in his awareness. Figure and ground had become indistinguishable as far as he was concerned.

Working through complex issues like these takes time, and later in this chapter we shall look at some of the skills which the Gestalt therapist can use to help clients deal with such problems.

<EXERCISE> ── Becoming aware ──────

Working individually, spend about five minutes becoming aware of your experiences at the present moment. What bodily sensations do you experience, for example? Are there any 'needs' which appear to be more pressing than other? If so, how does the pressing need affect your ability to attend to other factors in your present environment?

The here and now

The central focus of Gestalt therapy is on the *present*. Clients' present experiences, including their thoughts, feelings and actions, are – according to this approach – the most important point of interest in therapy. Even the experiences of remembering and planning are seen as present functions, regardless of the fact that they refer to the past and the future (Polster and Polster, 1974). Thus a client may be concerned about an issue from the past, but instead of focusing on a lengthy (and verbal) account of what happened, a Gestalt therapist would encourage the client to experience the past in the present. The following is an example of this idea.

CLIENT: It was a very long time ago, but I remember the feeling exactly. My father would expect me to be perfect at everything, and when I wasn't I was humiliated.

COUNSELLOR: The humiliation which you describe ... can you get in touch with that and feel it now.

CLIENT: [pausing] Yes, I can. I can feel it in my stomach like a dull sensation.

COUNSELLOR: If that sensation could talk to you, what would it say?

CLIENT: [surprised] That it is angry ... that it wants to be rid of the humiliation for good.

It can be seen from the example that the counsellor's emphasis on present experience enabled the client to access strong feelings which would have remained outside her awareness. Other forms of counselling and therapy encourage clients to talk about their problems and this, according to Gestalt therapists, can be counter-productive since it leads clients away from the actual experiences they describe. It is entirely possible to talk at length about something without ever feeling any real emotion in connection with it. It is possible also for people to hang on to past experiences and emotional traumas as a way of avoiding change. This tendency, which Gestalt therapy seeks to overcome, is one which may be encouraged (inadvertently) by other approaches. In Gestalt therapy the emphasis is on *experience* rather than on the counsellor's or client's interpretation of it.

Intellectualisation has always been regarded with suspicion by practitioners of Gestalt, and indeed Fritz Perls himself used very strong language in condemnation of this tendency (Perls, 1992). However, in view of the fact that Gestalt is a holistic approach to the person, there is now greater recognition of intellectual and cognitive experience and contemporary practitioners of the model are certainly less confrontative, sarcastic and cantankerous than Fritz Perls appears to have been (Miller, 1988). Gestalt therapy is quite different in many ways from some of the other theoretical models described in this book. There is an obvious contrast with the psychodynamic approach for example, since Gestalt emphasises present experience and the here and now, while the former encourages clients to look at the past and the childhood events which have shaped their lives.

Wholeness

The concept of wholeness is an important one in Gestalt therapy, and refers to the client's total experience – physical, sensory, emotional and intellectual. Integration of all these dimensions is a central aim of therapy, and to this end clients are encouraged to become more aware of themselves and to work towards a healthy assimilation of all their component parts. The client's non-verbal communication is often indicative of the real message which he seeks to convey, not just to the therapist but to himself as well. A client may, for example, express one view verbally while clearly indicating by his body language that the opposite is, in fact, the case. The following case study illustrates this point.

CASE STUDY — Eamonn

Eamonn, who was in his early thirties, received stress counselling because of problems at work and the break up of his marriage. He did not entirely believe in counselling, but decided to try it as a last resort. His friends and relatives were unable to give him the kind of help which he needed, so on the advice of his line manager he received counselling over a period of six sessions. In spite of his initial reservations, Eamonn found the experience helpful. At first he had some difficulty in expressing his feelings, and the counsellor who worked with him used a Gestalt approach to help him. Eamonn was emphatic that he has recovered from his marriage break up, but the counsellor noted that his body language was incongruent with this verbally expressed statement.

CLIENT: I am over the worst of it and I don't have grudges against Sian.

COUNSELLOR: I would like you to become aware for a moment, of your left hand and what you are doing with it.

CLIENT: My hand? [slightly disconcerted] I'm holding my neck with it, my throat.

COUNSELLOR: And what is it you throat wants to express.

CLIENT: I don't know what it wants to say ... but I know I had problems with my throat which the doctor said were due to stress.

COUNSELLOR: Your throat is you. Say what it is your throat is saying.

CLIENT: [slowly, and after a pause] I can't swallow it. That's it ... I have to say ... I can't swallow it yet. I suppose I've been fooling myself that I could get over something like that so quickly.

It can be seen that this case study is similar to the example given to illustrate the here and now. This is because the body, and the way it expresses itself, is regarded as the most significant vehicle for true meaning. Gestalt therapists are aware of the fact that people often refer to their own bodies, or parts of their bodies, as if these were in some way alien or separate from them. Thus, a client might speak about parts of himself as 'they' or 'it', and in doing so cut himself of from immediate experience and from a vital source of knowledge and information. In his book *Care of the Soul*, Thomas Moore points out that in the body we often see the inner spirit of the person presented in its clearest and most expressive form (Moore, 1994). Dress, gesture, movement, facial expression, mannerisms and tics are all indicative of inner psychological processes at work. This is why active listening, which we discussed in the early chapters of this book, is such an essential counsellor skill. Counsellors need to 'listen' to everything that the client expresses, which means that every form of expression needs to be monitored and observed.

EXERCISE — Language of the body

1 In groups of two to three, discuss the ways in which our inner problems may be reflected by our bodies. Has anyone in the group had personal experience of physical expression of feeling or conflict?
2 Think of your work with clients, and consider any examples of bodily expression of feeling which you have observed in them.
3 When you have completed your discussion, look at the following list of physical organs and say what you think are the most obvious emotions or conflicts associated with each:

◆ the heart
◆ the head
◆ the face
◆ the limbs
◆ the stomach
◆ the colon

◆ The use of language

The way in which clients use language is another important focus of attention in Gestalt therapy. As we have already noted, clients can use language to distance themselves from immediate experience. Clients may alienate themselves through the use of 'it', 'they', 'you' or 'one' statements, instead of owning their individual feelings through the use of the personal pronouns 'I' or 'me'. A client might say, for example, 'It seemed hot and stuffy', instead of 'I was hot and bothered', when referring to an uncomfortable encounter in the past. In Gestalt therapy such a client would be encouraged to 'own' his feeling by using the personal pronoun 'I' and by bringing the experience alive in the present. For example:

CLIENT: Yes, I was hot and bothered.

COUNSELLOR: Can you experience that feeling now, at this moment?

CLIENT: At the moment? Yes I feel it … hot and agitated.

Another example of the Gestalt focus on language is that clients who speak quickly may be asked to repeat slowly what they have said, in order to highlight and emphasise what it is they wish to convey. Clients who speak quietly may be encouraged to become louder, while those who hesitate might be asked to stay with the hesitation to discover its possible meaning. The use of certain words is also significant in the Gestalt approach, and clients might be asked to look more closely at the words they choose. A central tenet of Gestalt therapy is that linguistic habits say a lot more about the client, regardless of what he trying to convey (Polster and Polster, 1994). Communicating through jargon is another way in which people can distance themselves from others and from their own experience. The jargon which clients use in their work may be transferred by them into counselling too. When this happens, no real identification of personal feeling is possible. Some clients talk a great deal and this, in itself, is often a clue that things are carefully hidden, not only from the person who is listening but also from the client. Language can, after all, act as a smokescreen behind which important aspects of the real self are carefully guarded. There are many reasons for this kind of defence, and in most theoretical approaches counsellors are tentative in the way they respond to these. However, the Gestalt approach is somewhat more challenging in this respect although, as I have already indicated, contemporary practitioners are also sensitive in their responses to clients' defences.

Shoulds and shouldn'ts

Clients' frequently refer to behaviours, thoughts or feelings and use the words 'should and shouldn't' in relation to these. In these instances clients may simply be repeating outmoded rules and prohibitions which are inherited from childhood. These rules and prohibitions were probably accepted without question so that their suitability or otherwise to adult life is never seriously considered. Perls used the terms 'topdog/underdog' to refer to the conflicting parts of human personality (Perls, 1992). This concept is analogous to Freud's theory of personality, including Superego, Ego and Id, and the intrapsychic conflict which exists within this system. Topdog is defined by Perls as the righteous part of personality, while underdog is insecure, manipulative, ingratiating and lacking in conviction. Topdog is, according to Perls, a judge and a bully, and people can spend a great deal of time trying to please or placate this internalised 'parent' part of personality. The pressure of always trying to please can have the damaging effect of alienating people from their own feelings. Underdog, on the other hand, is incapable of dealing in a straightforward way with topdog's demands, and frequently resorts to procrastination or rationalisation in order to evade the strict demands being made. In Gestalt therapy the emphasis is on the integration of these conflicting parts, which means encouraging clients to accept that they are both valid parts of the self. If it is accepted by clients, that both these parts of personality can exist side by side, then pressure and conflict are diminished while insight and integration are increased.

EXERCISE — Topdog/underdog

Working individually, think of the rules (shoulds and shouldn'ts) which you have carried with you since childhood. Make a list of these, and consider how many of them still cause conflict within you. When you bring these rules into conscious awareness, you begin to understand their effects upon you in the present. You can also start to look at them in a more critical way, and in doing so lessen their inhibiting or damaging influences.

Layers of neurosis

Perls referred to the ways in which people avoid awareness of self, and described these as five layers of neurosis (Perls, 1992). These layers include the *phony*, the *phobic*, the *impasse*, the *implosive* and the *explosive*. In Perls' view these layers of neurosis need to be stripped away if clients are to achieve psychological growth and maturity.

The first layer – the phony – refers to the clichéd or inauthentic way in which we often relate to others. One example of this inauthenticity is reflected in the social games we play, and the daily rituals including small talk and role playing.

The phobic layer is the point at which we resist seeing aspects of ourselves which might cause emotional disturbance or pain. Thus aspects of the real person are denied, and self-acceptance is forfeited as a result.

A feeling of nothingness or emptiness is characteristic of the impasse layer, and marks an attitude of avoidance or a sense of being stuck. At the impasse layer people seek to manipulate the environment, including others, instead of acting with maturity and accepting personal responsibility. In Perls' view, however, it is impossible to overcome difficulties by resisting them, and he regarded the impasse layer as a source of many problems in therapy (Perls, 1992).

The implosive layer is activated when we allow ourselves to come into contact with feelings of deadness. Perls describes this layer as the 'death' layer, and he believed that behind it lies the explosive experience, which is, in effect, a connection or link with the 'real' or authentic person. Clients who access this layer of awareness often experience catharsis, either through grief, anger or great joy. Inability to experience appropriate feelings is a fundamental cause of emotional problems for many clients. However, catharsis on its own is not sufficient, and clients need to work through and make sense of this kind of experience. Perls himself was at pains to point out that the 'growth process' takes time, and that the aim of Gestalt is to enable clients to become independent, and to move from environmental to self support once the layers he describes have been uncovered by them.

Resistance

In Gestalt terminology the word *resistance* refers to the defences which people use to prevent real or authentic contact with others and with the environment in general. This resistance to real contact prevents us from identifying and mobilising our own innate resources and energy. It also prevents us from utilising our reserves of energy, and inhibits healthy participation in the present or the 'here and now'. Polster and Polster (1974) list five defences as follows:

◆ introjection
◆ projection
◆ retroflection
◆ deflection
◆ confluence

The word *introjection* refers to the internalised rules governing our thoughts, feelings and behaviour, which we absorb from parental and other influences from childhood onwards. Perls called this nagging inner voice 'topdog', a concept which we discussed earlier.

The second defence, *projection*, can be defined as a process of attributing aspects of ourselves to other people, as a result of which we disown them or fail to recognise them personally. Important aspects of the self are therefore not integrated or acknowledged. One example of this tendency is highlighted when some men refused to acknowledge the 'feminine' side of their own personalities, yet express forceful and negative views about 'effeminate' men in general (Harris, 1989).

Retroflection is a process whereby we do to ourselves what we would like to do to someone else. We may, for example, direct aggression inwards when we are fearful of directing it outwards towards others. This can result in depression or psychosomatic illness. It is also restrictive and stultifying. While Gestalt theory does not recommend that clients should actively be aggressive towards other people, it does suggest that there are other more positive and creative ways of expressing strong feelings.

The use of *deflection* as a defence, means that contact with others is diminished through a process of distraction. Humour and intellectualisation are two ways of avoiding real intimacy and contact. Asking questions, instead of making statements, is another way in which people can distance themselves, not just from others but from themselves as well.

Confluence describes a style of relating to other people which is based on an absence of conflict, and a conviction that everyone should be in agreement. People who are afraid to speak for themselves may use this particular defence, and in doing so protect against disagreement and the anxiety which might accompany it. This blending with others is negative when it precludes any recognition of one's real or personal feelings, and when it is evident in therapy clients are encouraged to focus on themselves in order to identify and express their own views.

These five defences have much in common with the Freudian defences discussed in Chapter

3, although the terminology is in some cases different. However, these similarities are understandable in view of the fact that Perls trained as a psychoanalyst, although he was certainly innovatory in his approach to clients and their problems.

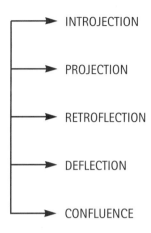

INTROJECTION

PROJECTION

RETROFLECTION

DEFLECTION

CONFLUENCE

Figure 6.1   *Gestalt Defences Indicating Resistance to Real Contact*

Dreams

In Gestalt therapy there is a special emphasis on working with clients' dreams. Perls described dreams as the 'royal road to integration' and he clearly regarded dreaming as a spontaneous art form through which the various fragmented parts of the self are expressed (Perls, 1992). In Perls' view each element of a dream represents an aspect of the dreamer, so any understanding of the dream must integrate or 'own' these projected parts. One way of doing this is to ask the dreamer to 'become' each part or element of the dream. This identification technique differs from techniques used in the psychodynamic model, where various parts of the dream are interpreted, usually by the dreamer, but with assistance from the therapist. In the Gestalt approach the dream is brought back to life by the client in the present. The following is an example of this technique:

CASE STUDY — Gestalt dreamwork

A client called Lois recounted her dream.

CLIENT: This is my dream. I am in my own bedroom at home, and I notice that a large hole has opened up around and beneath the wardrobe. I am very anxious about this and I try to draw my husband's attention to it, but he isn't listening.

COUNSELLOR: Become the wardrobe, and say what it is that the wardrobe is saying.

CLIENT: [after a long pause] I am on shaky ground and the floor is opening up beneath me. Michael [the client's husband] is not aware of what is happening.

Almost as soon as she said this the client knew what it meant. She and her husband were planning to move house, but he refused to discuss the fears she had in relation to this. The last time they moved house they had encountered many problems, and this time the client did indeed feel that she was on shaky ground. When the client explored the dream further she identified other relevant details of her relationship with her husband. These included the following:

CLIENT: I am a container for all the clothes, my husband's as well as my own. I am in charge of these and I'm keeping everything together.

The client was, in fact, keeping everything together, since she was the one in charge of the planned move.

The counsellor then asked the client to engage in a dialogue with parts of the dream, and from this exercise she was able to explore her relationship with her husband in greater depth.

COUNSELLOR: Stay as the wardrobe, and now speak to the floor.

CLIENT: You are letting me down ... I'm sinking. I have no support.

As a result of working through this dream the client realised that she would need to find a more effective way of communicating her needs to her husband. Perls believed that dreams contained important existential messages which, if recognised and assimilated, would provide the knowledge we need to help us understand and deal with problems in our lives.

The empty chair

There are other creative Gestalt approaches which can be used to help clients become acquainted with their dreams. Clients could, for example, use a 'two chair technique' as a means of addressing separate elements of the dream. This method involves the client sitting in one chair, while addressing a part of the dream which is 'sitting' in the other. The two chair technique is used quite extensively in Gestalt therapy, and can be used in other contexts apart from dreamwork. A client who has been bereaved, for example, might benefit from speaking to the deceased person who is present in another chair. This is one way in which clients can be helped to deal with complicated or unfinished grief reactions, including reactions of anger, guilt or resentment.

The client named Simon, referred to in the 'Unfinished business' Case Study on page 124 would probably have benefited from such an approach. Simon could also have conducted the dialogue by 'answering' for his brother who had died. Separate parts or aspects of a person can be addressed and re-integrated by means of the two chair, or empty chair technique. Thus a client who claims to be too anxious to socialise might be encouraged to talk to the anxious self in the opposite chair, and so on. The two chair technique is usually effective and quite often very powerful, and should, of course, only be used by therapists and counsellors who have received adequate training in this particular approach.

Groupwork

Gestalt therapy is often conducted in groups and, in fact, Fritz Perls himself was in favour of groupwork as a medium for therapy. There are many benefits for clients who participate in groupwork: these include the benefits of learning through participation, as well as the practical benefit of reduced cost. However Gestalt groups tended, in the past at least, to be different from other therapy groups. One reason for this is the way in which therapy was traditionally conducted. One member of the group was usually asked to take centre stage, while the rest of the group looked on. In *Gestalt Therapy Verbatim*, Perls outlined the essential tools of groupwork. These include what he called the 'hot seat', where people are invited to sit when they wish to address a personal issue or problem. In this situation, the group provides both feedback and support for the person who elects to use the seat. This approach to groupwork is one in which the therapist is placed in a central and quite powerful position. It is a role which obviously suited Fritz Perls, but it may not be a role which is attractive to every Gestalt therapist.

Harris and Philippson (1992), outline a new model of groupwork which is quite different from the 'hot seat' model used by Perls and many others. This new model is one which places the group, rather than the individual, centre stage. Attention is focused on group dynamics, although the experiences of individuals in the group are considered too. Such a model acknowledges the fact that many of the problems which bring people into therapy in the first place are relational or social in origin. People do not function in isolation, and contemporary Gestalt groupwork tends to reflect this fact. The Gestalt principle, that the Whole is more than the sum of its parts, is one which can certainly be applied to therapy groups. Harris and Philippson's book, *Gestalt: Working With Groups* (1992) offers a clear and comprehensive description of their approach and should be of interest to anyone wishing to find out more about developments in Gestalt therapy.

Skills and techniques

The basic counselling skills which were discussed at the beginning of this book are used in the Gestalt model, as in any other. There are, however, specific creative skills which are used in Gestalt therapy, although these are never slavishly followed. Creativity is a fundamental principle of this approach and therapists usually adapt their ideas to suit the needs of individual clients. Some Gestalt therapists regard the word 'technique' as limiting, and would prefer to discuss the different vehicles which can be used (Zinker, 1978). Some of these vehicles, like dreamwork and the two chairs, have already been discussed in this chapter. Others include the following:

◆ dialogue exercise (between topdog and underdog)
◆ role playing
◆ dialogue with opposites (these could be opposite parts of personality)
◆ staying with feelings (really experiencing a strong feeling which may have been evaded in the past)
◆ focus on language and the way it is used

◆ focus on the body, and what it conveys

◆ reliving unfinished business (incomplete gestalts)

◆ exaggeration (becoming aware of the obvious through exaggeration, including awareness of gestures, movements and speech)

◆ changing questions into statements (for example, instead of saying 'what's the time?' the client says 'I am worried about the time')

◆ being the projection (clients are encouraged to 'own' projected parts of themselves: a speaker who says 'you are dishonest' might be asked to play the role of the person who is supposed to be dishonest, which helps to clarify just exactly where the dishonesty lies)

◆ taking responsibility for self (clients are asked to take responsibility for statements they make, for example 'I find it difficult to get here on time, and I take responsibility for it')

◆ describing the group (group members are asked for a metaphor to describe the group, for example animal, situation, journey, building or vehicle)

This is just a selection of some of the creative ideas used in Gestalt therapy. There are obviously many others which have worked for individual therapists and their clients and have never been recorded. Certain techniques work for some clients while others may be quite unsuitable. Creativity, and sensitivity to clients needs, are essential components of Gestalt work, and counsellors who are interested in this approach need to be flexible, skilled and above all well trained to work from this perspective.

EXERCISE — Group metaphor

Working individually, think of a metaphor which describes your training group. Discuss this with other group members and identify any similarities which emerge.

The counselling relationship

Counsellors from a wide spectrum of theoretical backgrounds use Gestalt skills in their work with clients. In order to do this, however, they need to undertake specific training in Gestalt work. They will also (as a result of their training) realise that not all clients respond to this approach. There are, of course, specialist Gestalt therapists who work exclusively from this perspective, and in these instances clients who seek their help are usually well informed about Gestalt therapy and what it involves. These clients would, therefore, expect a fairly challenging approach and would be prepared to put a great deal of effort into the work. On the other hand, the idea that Gestalt therapy is always confrontative probably does it a disservice. Therapists are well aware of their clients' needs and will tailor the work they do with them accordingly. Clients are viewed as unique individuals who require individual approaches. This is an important point to remember, since clients often have deeply emotional responses to the work done. There is always a danger that techniques may come to dominate therapy, so that the actual relationship between counsellor and client takes second place. Clients should be informed and consulted about techniques used, and a trusting relationship between counsellor and client is certainly a prerequisite for successful therapy. Fritz Perls makes the point (1992) that what clients expect from a therapist can be done just as well by themselves. Helping clients to realise this places the relationship on an 'equal' footing, and helps to lessen the possibility that transference dependence will hamper therapy.

Clients who benefit from this approach

Gestalt therapy is suitable for clients who suffer from psychosomatic problems, with the proviso, of course, that they understand the approach and wish to get to the root of their problems. These problems may include tension headaches, Colitis, nervous stomach reactions, skin irritations, fatigue, breathlessness and indeed any other condition which has been medically investigated and found to have no underlying physical cause. People who suffer from inhibiting shyness may also benefit from a Gestalt approach, and people who have unresolved issues relating to bereavement and loss are likely to benefit as well. Clients who are out of touch with their emotions can gain a lot from Gestalt therapy, and those who are interested in dream work and self exploration tend to be attracted to it. An important point to remember is that the clients who benefit most from Gestalt therapy tend to be those who understand the approach, and feel they can gain help from it. Aspects of Gestalt therapy may be used in both family and marital work, and in certain behavioural problems in younger clients and children. Gestalt work is also applicable in training groups, especially those which value experiential learning for participants.

Some limitations

People who are frightened of groups, and those who are inhibited about expressing themselves in front of others, may not be suitable clients for Gestalt therapy. On the other hand, such clients might gain a great deal if their initial reluctance could be overcome. Clients who do not understand the links between the physical and emotional aspects of themselves are unlikely to benefit from Gestalt work. Some degree of imagination and creativity is necessary if clients are to be helped by this approach, and those who simply cannot express feeling may find Gestalt therapy very threatening. There are cultural limitations too, in the sense that the Gestalt emphasis on expression of feeling may run counter to what some people consider to be appropriate behaviour. Additionally, some clients might, for example, have deep reservations about the idea of holding a dialogue with a deceased relative.

The possibility of abuse is also, unfortunately, a consideration. Counsellors who are attracted to the approach, but not adequately trained in it, may be tempted to use techniques simply on account of their dramatic and highly-charged impact. It cannot be stated often enough that adequate training, both at theoretical and at an experiential level, is an absolute prerequisite for practice in Gestalt work. Regular supervision will act as an inbuilt safeguard too.

Finally, clients who are deeply disturbed, or detached from reality, are hardly likely to respond well to a challenging approach like Gestalt.

PSYCHODRAMA AND THE WORK OF J. L. MORENO

Jacob Levy Moreno (1889–1974)

J. L. Moreno, the founder of psychodrama, was a psychiatrist who worked in Vienna during the first part of the twentieth century. He became interested in the way children engage in play, and was especially impressed with their spontaneity and ability to role play various important figures in their lives. Moreno observed the therapeutic effects of this kind of acting, and he could see that children derived enormous emotional benefits from expressing their feelings, anxieties and concerns in this way. Through a process of role reversal, these children could 'become' the important authority figures in their lives, and this enabled them to view themselves, and their own behaviour, from a different and more informed, perspective.

In 1921 Moreno also founded the Theatre of Spontaneity in Vienna. This was, in fact, quite unlike the usual theatre where professional actors perform using scripts. Moreno's theatre was meant as a venue for ordinary people who wished to participate and act out, in a spontaneous way, events from everyday life, including news events which they had read in the papers. In 1925 Moreno emigrated to the USA where he set up the Moreno Institute, and continued his work in psychodrama. Although primarily interested in the therapeutic effects of his approach for emotionally disturbed people, Moreno was also concerned to show that psychodrama was a medium through which almost anyone would benefit. It is widely accepted that he coined the term 'group therapy' and he was certainly instrumental in promoting theatre as a medium for exploring emotional problems.

The theory of psychodrama

Moreno rejected the Freudian concept of psychoanalysis as a method of dealing with personal problems. Psychodrama, unlike Freudian therapy, is action based and conducted in a groupwork setting. Moreno opposed the notion of treating individuals in isolation by verbal methods alone. Instead, he proposed that people derive most benefit from experiential treatment conducted in the presence of others who are supportive and understanding. Moreno wished to give clients the opportunity to experience and rework important developmental stages of their lives which may have been problematic for them.

This repetition of past traumatic events, conducted in the safe environment of a supportive group, forms the basis of therapeutic psychodrama. When clients relive past events in this way new meaning is acquired, which can then be reintegrated in its more positive form. Psychodrama, therefore, allows people to correct original negative experience. It also allows clients to articulate those things which should have been said in the past but never were. In reference to this need to make sense of the past, Dayton (1994) makes the point that although society may not, at times, allow us to speak from the heart and to say what we most need to say, psychodrama does give us this opportunity.

Moreno's psychodramatic stages of development

Moreno described four stages of personality development, related in name to the action roles of psychodrama. These are quoted by Dayton (1994) and placed under the following headings:

◆ The double

◆ The mirror

◆ The auxiliary ego

◆ role reversal

The first stage of development, the double, is that phase during which the infant is symbiotically fused with the mother or caregiver. In this stage the baby feels at one with the parent, and the parent, in turn, senses the baby's needs. This relationship forms the basis of trust, and when good experiences are repeated often enough the child's development will proceed in a healthy way.

During the mirror stage of development information from the outside world is conveyed to the child, which may not, in fact, be congruent with what he/she actually feels. This process of mirroring helps to adjust a child's perceptions of self, and when it is provided in a supportive and caring environment will give important information about the way others see us from the outside. If the environment is harsh and unsympathetic, however, it becomes difficult for a child to feel located in the world. A sense of dislocation and weakened identity are the result of feeling oneself mirrored in a threatening and judgmental world.

The stage of the auxiliary Ego is one in which the developing child is aware that other people exist. Along with this realisation of the existence of other people there is, or should be, a willingness to fit in and be part of society. Through the first two stages of doubling and mirroring, most children will have learned that they are not alone, and that the world is a friendly place to live in. If a strong sense of self is in place, then an ability to empathise with other people is likely to follow at the third stage.

The stage of role reversal is reached when the individual is able to stand alone. If this is achieved, it becomes possible to 'take on' the role of another. One example is the way in which adult children take on roles of their own parents, once they themselves become parents. This stage can only be reached when people are sufficiently separate to stand on their own feet.

Roles and role playing

The terms 'role play' and 'roles' were actually invented by Moreno (Avery, 1996) and they form the basis of therapeutic psychodrama. The word roles refers to predictable patterns of behaviour which people use in order to cope with various situations in life. For example a woman may play many roles, including mother, sister, wife, teacher, nurse and works manager. When people are psychologically healthy they are able to move in and out of roles with some ease. On the other hand, psychological ill health is associated with rigidity and an inability to move out of certain roles. Another danger arises when the role dominates the person, so that spontaneity and a true sense of identity are lost. Psychodrama offers the opportunity to explore a variety of roles in a wide range of situations so that many alternatives and solutions become apparent. Participants in a psychodramatic group take it in turns to role play and to explore their conflicts and difficulties. This is carried out in a controlled and safe groupwork setting, in which all the people in the group are assigned certain roles. The following is a summary of those roles:

◆ The director

◆ The protagonist

◆ The auxiliary egos

◆ The audience

Another essential component of psychodramatic technique is the stage on which the action takes place.

EXERCISE — Roles

Working individually, make a list of the roles which you fulfil in everyday life. How easy or difficult is it for you to move from one role to another? Select one of the roles which you have listed, and identify any conflict which you experience in relation to it. Discuss your ideas with members of the group, and note any similarities of experience which emerge.

◆ The director

In psychodrama the director is the therapist whose task is to supervise the action, direct it and observe from a supportive distance. The therapist/director also selects the protagonist and decides which techniques are appropriate for individual clients. Preparation and planning are carried out by the director, and the selection of problems to be dealt with in sessions is part of her role too. An important aspect of the director's role is to help group participants become psychologically receptive to the work which is about to take place. This usually involves talking to the group about the nature and purpose of psychodrama, or it may take the form of preparatory exercises and techniques. Group members need to know that they are working in a safe environment, and the director needs to assure them of this. Additionally, participants should not feel pressured to take part if they don't wish to do so.

The director/therapist monitors all aspects of the psychodrama as it unfolds, clarifies when necessary, summarises at the end, observes the reactions of group members and facilitates group discussion when the work is over. All this requires a high level of skills, specialist training, creativity and substantial experience in working with groups.

◆ The protagonist

The protagonist is a volunteer from the group who selects the issues which he wishes to explore. These issues may be from the present or the past, and the protagonist's task is to re-enact the chosen scenarios. Both action and words are used by the protagonist in psychodrama. Relevant significant figures from the past are brought to life in the present, and important aspects of relationships are explored in the drama. The director's task is to follow the protagonist through the scenes which are re-enacted and to encourage, when necessary, greater focus on specific situation or events. The therapist/director is the person who, according to Dayton, holds the protagonist's hand with one hand while 'carrying a flashlight with the other' (Dayton, 1994).

◆ The auxiliary egos

The protagonist selects group members who will act as auxiliary egos. The function of the auxiliary egos is to play the parts assigned to them by the protagonist. These roles may include significant people, either alive or dead, in the protagonist's life. The protagonist presents himself as well as all the other characters in turn, according to his perceptions of them. Corey (1995) lists several functions of the auxiliary egos, and these include playing out the perceptions of the protagonist, looking at the interaction between their own roles and those of the protagonist, helping to interpret the various relationships, and acting as facilitators in the development of improved relationships for the protagonist.

◆ The audience

The audience is involved in the action which takes place on stage. Through a process of identification they are able to benefit from the psychodrama in progress. Because the atmosphere is heightened, and quite often intense, most people in the audience become absorbed in it. In this way learning by comparison takes place. Empathic responses, experienced by the audience, are often accompanied by insight and release of feelings. Feedback and support are also provided by the audience, and the protagonist is likely to receive helpful ideas concerning the issues being highlighted. General group discussion following action will provide further clarification, feedback and support.

◆ The stage

The stage is the physical area in which the action takes place. It should be large enough to accommodate some basic furniture, and it should also be comfortable, warm and private. The stage provides a platform from which the protagonist's story can be seen and heard by others.

◆ The double

The double is the person who plays the inner voice of the protagonist. This is an optional role and may be played by the director or any member of the group. The double's function is to move the action to a deeper level, so that material from the protagonist's unconscious is brought into focus. The protagonist thus sees himself portrayed simultaneously by someone else, and this helps to reveal aspects of himself which were outside his awareness.

The stages of psychodrama

Dayton (1994) lists the stages of psychodrama, and includes the *warm-up* stage, during which group members are helped to prepare for the action ahead. The purpose of this phase is to enable participants to become connected to the issues they need to work on. The second stage, *enactment,* is the action phase during which the protagonist's inner problems are structured and enacted before the audience. During the third stage, *sharing,* the protagonist is supported by the other group members and the director encourages a general sharing of experiences and feelings in the group. The final stage, *analysis,* takes place later when group members are less emotionally involved. It refers to cognitive appraisal of what has taken place, and it helps members to assess the emotional learning and insight they have gained. It also helps participants to bring into conscious awareness those destructive patterns and compulsions which have been problematic for them.

Skills and techniques of psychodrama

A variety of techniques is used in psychodrama. These include the following:

◆ role reversal (where the protagonist assumes the role of someone else in his personal drama)

◆ self presentation (the protagonist presents himself, and the other characters in the psychodrama)

◆ soliloquy (the protagonist is encouraged to think out loud and to talk freely about what is going on in his mind at any given time)

◆ mirror technique (one of the auxiliary egos takes on the role of the protagonist and mirrors his movements and words – the protagonist observes this and sees 'himself' more clearly)

◆ interview (the director asks the protagonist questions which help to clarify his thoughts and feelings)

◆ future projection (the protagonist is encouraged to play a future event in order to experience how it feels)

◆ vignettes (these are small scenes in which an empty chair is often used as an opportunity to express strong feelings like rage and anger)

◆ behavioural practice (the protagonist is encouraged to experiment with new ways of acting)

◆ dream presentation (the protagonist acts a dream instead of describing it)

CASE STUDY ▷— Expressing feelings

Annette was a member of a training group in which participants were given the opportunity to work through a personal issue. During the 'warm-up' phase the course trainer talked to the group about the nature and purpose of psychodrama. Each member of the group was interviewed in order to clarify any important issues which they might want to examine. Annette volunteered to work on a personal issue. She told the group about her difficult relationship with her father, and described the conflict she still felt in relation to this. Annette had been bullied at school over a period of some years, but her father refused to take her seriously when she plucked up the courage to tell him.

Annette's mother had died when she was young, so she felt isolated, vulnerable and very afraid of bullies. With the help of the director/trainer, she assembled the main players in the drama which she wished to re-enact. One member of the group represented Annette's father, another a teacher at her old school, while two other participants became the school bullies.

Throughout the presentation of the psychodrama the director supervised and directed the action. As a result of recreating the original drama, Annette experienced intense disappointment and anger with her father and his failure to protect her. This catharsis of feeling is important in psychodrama, and is regarded as the first step towards recovery and integration. However, catharsis, if it is to be properly effective, needs to be accompanied by both cognitive and emotional shifts in perspective (Dayton, 1994).

Annette was supported by the other group members, and was able to share her feelings and experiences with them. A week later, during another group meeting, participants assessed the events of the previous week and discussed what they had learned and the insights they had gained. The director/trainer highlighted several aspects of the psychodrama and clarified issues which were raised by some group members.

Clients who benefit from this approach

Because of its emphasis on spontaneity and creativity, psychodrama is suitable for clients who are inhibited in these areas but wish to do something about it. The approach is also useful for people who have experienced childhood traumas which have never been adequately addressed. In this context psychodrama may prove very helpful for adult children of alcoholic parents. Additionally, it may be used with clients who are themselves addicted to alcohol or other substances, since it provides support and a holding environment for strong feelings which emerge during recovery (Dayton, 1994). The format is highly structured, so participants feel safe and they know they will be listened to as well. New skills can be learned through interaction with others, and feelings of isolation are lessened. For those clients who have difficulty with verbal expression, psychodrama offers an alternative means of communication. Corey (1995) highlights an area in which psychodrama has special application: While working with people who spoke English as a second language, Corey found that emotions came quickly to the surface when clients spoke in their original tongue. This helped them to become more expressive and other group members responded positively to them.

Some limitations

There are clients who could not bear to explore difficulties in front of other people, and there are those for whom the idea of acting in front of other is unthinkable. Although psychodrama is a powerful and effective therapy, it is limited in some respects. Perls (1992) identified at least one of these limitations, which relates to the roles which other people play in the protagonist's drama. According to Perls, these auxiliary egos know very little about the protagonist, and they may even introduce their own fantasies and interpretation into the drama In this way the client's role is falsified and contaminated by others. Zinker (1978) highlights another limitation when he refers to psychodrama's commitment to a formal structure and to the drama, often at the expense of the process taking place within each. It is also possible for group members to hide behind roles, although this is something which the director/therapist should be able to identify. Psychodrama may be difficult to obtain in many areas, but it's occasionally available within the NHS.

SUMMARY

This chapter was concerned with two experiential and action based models of therapy. We discussed the work of Fritz Perls, and the psychology which influenced his approach. The terms gestalt, figure and ground, here and now, and wholeness were also discussed, and placed in the context of the Gestalt model of counselling. Defence mechanisms were identified and the importance of dreams in Gestalt work was emphasised. The benefits of group-work were also described, and the skills and techniques used in Gestalt counselling were outlined. Benefits and limitation of the approach were discussed, and aspects of the therapeutic relationship were highlighted. In the second half of the chapter we looked at psychodrama as a method of therapy, and placed it in its evolutionary context. The theory of psychodrama was explained, along with Moreno's psychodramatic stages of development. The terms role and role playing were examined, and participant's roles in the psychodrama were described. Stages of psychodrama were also outlined, and the skills and techniques central to it were listed. Finally, we looked at some of the areas of application and identified others where psychodrama might not be appropriate.

REFERENCES

Avery, B. (1996)	*Principles of Psychotherapy.* London: Thorsons.
Corey, G. (1995)	*Theory and Practice of Group Counselling.* California: Brookes/Cole.
Dayton, T. (1994)	*The Drama Within.* Florida: Health Communications Inc.
Harris, J. B. & Philippson, P. (1992)	*Gestalt: Working with Groups.* (2nd edn.). Manchester: The Manchester Gestalt Centre.
Harris, J. B. (1989)	*Gestalt: An Idiosyncratic Approach.* (2nd edn). Manchester: The Manchester Gestalt Centre.
Miller, M. V. (1988)	'Introduction to the Gestalt Journal', in Fritz Perls, *Gestalt Therapy Verbatim.* New York: The Centre for Gestalt Development (1992).

Moore, T. (1994)   *Care of the Soul.* New York: Harper Perennial.

Perls, F. S. (1992)   *Gestalt Therapy Verbatim.* New York: The Centre for Gestalt Development.

Polster, E. & Polster, M. (1994)   *Gestalt Therapy Integrated.* New York: Vintage Books.

Zinker, J. (1978)   *Creative Processes in Gestalt Therapy.* New York: Vintage Books (1997).

FURTHER READING

Clarkson, P. & MacKown, J. (1993)   *Fritz Perls.* London: Sage Publications.

Hare, A. P. & Hare, J. R. (1996)   *J. L. Moreno.* London: Sage Publications.

MacKewn, J. (1996)   *Developing Gestalt Counselling.* London: Sage Publications.

7 Transactional analysis

7

INTRODUCTION

The subject of this chapter is transactional analysis and its use in the context of counselling and therapy. Transactional analysis is a psychoanalytically inspired approach which links problem behaviour to early experience. According to the theory, this early experience exerts considerable influence in the present and is discernible in the 'ego states' each person feels and exhibits at any given time. In the course of this chapter we shall define and discuss these ego states, and we shall consider a number of other important concepts which are central to the theory of transactional analysis.

The approach also highlights each person's aptitude and capacity for change. This means, for example, that through awareness and insight the events of early childhood can be re-defined by the individual and self-defeating patterns of behaviour altered. These ideas are similar to those expressed in psychodynamic theory, where the emphasis is also on child-hood experience and the possibility of change through therapeutic intervention in later life.

The goals of psychodynamic counselling and transactional analysis have much in common, since both aim to help clients bring unconscious material into consciousness. In transactional analysis terms this means helping clients to become more autonomous and 'script' free. A similar view is implicit in the person-centred approach where the individual's 'actualising tendency' is seen as a powerful force for improvement and change. However, transactional analysis differs greatly from both the psychodynamic and humanistic approaches since it stresses the importance of social transactions – a dimension not emphasised by the other two.

ERIC BERNE (1910–1970)

Eric Berne, who was the founder of transactional analysis, completed his medical training in 1935 and later studied psychiatry at Yale University. In the 1940s he trained as a psychoanalyst at the New York Psychoanalytic Institute, and in 1956 applied for membership there. This request was refused, possibly because of Berne's divergence from, and criticism of, traditional Freudian teaching.

Berne was greatly influenced by his father (also a doctor) who died when his son Eric was eleven years old. This early bereavement had a lasting effect on Berne and when he came to formulate his own method of helping the patients in his care he dedicated his most important work to the memory of his father (Berne, 1961). It is worth mentioning this, because it serves to underline a degree of commitment to patients (or clients) which Berne shared with his father, a man who exemplified dedication to the poor and disadvantaged. Berne demonstrated his own concern for the patients in his care through the design and use of transactional analysis. As a method of communication, and as a psychotherapeutic tool, it was meant to translate complex ideas and concepts into more accessible and user-friendly language which could be understood by ordinary people. In addition to his work with patients, Eric Berne also wrote several very successful books. These include *Transactional Analysis In Psychotherapy* (1961), *Games People Play* (1964), *The Principles Of Group Treatment* (1966) and *What Do You Say After You Say Hello?* (1972) which was published after his death. The principles of transactional analysis are expressed very clearly in these books, and should be first choice for anyone wishing to specialise in this approach.

Terminology

Already we can see that the terminology used in transactional analysis is quite different from that used in any other approach. This is both a strength and a weakness of the model, because although the language is memorable and accessible, it is also regarded by some critics as simplistic and superficial. Berne was concerned to demystify the esoteric language of psychotherapy so that it could be grasped by anyone. He was especially interested in helping his patients to understand the basic principles of the approach and the origins of the psychological problems which they had come to experience. In this respect Berne was certainly successful, not least because transactional analysis does appear to help clients and patients to participate more fully in their own therapy. Since its inception, however, Berne's model has been extended considerably by different schools and theorists, and new and more complex ideas have been added to it. While the fundamental principles of transactional analysis remains intact, the accessibility which Berne valued so much is often obscured.

Apart from these criticisms, however, transactional analysis continues to gain popularity, not only as a theoretical approach to counselling and therapy but also as a communications skills model which is used extensively in education, management, industry, health care and many of the caring professions. The International Transactional Analysis Association (ITAA) was formed in 1964 as a training and accreditation body, while the European Association for Transactional Analysis (EATA) performs a similar function. Many of the people who become involved in transactional analysis do so because they are interested in it as a communications model. It is important to remember this fact, since it highlights the point that transactional analysis is first and foremost about the development of effective interpersonal skills.

Groupwork

Transactional analysis therapy usually takes place in a group setting. Berne believed that many problems could be addressed more readily in groups, since such a format lends itself to the identification and analysis of faulty social interactions and communication styles. He himself had gained a great deal of experience of groupwork in the 1940s while working as a psychiatrist in the United States Army Corps, and he set up the first transactional analysis group in 1954. Invaluable information about the way people relate to each other is readily available when clients work together in groups. Each participant is afforded the opportunity to monitor and perhaps change the interactive styles they habitually use. As we shall see, Berne formulated his user-friendly theory of personality in a way which seems to owe something to Freud's concept of Id, Ego and Superego, although Berne did point out that his concept of personality was different in the sense that his ego states represent 'phenomological realities' (Berne, 1961). In simple terms, this means that the three ego states are real and observable, whereas the parts of personality which Freud described were not always clearly seen in this way. Group participants can, therefore, learn about personal styles of social interaction and any problems associated with these, while at the same time becoming aware of the intent behind their ways of relating to others.

EGO STATES

An idea fundamental to transactional analysis is that of ego states. Berne suggested that human personality is made up of three elements which he referred to as Parent, Adult and Child. These familiar words were used by him to describe states of 'self' or states of mind which he believed gave rise to their own individual patterns of behaviour. In transactional analysis Parent, Adult and Child are always spelt with capital letters in order to distinguish between their usual meaning and that which Berne assigned to them. Ego states are, of course, common to all of us and govern our thoughts, feelings and behaviour. In any given situation an individual will exhibit a certain pattern of behaviour which corresponds to the way that person is actually feeling at the time. As feelings change, so also do the patterns of behaviour which the person displays. As a result of his experience with groups, Berne observed that these patterns included noticeable changes in voice, posture, vocabulary, viewpoint 'and other aspects of behaviour' (Berne, 1964). The principles of transactional analysis are illustrated in diagrammatic form, the most basic of which is the structural diagram illustrated in Figure 7.1.

Each of these states, Parent, Adult and Child, is present from early childhood, and all are described by Berne as 'psychological realities' (Berne, 1964). In the structural diagram

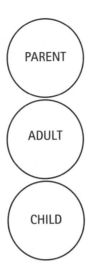

Figure 7.1 *Structural Diagram of Personality*

Figure 7.1, the ego states are separated from each other because they are incompatible and differ considerably.

Parent ego state

The Parent ego state represents a set of thoughts, feelings and behaviour which are derived from parental figures. According to Berne (1964) the Parent ego state is exhibited in both indirect and direct form. A person may, for example, respond as one of his parents actually responded in a given situation. When this occurs, the ego state is directly shown. When the parental influence is an indirect one, then the person is likely to respond as his parents would have wished him to respond. A distinction between these two forms is important, and explains how:

1   people can sometimes 'become' one of their own parents when the Parent ego state is directly active, and

2   how people exhibit the kind of response which parents required in the past.

A client called Viv recounted the following experience.

 Parent Ego State

Sometimes I feel that the children are driving me crazy. Most of the time I cope quite well, and my husband is supportive and helpful. At other times, especially when I have just got in from work, I simply don't know where to start. Then I find myself getting into a panic and I start to shout at them. When this happened to me yesterday I suddenly realised that I sounded exactly like my mother. It wasn't just the tone of my voice ... it was the words as well. I actually used the word 'weary' as she used to do, and later on I used another expression of hers as well. I'm sure I looked like her too, standing there with my hands on my hips glaring at the children. It pulled me up short and made me really think ... do I want to become old before my time and end up hassled and bad tempered the way she always seemed to be?

In the example just given, the client described a situation in which she felt she had 'become' her own mother in her response to her children. Her actions and her state of mind were the same as her mother's used to be in a similar situation. It is important to point out here that the word Parent refers to parental substitutes as well as to actual parents, and could include, for example, teachers and others who exerted influence on a person's early life.

Do as I say: Indirect Parent

The second category of Parent which Berne identifies actually operates in conjunction with a person's Child ego state. Stewart (1992) describes this as an 'internal dialogue' taking place between ego states. When a person responds in this way, the parental 'influence' is evident. Another way of saying this is that the response shown is one which clearly stems from the instruction 'this is how one should behave' or 'do as I say'. This adaptation to parental influence is evidence in the 'adapted Child' ego state which we shall consider later in this section.

◆ Aspects of socialisation

Whether shown in direct or indirect form, the Parent ego state resembles a compendium of the entire socialisation process which each person has received in early life. This early socialisation is passed from parents, teachers and other significant people in childhood, and is usually absorbed without question by the growing child. However, it is not just parental pronouncements and injunctions which are recorded in this way; the example which parents and other significant people give is also relevant here. Both negative and positive influences are recorded in the Parent ego state, and everything which is experienced by the child is internalised to become part of the personality. Once again Berne's psychoanalytic training is evident in his theory, since the idea of parental internalisation is common to all branches of psychodynamic teaching, including object relations theory.

There is an important point of difference, however, between Berne's theory of personality and those described by the various branches of psychodynamic theory. This difference concerns the 'paternal' influence which, in Berne's formulation, is potentially just as influential as the 'maternal'. If we consider the theories discussed in Chapters 3 and 4 it is clear that such an equal emphasis is absent from many of the psychodynamic approaches. In transactional analysis, therefore, both parents are believed to impart information explicitly and implicitly to the developing child's Parent ego state.

◆ Information from the past

Information which is recorded in the Parent ego state enables us to cope with all aspects of living. It also provides all the data necessary to enable people to function as parents themselves and raise their own children. Another significant aspect of the Parent ego state is that it enables people to respond automatically in many situations, so that many 'routine matters' as Berne describes them can be dealt with without unnecessary expenditure of energy (Berne, 1964). Problems arise, though, when the Parent ego state is inappropriate or counter-productive in a given situation. One example of this is the bank cashier who adopts a certain 'superior' stance in relation to the account holders she is meant to serve. Her critical parental attitude is likely to stem from a childhood in which attitudes to money (and especially those who borrow it) are fraught with ambiguity and moral disapproval. In the present situation, however, the bank cashier's Parent ego state is liable to cause problems, since it is sure to encourage a 'Child' response from the customer and an end to real productive communication.

Berne (1972) elaborated on his structural diagram of personality, so that the Parent ego state is now commonly divided into 'Nurturing Parent' and 'Critical' or 'Controlling' Parent – see Figure 7.2. This diagram also illustrates the subdivision of the Child ego state into 'Free' or 'Rebellious' Child, and 'Adapted' Child.

> **EXERCISE** — Parent ego state
>
> Working individually, try to identify as many situations as possible where you respond in a Parent ego state. How do you think, feel and act when you respond in this way? Think carefully about your tone of voice, your gestures, your facial expressions and any other observable features which are manifest in your Parent Ego state.

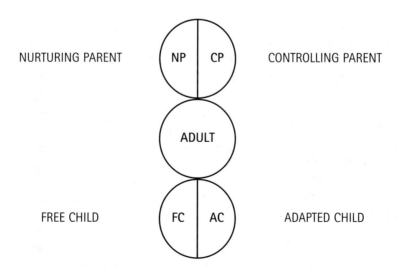

Figure 7.2 *Descriptive Diagram of Personality*

◆ Nurturing Parent and Controlling Parent

The terms 'Nurturing Parent' and 'Controlling Parent' refer to two different sets of influence which are absorbed in early childhood and are clearly distinguishable from each other when they are manifest. Berne originally used the word 'prejudicial' instead of controlling to describe the second form in which the Parent ego state is exhibited (Berne, 1961). However both these words, 'Controlling' and 'Prejudicial', are meant to denote arbitrary and pro-hibitive attitudes which are borrowed from parental figures and are usually exhibited auto-matically and without question in certain situations. The example of the bank cashier is a case in point here, and serves to illustrate the way in which some people respond to par-ticular situations exactly as a parent or parents would have done. The 'Nurturing' Parent ego state is shown in a completely different way, and is usually manifest as sympathy or support for others in need or distress. It is important to remember that children are also capable of responding in all three ego states, and when they are in 'Nurturing Parent' it tends to be demonstrated as concern for someone or something smaller, weaker and more vulnerable, including toys and dolls.

Child ego state

While information is being recorded in the Parent ego state, another recording is taking place simultaneously. This second recording also derives from the past and represents a young child's actual reactions to what is going on in the environment. Later on in adult life the Child ego state is evident when the emotions which the original situation produced are felt once again. Harris (1967) makes the point that a young child has no vocabulary in the critical early years, so most experience is recorded as 'feelings'. These feelings responses can be evoked at any time in adult life, and often the individual concerned is unaware that the response is an archaic one. The following is an example of this.

◁ **CASE STUDY** ▷— Child ego state ─────────────────

Gwyneth, who was in her early forties, received counselling because she was unable to cope at work. Her problems arose when she had to deal with complaints from staff or customers, or when any situation arose in which there was conflict. When things became difficult, Gwyneth either felt angry and defensive or extremely tearful. She was aware that her responses were inappropriate, but was unable to modify the strong feelings which certain people and situation evoked. In the course of counselling she revealed that her parents had been habitually critical, so that she reached a point in her childhood where she despaired of ever pleasing them. Her transferential responses to staff and cus-tomers, was an exact replica of the way she responded to parental criticism in the past. When she understood this Gwyneth was in a position to alter her responses and access her Adult ego state when conflict or disagreement arose. This was not something she achieved immediately, however. Understanding and practise are necessary before long established ways of responding are changed in this way. Gwyneth's counsellor taught her the basic principles of transactional analysis and showed her how 'complementary' and 'crossed' transactions work in practice (see also Figures 7.3, 7.4 and 7.5).

◆ Adapted Child and Free Child

We have seen that the Child ego state is preserved from childhood, so that a person functioning in this way behaves as he or she did at a very early age. Like the Parent ego state, the Child is demonstrated in speech, stance, demeanour and overall appearance. In addition to these outward signs and behaviour, there are what Steiner (1974) refers to as accompanying 'perceptions, thoughts and feelings' which correspond to the visible indicators. In referring to the Child ego state, Berne stressed that it was not intended to mean 'childish' or 'immature' (Berne, 1961). Berne was aware of the danger that his terminology could be misinterpreted and used in a disparaging way. In his early writing he uses the terms 'Adapted' and 'Natural' Child to describe the two broad manifestations of that particular ego state, though the word 'Free' is now often substituted for 'Natural'.

◆ Adapted Child

In the section entitled 'Do as I say' we looked briefly at how people adapt to parental influence, and the way in which this adaptation is revealed through the Child ego state in adult life.

The person who is functioning in Adapted Child will demonstrate behaviour meant to conform to the expectations of parents and parental figures. Different parents have different expectations, however, and behaviours which please one will not necessarily please the other. This means that people learn to respond or adapt to both parents, and in later life these responses will be triggered in situations which are reminiscent of earlier ones. A young woman who has received poor grades in college assignments, for example, might respond to a male lecturer by becoming silent and withdrawn since that was the way she responded to her father's disapproval when she was a child. A woman teacher might, on the other hand, evoke a different, perhaps more combative response, which stems from the relationship the student had with her mother. The point to make here is that both these 'adapted' responses are outmoded and archaic, because in each case the student is communicating in the way that she would have done at a much earlier time with the important people in her life. The Adult ego state, which we shall consider later, represents a much more effective way of communicating.

◆ Free Child

The Free Child ego state is the source of strong feelings and can be classified as either positive or negative. Spontaneous expressions of joy, anger, sorrow and a sense of fun are characteristic of Free Child. These are all feelings which have escaped the inhibiting influence of parents, but when they are expressed inappropriately these uncensored impulses can be problematic. On the other hand, positive Free Child ego states are often observed in social situations or contexts where such expressions are permitted. Steiner (1974) lists sports events and parties as examples of structured situations in which the Free Child ego state is given unlimited opportunity for expression. Apart from aspects of behaviour which can be identified with Free Child, there are also words and phrases like 'super' and 'wow', for example, which are associated with it.

Adult ego state

The adult ego state denotes the feelings, attitudes and behaviour patterns which belong exclusively to the individual, and which are in touch with current reality and relationships in the present. Once again it is possible to detect similarities between Berne's description of personality and aspects of psychodynamic theory, since the Adult ego state appears to have much in common with the Freudian concept of the 'Ego'. Like the Ego, the Adult ego state represents reason, and common sense. It is that part of the personality which can truly be described as autonomous and free from parental influence, or strong feelings emanating from the Child ego state. The Adult ego state is characterised by objective, logical thinking, and an ability to make independent judgments and decisions in any situation. Experiences gained throughout life are examined and used by the individual when in Adult, so that realistic choices can be freely made. Every so often the material which is stored in the Adult ego state is re-assessed and updated, in order to keep in touch with changing circumstances and needs. Children too have an Adult ego state, which represents that part of personality which has absorbed and tested information passed to them from parents and other significant people. The central concern for the Adult ego state is the development of individual autonomy and the ability to make informed and realistic decisions on one's own.

EXERCISE — Looking at ego states

Working individually, look at the responses given to the situations described. Say whether you think these responses come from each person's Parent, Adult or Child ego states.

1   Helen has been asked by her manager to work extra hours at the weekend. She asks for some time to consider the situation. Next day she replies that she has given it some thought and is willing to do the overtime.

2   Bruce has been admitted to hospital for an operation. He is approached by a doctor who wishes to carry out some diagnostic procedures which Bruce does not understand. Instead of asking, however, he keeps silent and worries for the rest of the day.

3   Catherine has just learned that she has not got the promotion she hoped for. She has a confrontation with her boss and finds herself becoming angry and tearful.

4   Joanne and Lyn are friends and attend the same university. Joanne has a row with her boyfriend and Lyn responds in the following way:

   'He's not worth it. I never thought he was good enough for you. To be quite honest, I thought you were wasting your time.'

5   Phil and Simon are friends who share the same office at work. Phil's girlfriend breaks off their relationship and Simon responds in the following way:

   'Look, I know you must be feeling rotten. If you like, I'll clear up those files for you and you could leave a bit early.'

6   Karen's husband asks her to consider changing their next year's holiday plans. They

had planned a sightseeing holiday, including visits to the local art galleries and museums. He suggests they need a more relaxing break. Karen responds by pointing out that they had both resolved to improve their knowledge of art and anyway, she has better things to do than waste time on the beach.

7   Mrs Rae is an eighty year-old resident in a nursing home. One of the attendants asks her if she would like to go out for a walk since the day is warm and sunny. Mrs Rae is enthusiastic about the suggestion, and adds that she wouldn't mind paddling at the local beach as well.

8   James, who is eight, has been told by his parents that he must not play in the sun without wearing sunscreen lotion. He replies that he knows not to do this because he got burned on holiday last year.

9   Carolyn's mother has asked her to visit home more often. Carolyn, who is twenty and sharing an apartment with some friends, replies that her mother needs to get out and about more so that she can have a life of her own.

10   The manager of a small firm is concerned that her secretary is repeatedly late for work. The manager, Mrs Burrows, waits until her irritation is under control then makes an appointment to speak to her secretary. She expresses her concern and asks for an explanation.

ANSWERS

It should be stressed that it is not possible to be totally accurate about the correct answers to this questionnaire. This is because so much depends on the manner and tone of voice of the person responding in each case. However, from the evidence given, the answers are shown on page 169.

Application to counselling

Berne's main objective in formulating transactional analysis was that it should provide a frame of reference for helping clients in therapy. He developed his theories as a result of working directly with patients, whose behavioural changes he observed and then identified in the ego state model. The behavioural changes he noted included alterations in voice tone, gesture, choice of words, facial expression, posture, body movement and even sentence construction (James and Jongeward, 1971). Berne was intrigued by this phenomenon, and observed that people seemed to be governed by different 'inner' personalities whose influences were manifest at different times and according to circumstances. He also observed that people communicated in a variety of ways, depending on the ego state which dominated the personality at any given time. These 'transactions', as he called them, could be analysed in order to help people identify some of the problems they experienced in communicating with others. Transactional analysis, therefore, is meant to help clients gain intellectual insight through analysis of the way they relate to other people. It is concerned with four major areas of analysis.

◆ structural analysis – this is the analysis of individual personality or ego states
◆ transactional analysis – refers to the analysis of communication styles or social behaviour
◆ game analysis – this is analysis of the psychological games which people play
◆ script analysis – analysis of a complex set of transactions which people act out compulsively

◆ Structural analysis

We have considered Berne's structure of personality which was shown in diagram from (see Figure 7.1). Berne believed that structural analysis should always come before transactional analysis, and can be taught to clients in either group or individual settings (Berne, 1961). It is important for clients to understand the ego state model before they can move on to consider the way they conduct transactions with other people.

◆ Transactions

While structural analysis refers to the individual, analysis of transactions refers to social behaviour. The work 'stroking' is used by Berne to describe the social exchanges which take place between people. Stroking implies recognition of another person and is defined by Berne as 'the fundamental unit of social action' (Berne, 1964). Any exchange of strokes is called a 'transaction' and is the basic unit of social interaction. We exchange strokes through verbal greetings, non-verbal recognition, touching, kissing, hugging and so on. According to Berne, strokes are a necessary and integral part of human interaction, and we all need them even when they are negative. Children will, for example, seek recognition from parental or other important figures, and when positive recognition is not forthcoming negative strokes are seen as preferable to none at all. When patterns like this are established in early life, it may take some time for people to change them. Transactional analysis counselling is one way in which clients can learn to change the way they communicate with, and seek approval and recognition from, other people.

◆ Complementary transactions

People communicate with others from either the Parent, Adult or Child ego state. The person making the response will also do so from either of the three ego states. A complementary transaction will take place when, for example, one person addresses another from the Adult ego state, and the second person replies from Adult (see Figure 7.3).

STIMULUS: Have you seen my glasses?
(Adult to Adult)

RESPONSE: Yes, they're on the dining room table.
(Adult to Adult)

Berne illustrated his theory of transactional analysis in diagram form in order to make it easier to understand. He also stressed the point that when transactions remain complementary, communication proceeds indefinitely. Complementary transactions don't just

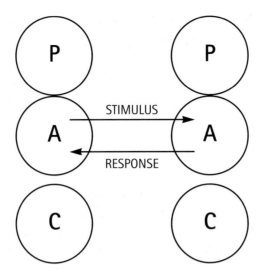

Figure 7.3   *Complementary Transaction*

take place between Adult to Adult ego states. Berne (1972) identifies nine possible types of complementary transactions, in which the responses given were those which the question or stimulus intended. Figure 7.4 is an example of one.

STIMULUS: Isn't it dreadful how long it takes to get through these checkouts?
(Parent to Parent)

RESPONSE: Yes, it's disgraceful. They should have more staff.
(Parent to Parent)

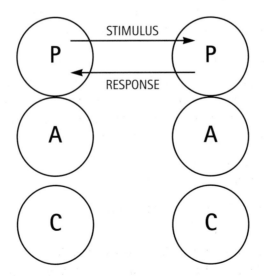

Figure 7.4   *Complementary Transaction*

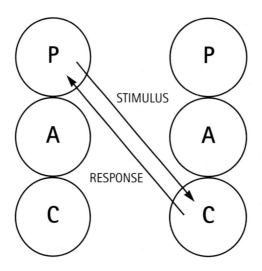

Figure 7.5 *Complementary Transaction*

The following is another example of a complementary transaction, this time Parent to Child.

STIMULUS: That's twice this week you've kept me waiting.
           (Parent to Child)

RESPONSE: I'm sorry, to be such a nuisance.
           (Child to Parent)

◆ Crossed transactions

A crossed transaction occurs when the response given is not the one which the stimulus intended. When such a situation arises, communication tends to break down. Figure 7.6 illustrates this.

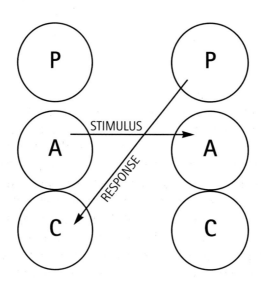

Figure 7.6 *Crossed Transaction*

STIMULUS: Have you seen my glasses?
(Adult to Adult)

RESPONSE: Oh you haven't lost them again!
(Parent to Child)

The response to the question 'Have you seen my glasses' might have been given from a Child ego state as follows:

STIMULUS: Have you seen my glasses?
(Adult to Adult)

RESPONSE: You can't expect me to look after your things.
(Child to Parent)

Once again this is illustrated in diagrammatic form (see Figure 7.7).

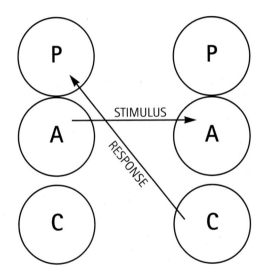

Figure 7.7   *Crossed Transaction*

◆ Ulterior transactions

Both complementary and crossed transactions are relatively simple, and operate on one level. However, Berne describes another, more complicated, transaction which operates on two levels and conveys a double set of messages. These are referred to as 'ulterior' transactions because they contain a hidden agenda. Another way of stating this is to say that one of the messages occurs at a psychological level, while the other takes place at a social level. The psychological aspect of the transaction is conveyed subtly, and is often picked up via non-verbal clues. It is by far the stronger of the two messages, and dominates the social message which is conveyed verbally. Ulterior transactions are frequently contained in exchanges between people who wish to become more intimate and are wary of stating their intentions openly. However, they are also common in many other situations. The following is an example.

PATIENT: My back is less painful, although it does tend to play up when I'm sitting at my desk.
           (Adult to Adult)

DOCTOR: Certain situations make it worse for you.
           (Adult to Adult)

On the surface this is a straightforward transaction between two people who are discussing a medical condition. At a psychological level, however, the transaction is likely to be more complex, with a subtle testing of responses taking place on both sides. Depending on voice tone, body language and other non-verbal clues, the ulterior message may be as follows:

PATIENT: I'm not ready to go back to work and I need your help.
           (Child to Parent)

DOCTOR: I'll take care of you and give you extra time.
           (Parent to Child)

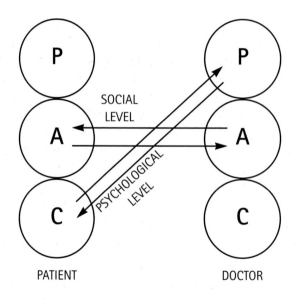

Figure 7.8 *Ulterior Transaction*

EXERCISE — Ulterior Transactions

Working individually, identify any ulterior transactions you have experienced either at work or at home. Illustrate these in diagram form and discuss the way they work with other members of the training group. Are there some transactions which are common to a number of people in the group?

◆ Game analysis

Berne (1964) defines the psychological games which people play as follows:

◆ they are extensions of ulterior transactions

◆ they progress to an expected and definite outcome

◆ superficially, they appear to be straightforward transactions

◆ what is said is not what is felt

◆ all games have some common elements, including a hidden agenda and a negative payoff

Berne also makes a useful distinction between an 'operation' – a simple transaction or transactions set in motion for a specific purpose – and a game – a dishonest 'manoeuvre' (Berne, 1964). If someone asks for help and gets it, for example, then that is an operation. If, on the other hand, the person who gives the help is adversely affected in doing so, then that is a game. The following is an example of a game.

⊂ CASE STUDY ⊃— Mr Phillips

Mr Phillips was a thirty-six year-old man who had been out of work for several years. He had a number of minor health problems which meant that he had visited his doctor on many occasions. However, his GP had some difficulty in persuading Mr Phillips that he had no serious health problems, an assessment which was confirmed by the many diagnostic procedures which had been carried out. Mr Phillips had also visited several alternative practitioners, all of whom he described as 'hopeless' and incapable of giving him the help he needed. At a later date he requested counselling, and during his first sessions informed his counsellor that no one had been able to help him so far. The counsellor observed that Mr Phillips smiled as he described all the failed attempts to understand and assist him. Nevertheless, she worked with him over a period of ten weeks, and during that time was able to help him identify the game he was playing over and over again, and the payoff he received on each occasion.

We can see that Mr Phillips was receiving a great deal of attention as a result of his repeated visits to helpers. Gaining attention in this way was a continuation of the strategy he had employed as a small child. However, the kind of attention this client received effectively prevented him from achieving any real intimacy in relation to other people. In transactional analysis terms, games are designed to confirm and support the original decisions which people make in early life about the best way to relate to others. As far as Mr Phillips was concerned, real intimacy was fraught with danger. This was a lesson he had learned in childhood, at the hands of neglectful and often abusive parents. In response to these early events, he had devised his own method of gaining the 'strokes' or recognition he desperately needed. As a result, he was also able to experience the familiar, and what Berne (1972) referred to as 'racket', feelings of hurt and satisfaction associated with his own special game. The fact that he was sabotaging his own best interests did not occur to him. In the chapters dealing with psychodynamic approaches to counselling, we noted that Freud (and other Freudian theorists) believed that people frequently repeat early patterns of behaviour in an unconscious and repetitive way. This idea is taken up by Berne, and is integral to his theory of games and life scripts.

SCRIPTS

The theory of life scripts has a central place in transactional analysis. Berne (1961) defines a script as a 'preconscious life plan' to which people construct their activities, lives and relationships. According to this theory, fundamental decisions about an individual's entire lifespan are formulated at a very early age. Scripts are based on parental conditioning and influence, and they come under two headings or categories, 'winning' and 'losing' (Berne, 1972). These script types are closely associated with another transactional analysis concept – the OK positions. The OK positions represent a variety of convictions which people adopt and adhere to from childhood through life. There are four basic OK positions from which games and scripts originate. They are as follows:

◆ I'm OK – You're OK

◆ I'm OK – You're not OK

◆ I'm not OK – You're OK

◆ I'm not OK – You're not OK

What the positions mean

The first position is the most positive one, and is based on the conviction that every person has worth and value. An infant who is loved and cared for is likely to imbibe feelings of goodness which, if the quality of care continues, will last a lifetime. Feelings of goodness about 'self' are then translated into feelings of goodness about other people too. Once again it is possible to detect echoes of psychodynamic theory, in particular object relations theory, in Berne's ideas. Unfortunately, problems tend to arise in later childhood when the parents and others become more critical and demanding. When this happens the I'm OK – You're OK position of an earlier era may be questioned, and the original conviction of worth may then be lost.

Some fortunate people retain the I'm OK – You're OK position throughout life, but the majority of others probably fall into the depressive I'm not OK – You're OK group. This is because so much learning has to be done in childhood, and so many obstacles have to be overcome. Negative feedback is often given by parents, and in extreme cases they may even be abusive or neglectful.

When this last situation obtains, some children respond by adopting the I'm not OK – You're not OK 'futility' position. Another group of people, those who are arrogant and distrustful of others, will slot into the I'm OK – You're not OK 'paranoid' position. An important point to make in relation to OK positions is that it is possible for all of us to move from one to the other at different stages of life depending on changing circumstances. However, a fundamental I'm OK – You're OK position which is established in childhood is never totally obscured, even in the most adverse conditions of life.

Focus on counselling

Achieving the I'm OK – You're OK position often requires a conscious decision (and some effort) in adult life. People who do achieve it tend to respect themselves, and all those other people with whom they are in contact. In his writing Berne makes it quite clear that personal change cannot simply be effected by external circumstances, but must come from *within* the individual.

An important objective in counselling is to help clients identify and use their own resources so that therapeutic change becomes possible. In transactional analysis people are viewed in a positive way, and a basic principle of the approach is that people can be helped to locate their innate (though often neglected) coping abilities). Clients are encouraged to make new decisions about their lives, and alternative ways of behaving are explored in therapy. The OK positions which were adopted in early childhood can be challenged and changed, and negative life scripts can be re-constructed to become more positive.

Earlier in this chapter we noted that transactional analysis is frequently conducted in groups. The group is, in fact, the ideal medium for clients who wish to become more aware about their personal life scripts and how they originated. Understanding must always precede change, and in transactional analysis groupwork clients receive feedback from other participants. This practice is of considerable help in increasing self knowledge for individual clients. The following is a summary of objectives in transactional analysis therapy:

◆ that clients should become more autonomous and 'script free'
◆ that clients work towards the I'm OK – You're OK life position
◆ that clients learn to state their needs and views clearly without game playing
◆ that clients take responsibility for their own feelings

> **EXERCISE** — Life positions
>
> Working either individually or as a group, look at the four life positions listed below and identify any situations in your own life when you experienced each of them. What were the circumstances in each case, and how did you resolve any difficulties you had?
>
> I'm OK – You're OK
> I'm OK – You're not OK
> I'm not OK – You're OK
> I'm not OK – You're not OK

Contracts and goals

In transactional analysis, client and counsellor establish a specific contract which must be agreed by both. We have noted that other models of counselling use contracts as well, but these tend to be less detailed than those favoured by the transactional approach. All administrative and business aspects of the counsellor/client relationship are included in a transactional analysis contract, but a much wider agreement on the goals of therapy, and the way these will be achieved, is included too. Goals, which are always stated in positive terms, are also revised and updated when necessary. This means that attention is directed towards a wide view of personal development and away from a superficial problem solving approach. However, this does not imply that therapy should always be lengthy. Clients state the specific beliefs and behaviours they wish to change and both client and counsellor work towards these objectives. This joint approach does serve to strengthen the equality of the relationship, and encourages the clients to experience themselves as active participants in their own therapy.

The relationship

The relationship itself is based on the concept of equality between the two people involved, and all information, including any notes taken, is shared openly. Clients in transactional analysis counselling are helped to achieve emotional and intellectual insight, but the primary focus of therapy is certainly cognitive. This refers to the understanding which we have already mentioned, as a necessary component in the progress towards autonomy and script free independence. However, creativity and flexibility are further attributes which transactional analysis counsellors need to have.

Clients are also encouraged to become more aware of all aspects of everyday life, and to live with spontaneity in the present. Spontaneous living in the here and now implies freedom from outdated scripts, as well as an ability to choose appropriate responses in personal and social situations. The ability to form relationships without resorting to games or subterfuge is another desired outcome in counselling. Communication between client and counsellor should be clear, and this clarity is facilitated when clients are familiar with the theoretical framework of transactional analysis and its terminology. Clients are encouraged to learn about transactional analysis and to attend courses if possible. When therapy is taking place in a group context, its aims and objectives are discussed so that all participants are clear about purpose and progress.

Permission

In the transactional analysis model of counselling, the concept of 'permissions' has an important place although, as Stewart (1996) points out, some transactional analysis counsellors now tend to de-emphasise this. The word 'permission' refers to the counsellor's role in encouraging clients to abandon unhealthy or destructive behaviours in favour of more positive and life affirming action. Giving permission may take the form of simply telling clients that they need not continue with certain types of behaviour which stem from childhood beliefs still operating at an unconscious level. Many of these beliefs have been passed on from parents, and become absorbed into the client's own Parent ego state. The rationale underlining the concept of permission is that it is possible for the counsellor or therapist to switch off the parental recording which is responsible for the client's problems. However, there is another much more important reason for helping clients become free of negative parental messages. Clients need to learn to trust their own judgment before they can experience true autonomy and freedom from outdated scripts. The following case study highlights the therapeutic effects of permission in counselling.

> ⊂ **CASE STUDY** ⊃— Shelly ─────────────────────────────

Shelly was a middle-aged client whose mother had died two years before she started counselling. She was now living alone, and complained of an inability to enjoy herself which she described in the following way:

I make plans to go out with Freda [her best friend] and I'm really looking forward to it. Then when I get to the cinema or the restaurant, a black cloud seems to descend on me and something inside me says that I should not enjoy myself. After that I start to feel guilty that I am out on the town, when so many other people can't afford to socialise in that way. I think something bad will happen to me if I enjoy myself.

───

The counsellor who helped this client agreed and established a specific contract with her. Background details about Shelly's lifestyle and general health were also discussed, and after this a treatment contract was devised. Shelly stated what it was she wished to achieve through counselling, and later on goals were agreed between client and counsellor. The treatment contract was outlined in positive terms, and Shelly stated that she wished to become more confident about going out. She also wished to be free of the guilt feelings which had plagued her for so long. Her parents had been very religious, and the idea that enjoyment was sinful was accepted in the family when Shelly was a child. These strong messages were stored, therefore, in her Parent ego state, and she was unable to dislodge them without someone to encourage her. The counsellor told Shelly that she need not feel guilty on the next social outing. In order to reinforce this permission she asked Shelly to picture their present conversation each time pangs of guilty assailed her. This worked very well for the client who then learned to give herself permission when she needed it. Eventually, even this conscious self permission was no longer necessary, as Shelly started to feel more independent and free to think for herself.

Potency and protection

Offering permission to clients, in the way just described, can only be done when the other important conditions of potency and protection are also present. The word 'potency' refers to the counsellor's strength or conviction, which must be felt by the client if parental injunctions and outdated rules are to be challenged. In other words, the counsellor must, as Berne describes it, feel sufficiently potent to deal with the client's 'Parent'. Furthermore, the client's 'Child' must be convinced that the counsellor is potent enough to give 'protection' against parental anger (Berne, 1972). Protection can often take the form of assurance from the counsellor that she is available if the client should need her. This highlights an aspect of transactional analysis which sets it apart from many other models, for although there is an emphasis on client/counsellor equality, there is also a recognition that clients frequently need strong support and protection at certain stages of therapy. This means that counsellors need to be aware of their own strength and protective position within the relationship, as well as the need to be directive when necessary. The client is there to receive help, and the counsellor is there to give it. However, clients are not encouraged to become dependent in transactional analysis therapy, and the emphasis throughout is on helping the client to get well and become more autonomous.

Transference

We have considered the concept of transference in the chapters dealing with psychodynamic approaches to counselling, and it is discussed in Chapter 10 alongside other important issues in counselling. Individual approaches to therapy have their own views about transference, but all are aware of its existence or potential existence in the counselling relationship. Transactional analysis is no exception, and indeed Berne (1972) believed that it was a common cause of many problems, both inside and outside therapy. In the context of transactional analysis, the most effective way of illustrating transference (and counter-transference) is in diagram form. When clients transfer to counsellors feelings and attitudes stemming from childhood, then the counsellor is cast in the role of a parent figure. The following diagram, Figure 7.9, is an example.

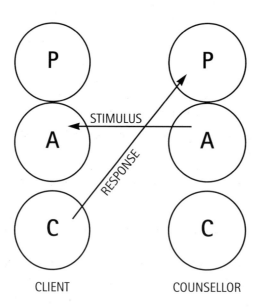

Figure 7.9 *Transference (Crossed Transaction)*

The conversation taking place between counsellor and client was as follows:

COUNSELLOR: Last week we talked about the changes you wanted to make ...
(Adult to Adult)

CLIENT: I'm going to need a lot of help to get started.
(Child to Parent)

Transference dependence on the counsellor is something which is certainly not encouraged in transactional analysis, and the equality of the relationship tends to work against its continuing development in any case.

Countertransference

Countertransference can also be illustrated in diagram form. Figure 7.10 shows the counsellor's Parent response to a statement the client has made.

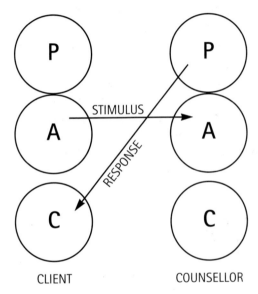

Figure 7.10   *Countertransference*

The conversation during this exchange was as follows:

CLIENT: I want to refer to one point in the contract we discussed last week
(Adult to Adult)

COUNSELLOR: Is there something that worries you ... something I can help you with?

┌───┐
│ ◀ **EXERCISE** ▶ ── Exercise Transference/countertransference ── │
│   │
│ Using the ego state model described in this chapter, illustrate in diagram form any examples │
│ of transference or countertransference you can identify from personal experience of help- │
│ ing, or being helped.   │
└───┘

(Parent to Child)

Early and more recent developments in transactional analysis

Transactional analysis continues to grow in popularity, both as communications models and as a model of therapy. In the psychotherapeutic context, new ideas are constantly emerging. Perhaps one of the most interesting of these is the way in which Gestalt techniques are incorporated into transactional analysis by some counsellors and therapists. This approach is illustrated clearly by James and Jongeward in their book *Born to Win* (1971). Here Gestalt experiments and exercises are incorporated into the theory of transactional analysis, with the underlying assumption that both methods are concerned with what is happening at the present moment. The 'redecision school', founded by the Gouldings, also integrates the theory and practice of transactional analysis with Gestalt therapy (Goulding and Goulding, 1979). Counsellors from a variety of theoretical backgrounds also use aspects of transactional analysis in their work with clients, although it should be pointed out that they need proper training in order to do this. Other important developments of the model are listed below.

◆ The Cathexis school

This refers to a school of transactional analysis which is designed to help disturbed clients in residential care. It uses the concept of 'reparenting', an idea developed by Schiff (1975) who worked with psychotic patients. Those patients who had experienced poor parenting in childhood were given a new experience of good parenting by the helpers who cared for them.

◆ Egograms

The egogram is a diagram or graph designed by Dusay (1977) to indicate the relative importance of each ego state within an individual's personality. This is based on the premise that we all have different amounts of psychic energy invested in the three ego states. It is possible to chart your own egogram by drawing a graph of your feelings over a period of time, indicating the ego states operating as feelings and behaviour change.

◆ Personality adaptations

Stewart (1996) refers to the work of Ware (1983), and the concept of personality developments. Ware's ideas extend the theory of script formation, and indicate the ways in which children decide on the best possible means of surviving and getting what they need. These methods of responding are called 'adaptations', and Ware identified six of these. Stewart describes these ideas in his book *Developing Transactional Analysis Counselling*, along with other interesting extensions of the model.

Clients who benefit from this approach

Transactional analysis is a model of counselling which has potential benefit for most clients. Its strength lies in its accessibility as a communications skills model, and it is especially helpful to those clients who have relationship problems (whether at home or in the workplace). In either of these two situations, clients can be helped through the use of the structural and descriptive diagrams of personality in order to identify the source of their difficulties in communicating effectively with others. Transactional analysis can also encourage clients to abandon outdated ways of relating to others through game playing. The unpleasant feelings like anger, hurt, fear and guilt which are associated with games, and referred to as 'rackets' by Berne (1972), are highlighted in therapy too. When such feelings are identified in this way, clients are then able to make the changes necessary to become more open and spontaneous in relation to other people.

The concept of scripts is useful too since it serves to illuminate the early events and formative influence which tend to govern the course of our lives and behaviour. Clients who experience a compulsion to repeat certain patterns of behaviour, for example, can learn a great deal through transactional analysis, and those clients who are simply interested in personal growth can also benefit from it. The approach has many applications to everyday life, and since it is often conducted in groups it has special relevance for clients who experience problems in relation to groups. The group approach tends to make therapy cheaper for clients as well, and because transactional analysis training is well established and thorough, with an emphasis on professionalism and accreditation, clients are likely to get quality service from the counsellors who help them.

Some limitations

At the beginning of this chapter we noted that the specialised terminology of transactional analysis is both its strength and its weakness. The language of the approach is attractive to many people, but there are others for whom it is too simplistic or even irritating. In addition to this, there are clients whose cultural background might not fit so easily into the paradigm of scripts described by Berne and others. Cultural considerations aside, the language of transactional analysis may also seem contrived and inhibiting to certain clients. The cognitive emphasis in transactional analysis may also limit it for some clients who place more value on the expression of emotion (although the integration of Gestalt with the model is an effective method of obtaining a balance). An important point to make here is that practitioners of transactional analysis should, ideally, have a thorough knowledge of Freudian and psychodynamic theory if their work is to avoid the kind of superficiality for which it is sometimes criticised.

Clients who receive transactional analysis counselling may also respond to its instant appeal, resulting in a superficial understanding of themselves and others. There are some situations, including crisis counselling, for which the approach is probably not suitable, initially at least. Specific problems like sexual abuse, eating disorders, serious depression and childhood trauma may also require a different, more affective, emphasis.

SUMMARY

In this chapter we looked at transactional analysis, and considered its application to therapeutic counselling. The first part of the chapter dealt with some aspects of the specialised terminology used in the approach, and its groupwork format was also discussed. A brief history of Eric Berne was provided, and his ego state model was described in some detail. The four major areas of transactional analysis (structural, transactional, game and script) were outlined. The four basic OK positions were also described, and the way in which games and scripts originate from these was discussed. We looked at the objectives in transactional analysis counselling, the importance of contracts and goals and at the therapeutic relationship between client and counsellor. Transference and counter-transference were shown in diagram form, and the dialogue was included to illustrate these concepts. Early and more recent developments in transactional analysis were outlined, along with some discussion about the advantages and disadvantages of the approach in relation to clients.

REFERENCES

Berne, E. (1961)   *Transactional Analysis in Psychotherapy.* London: Souvenir Press (1991).

Berne, E. (1964)   *Games People Play.* London: Penguin Books (1968).

Berne, E. (1972)   *What Do You Say After You Say Hello?.* London: Corgi Books (1992).

Berne, E. (1996)   *Principles of Group Treatment.* New York: Grove Press (1966).

Dusay, J. M. (1977)   *Egograms.* New York: Harper and Row.

Goulding M. & Goulding, R. (1979)   *Changing Lives Through Redecision Therapy.* New York: Brunner Mazel.

Harris, T. A. (1967)   *I'm OK – You're OK.* London: Pan Books (1973).

James, M. & Jongeward, D. (1971)   *Born to Win.* London: Signet Penguin (1978).

Schiff, J. et al (1975)   *The Cathexis Reader.* New York: Harper and Row.

Steiner, C. (1974)   *Scripts People Live.* New York: Grove Press (1995).

Stewart, I. (1992)   *Eric Berne: Key Figures in Counselling and Psychotherapy.* London: Sage Publications.

Stewart, I. (1996)   *Developing Transactional Analysis Counselling.* London: Sage Publications.

FURTHER READING

Stewart, I. (1989)   *Transactional Analysis Counselling In Action.* London: Sage
                      Publications.

Stewart, I. (1992)   *Eric Berne (Key Figures In Counselling And Psychotherapy Series).*
                      London: Sage Publications.

Stewart, I. &   *T. A. Today.* Nottingham: Lifespan Publishing
Joines, V. (1987)

◆ **Answers (from page 153)**

   1   Adult
   2   Adapted Child
   3   Free Child (Negative)
   4   Controlling Parent
   5   Nurturing Parent
   6   Controlling Parent
   7   Free Child (Positive)
   8   Adult
   9   Controlling Parent
  10   Adult

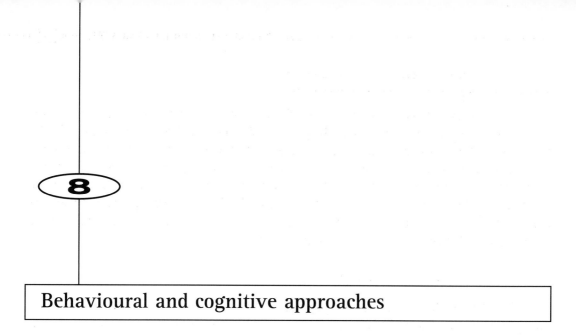

Behavioural and cognitive approaches

INTRODUCTION

In Chapter 2 we identified the major theoretical approaches to counselling from which all the contemporary models described in this book have evolved. Of the three perspectives – psychodynamic, humanistic and behavioural – only the behavioural school, and the approaches derived from it, remain to be discussed in more detail.

Many of the counselling models we have looked at are concerned to describe the internal or unseen characteristics said to govern human behaviour. The structure of personality outlined by Freud, and the actualising tendency or potential for growth which both Rogers and Maslow upheld, are firmly located within the person. In contrast to this, the behavioural tradition looks at overt behaviour and the processes whereby human learning takes place. Within recent years another important dimension – the cognitive – has been added to the behavioural tradition. While the focus remains on outward behaviour, there is an increasing emphasis on internal or covert human behaviour as well. This new focus has occurred because behaviour therapists have gradually recognised the significance of thinking, reasoning and other cognitive processes in determining a person's actions and behaviour.

In this chapter we shall consider both the behavioural and cognitive approaches, with special reference to the principles of experimental psychology and their application to therapy and counselling. The work of Albert Ellis, and the cognitive approach (now called Rational Emotive Behaviour Therapy) which he pioneered, will also be discussed in some detail.

EVOLUTION OF BEHAVIOUR THERAPY

Behaviour therapy has evolved from the theories of human learning which were formulated at the beginning of the twentieth century. The first studies of learning took place in the laboratory and animals, not humans, were used in the experiments. In order to understand the theory and practice of behavioural counselling and therapy, it is necessary to appreciate the relevance of the research which prompted this approach. In the following section we shall consider some of the main contributors in the field of learning theory. Important names include Pavlov, Watson, Thorndike and Skinner, although other psychologists have also contributed their ideas and research in this area.

Ivan Pavlov and classical conditioning

Ivan Pavlov (1849–1936) was a Russian psychologist whose main area of study was the digestive system. In the course of his work he observed that dogs would salivate at the sight of food, an observation which led eventually to the concept of 'Classical conditioning'. Pavlov's dogs appear to have learned that the appearance of an assistant carrying a tray meant they were going to be fed. In the ordinary course of events dogs will salivate when they smell or taste food, a response known as an 'unconditioned reflex'. However, Pavlov showed through further experiments that it was possible to condition the animals to salivate when they heard the sound of a bell prior to eating. In the final part of his experiment Pavlov demonstrated that his dogs would salivate at the sound of a bell, which he called the 'conditioned stimulus', even when no food followed. This proved to him that the animals had 'learned' to associate the bell with the food, also known as the 'unconditioned stimulus'. Pavlov called this sequence of events the 'conditioned response'. This 'associative learning' offers some explanation about the way humans respond in certain situations too. The development of a phobia can be illustrated in the light of Pavlov's theory, as the next example shows.

CASE STUDY — Vanessa

Vanessa, who was five years old, liked furry toys and stories about animals. In the context of classical conditioning, the toys and stories are the 'unconditioned stimulus', while the pleasure she derived from these is known as the 'unconditioned response'. On a number of occasions Vanessa was taken to visit friends in the country who owned a large and rather noisy dog. After a period of time she began to fear the dog, especially when it came close to her and barked aggressively. Eventually the dog became, for her, a 'conditioned stimulus' that was then linked to the 'unconditioned response' of fear in the face of aggression.

Over a period of time all dogs and furry animals became the 'conditioned stimulus' which then produced the 'conditioned response' of intense anxiety (see Figure 8.1) This maladaptive response extended itself over a period of time, so that Vanessa was unable, in the end, to derive any pleasure from her toys or stories about dogs and other furry animals. This latter effect is called 'stimulus generalisation' and occurs when a stimulus which is similar

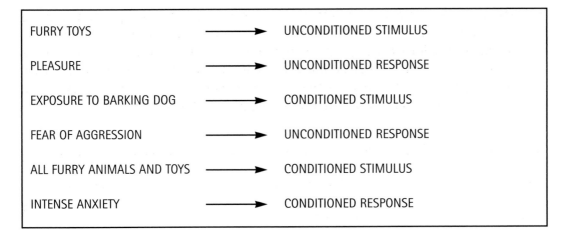

Figure 8.1 *Development of a phobia*

to the original one (in Vanessa's case the barking dog) is encountered. Conditioned responses vary in other ways too, including the following:

◆ **Stimulus discrimination**

Vanessa's response to the dog extended itself to other dogs and furry animals. However, it did not develop into a fear of birds because she was able to identify these as belonging to another species. Pavlov's dogs were also able to discriminate, and after a while responded only to the specific bells which were used to condition them.

◆ **Stimulus extinction**

When responses are not reinforced, at least occasionally, they will cease eventually. The total elimination of a response is known as 'extinction'. Again, Pavlov proved this in his experiments with dogs. When a bell was repeatedly rung without any appearance of food, they simply stopped salivating.

◆ **Spontaneous recovery**

However, even when a response has been extinguished, it can be reactivated. This happens at a later date when the conditioned stimulus is presented once again. Pavlov's dogs began to salivate at the sound of a bell, which was rung long after their learned response had been 'extinguished'. This response suggests that they had retained some memory of the association between food and the bell.

◆ **Phobias**

It is important to link Pavlov's research and findings to the actual practice of behavioural counselling and therapy. If this connection is not made, the theory of classical conditioning tends to appear almost meaningless in the human context. Pavlov's work was carried out on animals, but it does have direct application to human behaviour and to some of the psychological problems people experience. The case study of the five year-old Vanessa serves to illustrate the significance of learning theory in relation to phobias and the way they develop. Phobias are strong irrational fears, which interfere with a person's ability to cope with everyday life, and they are remarkably common. Later in this chapter we shall look at ways of helping clients overcome their phobias. However, classic conditioning has application to other conditions too. People with high blood pressure, for example, may have been conditioned by stressful events, either at work or in the home environment. This is also true of other stress related illnesses, like skin conditions such as eczema, and ulcers.

< **EXERCISE** > ── Individual phobias ──────────

Working in pairs, look at the following list of phobias and discuss ways in which you think they may have developed.

Fear of:

◆ The dark
◆ Spiders
◆ Public speaking
◆ Going out
◆ Being alone
◆ Cats
◆ Flying
◆ Snakes
◆ Confined places
◆ Blood

These are some of the most commonly experienced phobias, but it is possible to develop specific fears about almost anything. Do you have a specific phobia, not included in this list? If so, say how you think you may have acquired it and in what ways, if any, it bothers you in everyday life.

J. B. Watson (1878–1958)

While Pavlov was conducting his research in Russia another psychologist, J. B. Watson, was involved in similar work in America. Watson's contribution to learning theory extended beyond animal experiments, and at one stage he actually conditioned a small child to fear a pet rat. This was achieved by frightening the child with a loud noise each time he played with the animal. In the long term this fear was extended to furry toys, and even fur coats. Watson's work supported the view that human emotional response, like phobias, are indeed the result of conditioning. If we accept that this is the case, then it seems logical to suppose that conditioning can be reversed through a process of unconditioning. Such a process is fundamental to many of the methods traditionally used in behaviour therapy. It should be added, however, that the behavioural viewpoint offers one explanation about the cause of phobias. The Freudian or psychodynamic interpretation is quite different, and suggests that the phobic object represents an impulse, wish or part of the Self which is unacceptable to the individual (Rycroft, 1972).

E. L. Thorndike and the law of effect

Learning theory was enhanced by the work of another American psychologist, E. L. Thorndike (1874–1949) who also carried out work with animals. Thorndike formulated the 'law of effect' which states that when a response to a specific stimulus is followed by a reward, the bond between the stimulus and the response will be strengthened. On the other hand, when the response is followed by a negative outcome, the bond will be weakened. Thorndike's research enhanced the status of learning in psychology, and showed that it is possible to predict behaviour through an understanding of its laws. In simple terms, we could say that a satisfying experience is one which induces movement towards it, while an unsatisfying experience has the opposite effect. Behaviour is therefore dependent on its consequences, which may be either rewards or punishments.

B. F. Skinner and instrumental learning or operant conditioning

Thorndike's law of effect was developed further by B. F. Skinner (1904–1990) whose work on 'operant conditioning' was conducted in the 1930s. Skinner, who was born in Pennsylvania, carried out much of his research at the University of Minnesota. He first used the world 'reinforcement' in connection with animal experiments. In order to ensure that responses will be repeated, an animal needs to be rewarded so that its behaviour is reinforced. Skinner's laboratory animals learned by trial and error that there is a link between behaviour (for example pressing a lever) and the reward (for example food). If a certain type of behaviour leads to discomfort however, or an expected reward is not forthcoming, then the behaviour becomes less likely in future.

Skinner identified two kinds of reinforcers: positive and negative. As far as animals are concerned, positive reinforcement is usually food. In relation to people, food and material comforts can act as reinforcers. Negative reinforcement for animals involve the removal of discomfort when a correct response is made. The same principle of negative reinforcement applies to humans as well. A person under stress might, for example, take up exercise in order to reduce pressure – both mental and physical. If this course of action is successful, then it is likely to be repeated in the future when stress levels rise. The principle of reinforcement is important in relation to behaviour therapy, as we shall see later in this chapter.

APPLICATION TO PRACTICE

While classical and instrumental learning can be separated in theory, they are not, as Richards and McDonald (1990) point out, as easily segregated in practice. Both viewpoints have, however, contributed a great deal to our understanding of the way certain human behaviours originate and are perpetuated. The establishment of more desirable forms of behaviour (a fundamental goal of behavioural counselling) becomes possible once we appreciate the principles of reinforcement.

The conclusions drawn by both Thorndike and Skinner leave very little room for the concept of free will or choice, and they certainly reject the Freudian idea of personality structure or any other mental entities which might affect behaviour. Instead, Skinner in particular subscribed to the view that all behaviour is 'determined' by stimulus-response associations beyond the conscious control of the individual. In addition to this he placed little value on rationality as an explanation for human behaviour. It is important to remember that in learning theory the principles of behaviour apply to animals as well as people. So rationality is certainly not stressed or even acknowledged. As Phares (1988) indicates, such a view leads to the corollary belief that 'behaviour can be controlled'. Whether or not we agree with these strict behaviourist ideas, we can at least learn from them. It is probably true to say that in the history of psychotherapy a great deal of emphasis has been placed on the inner life of the person, without too much attention being focussed on overt observable behaviour and its environmental influences. The work of the behavioural psychologists has served to redress this balance. In Skinner's opinion 'almost all our human problems involve human behaviour' (Skinner, 1971) – a view which is difficult to dispute.

Social learning theory

Another group of psychologists, the social learning theorists, also accept that human learning takes place according to the principles of reinforcement and punishment. However, they go beyond this, and suggest that children learn from others too, through the process of observation and imitation. Children who observe others being punished for certain behaviour, for example, are unlikely to engage in that behaviour themselves. By the same token, behaviour which is clearly rewarded in others is likely to prompt imitation in the hope of similar rewards. The social learning theory of Albert Bandura (1925–) helps to explain how people acquire complex behaviours in social settings. For Bandura, both the psychodynamic and learning theory approaches are limited in their assessment of human behaviour because they do not pay sufficient attention to this important social dimension. Bandura's position makes so much sense that it is difficult to see how it could possibly have been overlooked.

Observational learning

By observing others we learn to do things we were unable to do before, but according to Bandura the behaviour we observe is already in our repertoire. The effect of observation is to encourage us to do that which we know anyway. In this instance, the role of the model is a 'facilitative one' (Phares, 1988). This last point is important since it links Bandura's theory to the practice of therapy, and in particular to the use of 'modelling' as a technique in the behavioural approach. This is a point we shall explore later in this chapter.

Bandura's experiments support the idea that learning may take place through a process of 'vicarious conditioning', and that we are influenced by those people with whom we are most in contact. Bandura also described four requirements for successful observational learning to take place. These include the ability to pay attention, the ability to remember or 'retain' what is observed, the ability to reproduce behaviour and the motivation to perform or act. From the point of view of therapy these requirements are important too, quite simply because they are often absent in emotionally distressed clients (especially those who are in crisis). This does not mean that such clients cannot be helped by behavioural methods, however. What it does imply is that it may take some time for certain clients to respond *positively* to such an approach.

Other contributions

Joseph Wople, a South African psychiatrist, also contributed significantly to the field of behaviour therapy. In 1958 he developed behavioural methods which were effective in relieving a number of psychological problems, including stress, anxiety and irrational fears. 'Systematic desensitisation', a process he pioneered for the treatment of phobias, is now widely used in therapy. In addition to this he developed the technique of 'progressive relaxation training', which is used in conjunction with systematic desensitisation. These behavioural methods will be discussed later in the chapter.

In 1966 Hans J. Eysenck, a psychologist who worked at the Maudsley Hospital in London, produced a study of the effectiveness of psychoanalysis as a treatment for psychological problems. He compared people who were receiving this treatment with others who had similar problems but received no treatment at all. The results of this study are interesting, and suggest that psychoanalysis achieved very little. In fact, those people receiving no treatment did just as well. The effect of this research was that more attention was focussed on the worked of clinical psychologists, and the behavioural work they were doing to help people with emotional problems. Behaviour therapy as a method of treatment was certainly enhanced by Eysenck's intervention.

BEHAVIOUR THERAPY AND ITS VIEW OF THE PERSON

The behavioural tradition in therapy has been effective in shifting attention away from the intensely introspective approach to clients. The Freudian approach, especially, was emphatic in the belief that unconscious forces and unseen impulses were at the root of most human problems. In order to deal with these problems it was necessary to engage in a series of verbal transactions between client and therapist, which would shed light on these hidden areas of personality.

In contrast to this, the behavioural approach encourages us to focus directly on the client's undesirable behaviour, and to make them the target of various methods which will stimulate relearning and healthy behavioural change. According to the behavioural approach, it is simply not enough to talk about problems, for clients need to 'learn' their way out of them too. The rationale behind such a view is that maladaptive and neurotic problems which have been learned can, according to the same principles of acquisition, be unlearned.

The counsellor or therapist is concerned with a person's visible and observable behaviour, as well as with the environmental context in which behaviour takes place. Details of the past are important only insofar as they relate to present behaviour, and aspects of the client's emotional life, though certainly acknowledged, are not especially highlighted. The term 'counter-conditioning' is sometimes used to describe the processes and techniques which are central to behaviour therapy.

The therapeutic relationship

In common with all other models of counselling, the behavioural approach places some emphasis on the quality of the client/counsellor relationship. However, since behaviourists have always valued their scientific credentials and the substantial body of research which underpins the approach, attitudes of objectivity in relation to clients have traditionally been the norm. There has been some change in these attitudes in recent years, and the importance of rapport and partnership within the therapeutic relationship is now recognised. Richards and McDonald (1990) refer to this 'joint approach' which they see as necessary, especially in the early stages of counselling. In relation to handling strong emotions expressed by clients, they also stress the value of using 'empathic statements' which will convey the counsellor's attitudes of acceptance and understanding. Empathy, therefore, has some place in behavioural counselling, but is not especially highlighted nor deliberately fostered.

Clients are encouraged to become active participants in their own therapy, and indeed a fundamental goal of the behavioural approach is to encourage a sense of personal control in clients. Clear communication between counsellor and client is valued, and this is especially relevant in relation to specific problem behaviour which needs to be changed, and the goals which the client wishes to achieve. Behavioural counsellors use all the skills described in the first part of this book, along with attitudes of respect and acceptance towards the people the help. They are also directive in formulating and maintaining individual programmes of therapy for clients.

Focus of therapy

In behavioural counselling there is strict adherence to principles and procedures, which have been scientifically tested for their effectiveness in relation to specific problems. Techniques and methods used are adapted to meet the individual needs of clients, although there is a definite educational bias within the approach. A basic aim of counselling is to enable clients to exercise more control over their own behaviour, and the environment. Another aim is, quite simply, to help clients reduce the distress, anxiety and inconvenience central to most behavioural problems.

◆ Groups

Behavioural counselling is often conducted in groups, and indeed this forum is highly successful for therapy since many clients experience problems in their social and family relationships. The group becomes a source of support and feedback for clients, and provides valuable training opportunities for overcoming limited skills and changing problem behaviour in a safe environment.

The initial assessment

The initial assessment of the client's problems should be accurate and comprehensive so that an individual action plan can be devised. In order to do this well, the counsellor needs to be skilled in gathering and collating information, especially with anxious or emotionally upset clients. The client's problems should be identified early on, and these should also be set in the context in which they occur. In addition, the client's physical and emotional responses in these situations need to be identified. The following considerations are also important:

◆ The nature of the problem
◆ The client's first experience of the problem and where it occurred
◆ The sequence of events following the experience
◆ Factors which may have prompted the problem
◆ The client's actions and thoughts in the problem situation described
◆ How frequently the problem behaviour occurs
◆ The duration and intensity of the problem behaviour
◆ Any factors which worsen or relive the problem
◆ Effects of the problem on aspects of everyday life, including work, social life and family
◆ Identification of other people associated with the problem

EXERCISE — Problem assessment

Working individually, think of a personal problem you have had in the past. Describe your experiences in relation to the problem, using the list of considerations just described. Start by stating the nature of the problem, and then work through the other points above. Afterwards, discuss your findings in groups of three to four, paying special attention to any aspect of your experience not included in the list.

Observation of clients

Apart from the information clients convey verbally at the initial assessment, they also provide non-verbal clues about the nature and severity of their problems. Changes in voice tone and general demeanour will, for example, say much about the level of distress a specific problem causes to a client. It is also possible to see just how socially inept or otherwise a client may be and as Nelson-Jones (1996) indicates, interview assessment affords an opportunity to identify the factors which individual clients find personally reinforcing.

These factors include praise, attention and encouragement, and they can prove useful in helping clients to change problem behaviour.

Setting and implementing goals

The setting of specific goals follows the initial assessment or behavioural analysis. These goals need to be considered jointly by both client and counsellor, and the client in particular should be fully aware of the purpose of these goals. Commitment to objectives is important too, and one way of achieving this is to establish a contract between counsellor and client in which desired changes are clearly stated. It is essential that clients experience some measure of control in the setting and implementation of goals, and to this end on-going communication and negotiation between client and counsellor is the norm. When goals have been discussed and correctly defined, an action plan is set up and a definite decision is made by both client and counsellor to work together – unless it has become obvious that a different form of therapy would be in the client's best interests. There are some clients who do not respond well to a behavioural approach, and these and other limitations will be discussed later in the chapter. In behavioural therapy assessment continues throughout all the sessions. This is important in order to ensure that goals are either being met or altered in the light of changing situations.

Behavioural methods and procedures

The methods and procedures used in behavioural therapy are all designed to meet the needs of individual clients. There is no rigid set of techniques and the view of helpers in this field is that since each client is unique, all helping procedures must reflect and address this. However, behaviourism does have within its repertoire a wide range of methods which can be used wtih clients, and counsellors creativity and innovation are valued as well. The following is a summary of established behavioural techniques, which are frequently used successfully in therapy.

◆ Relaxation training
◆ Systematic desensitisation
◆ Client self monitoring
◆ Practising and planning behaviour
◆ Assertiveness training
◆ Social skills training
◆ Reinforcement methods
◆ Modelling
◆ Focus on physical exercise and nutrition
◆ Imagery and visualisation

Relaxation training

Anxiety and stress are common problems for many clients who seek behavioural counselling. In view of this relaxation training is a central focus of the approach and is used extensively for a variety of problems. Anxiety, which is quite different from fear, affects people on three levels – psychological, physiological and behavioural. Whereas fear tends to have a definite external focus, anxiety is usually internal and often unrelated to a specific identifiable cause. When clients talk about anxiety they sometimes describe it as a 'vague feeling of losing control' or as a 'sense that something awful will happen'. In order to combat the cycle of anxiety, it is useful to start by explaining its effect to clients. When this is done, relaxation techniques make much more sense, and clients are likely to engage in this approach with greater commitment.

Anxiety tends to increase the heart and breathing rates and may cause a variety of other symptoms including muscle tension, irritability, sleep problems and difficulty in concentrating. Counsellors can show clients how to reduce these effects by teaching concentration on the following key areas:

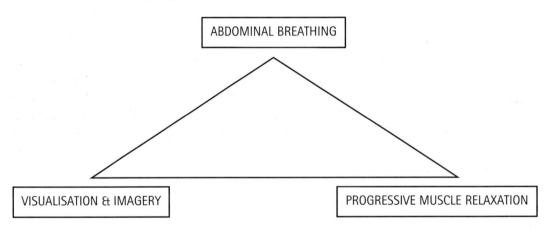

Figure 8.2 *Aids to relaxation*

Many anxious people tend to breathe in a shallow fashion from the chest, and clients can be taught to change this pattern so that deeper abdominal breathing is learned. This has the effect of increasing oxygen supply to the brain and muscles which, in turn, helps to improve concentration, promote a state of calmness along with deeper feelings of connectedness between mind and body. These feelings are exactly the opposite of those experienced in anxiety and stress, and when deep breathing is accompanied by progressive relaxation of body muscles, and visualisation of a peaceful scene, reduction of general anxiety is bound to follow.

There are numerous instruction manuals and tapes for teaching these techniques, and anyone interested in helping clients in this approach should become familiar with them. Clients can be taught to set aside time each day for relaxation, and this is especially beneficial for those people who suffer from stress-related conditions such as tension headaches, poor sleep patterns and high blood pressure.

Systematic desensitisation

Systematic desensitisation is a technique devised by Joseph Wolpe, whose research was outlined earlier in this chapter. It is used in behavioural counselling as a means of helping clients deal with irrational fears and phobias. Wolpe believed that it is impossible for a person to be anxious and relaxed at the same time, since these two states are mutually exclusive. He also believed that anxiety responses are learned or conditioned, and that it is possible to eliminate these responses if the anxious individual is helped to relax in the face of the anxiety-producing stimulus. The person is, therefore, 'systematically desensitised' to the fearful object or situation through a process of exposure to it, while in a relaxed state. Progressive muscle relaxation methods and deep breathing are integral to this technique, and clients are taught how to reduce anxiety in this way before they confront their fear. Constructing an appropriate 'hierarchy' is another important feature of systematic de-sensitisation, and involves outlining a series of situations or scenes relating to the phobia. Each scene in the hierarchy is ranked from mildly anxiety-provoking to extremely anxiety-provoking.

─◁ **CASE STUDY** ▷─ Constructing a hierarchy ─────────────

The following is an example of a hierarchy which was used to help a client called Isobel, aged twenty, who had a phobia about eating in front of strangers. Isobel's phobia was embarrassing and inconvenient because it meant that she refused to socialise on many occasions. She also found herself increasingly isolated at work, and decided to seek help when she no longer felt able to accompany her friends to the lunch canteen. The counsellor taught Isobel the relaxation procedure and breathing methods already discussed, and then helped her to design and work though the following hierarchy, which she was encouraged to practise on a regular basis:

Visualise

◆ Asking a close friend to accompany you on a visit to a restaurant
◆ Phoning a restaurant to make a reservation
◆ Getting dressed for your evening out
◆ Doing your hair and putting on make up
◆ Opening the door to greet your friend
◆ Walking to the restaurant a short distance away
◆ Meeting people along the way
◆ Passing other cafés and restaurants as you walk along
◆ Arriving at the door of the restaurant
◆ Speaking to the waiter about your reservation
◆ Walking to the table with your friend and the waiter
◆ Looking at the menu and discussing it with your friend
◆ Placing an order with the waiter

- Looking at your food when it arrives
- Picking up the knife and fork and starting to eat
- Tasting the food and enjoying it
- Looking around at the other diners
- Noting that other people are enjoying themselves
- Becoming aware that other people occasionally glance at your table
- Continuing your meal and the conversation with your friend

Designing the hierarchy

Clients need to give a detailed history of the phobia, with special emphasis on those aspects of it which cause the most anxiety. What made this client most anxious was the thought of being observed while eating. For this reason, observation was presented towards the end of the hierarchy which meant that Isobel could work very gradually towards it.

Real-life desensitisation

It should be emphasised that this exercise was based on imagery, and that later on the client and counsellor constructed a hierarchy for 'real-life' exposure. Real-life desensitisation is perhaps the most effective method of dealing with phobias, and is quite often used following a period of visual or imagery desensitisation. 'Exposure therapy' is another term used to describe this form of treatment (Bourne, 1995), and it is especially effective for phobias which include a 'social' element, as Isobel's did. However, real-life exposure does take time, because the introduction of anxiety-provoking stimuli needs to be very gradual. Not all clients with phobias are willing to undertake real-life exposure, since the process causes some degree of initial discomfort at least. It also needs to be practised over a period of time, on a regular basis and in spite of probable setbacks.

Client self-monitoring

In behaviour therapy clients are sometimes asked to maintain records of their behaviour, with particular references to those aspects of it which are problematic along with any attendant conditions. A self record may take the form of a daily diary, and one of the benefits of this kind of self monitoring is that clients often react to their own observations by reducing the frequency of their own problem behaviour (Phares, 1988). People who smoke, for example, may not realise quite how many cigarettes they consume in a day, until they see the evidence on record. Client self monitoring does have great therapeutic potential, though clients need to be well motivated to pursue it.

Assertiveness training

Assertiveness training is widely used in behaviour therapy and counselling. Clients often experience difficulties in several key areas. These include:

◆ Expressing their feelings

◆ Asking for what they need or want

◆ Saying no to requests from others

The most important aspect of assertiveness training is in helping clients differentiate between 'submissive', 'aggressive' and assertive styles of communication. When people are submissive they tend to ignore their own rights and needs, and this can result in feelings of depression and anger which are never really expressed. Aggressive people may be bullying and demanding, characteristics which inevitably alienate others. On the other hand, assertive behaviour involves direct person-to-person communication, without manipulation, hostility or self abnegation. Assertiveness training is often conducted in a group setting, and non-assertive clients who express an interest are sometimes referred to them so that they can increase their self awareness and confidence generally.

◆ Social skills training

Clients also frequently experience difficulties in social situations, and this is another area in which behavioural counselling offers some support to clients. In many ways there is an overlap with assertiveness training here which incorporates the social skills dimension, but it is also possible for counsellors to offer some individual skills training to those clients who request help in this way. 'Practising and planning behaviour' is one aspect of social skills training, and this may take the form of role play of a specific situation seen as problematic or daunting by the client. The practice of interview techniques is one example of this kind of approach, and in behavioural counselling such methods and techniques are commonly used. In social skills training there is an emphasis on setting achievable goals so that maximum positive reinforcement is obtained for new behaviours early on.

◆ Modelling

Observational learning or modelling is sometimes used to help clients acquire new forms of behaviour. The emphasis in this technique is on showing clients that certain behaviours can be undertaken (in this case by the counsellor) in a calm and non-threatening way. This is especially effective when used in conjunction with systematic desensitisation, especially when the counsellor 'models' the behaviour which the client associates with anxiety and stress. Videotapes are sometimes used as part of a modelling programme, and 'participation modelling' is another variant.

This technique refers to a process in which both client and counsellor participate. A counsellor might, for example, model attitudes of composure and calm while walking into a restaurant. Later on, the client can practise this behaviour in the company of the counsellor.

Reinforcement

Understanding of reinforcement principles is essential in behavioural counselling. Certain problems, such as persistent cleansing rituals or hypochondria, require environmental reinforcement to make them continue. As Avery (1996) points out, people who look for dirt will always find it, and those who seek reassurances about their health are likely to get it from friends and family. In these two problem situations the environmental reinforcement can be broken, in the first instance, by helping the client to interrupt the cleansing ritual and substituting something else. In the second instance they can enlist the help of the client's friends and persuade them to 'withhold reassurance' (Avery, 1996).

◆ Positive reinforcement

Positive reinforcement is based on the work of Skinner and his theory of operant conditioning. The behavioural approach to counselling places considerable emphasis on the practice of systematically reinforcing a client's desired behaviour, while at the same time ignoring any problematic behaviour. If positive reinforcement is continued over a period of time, then maladaptive behaviour should become extinct. Clients can also be encouraged to identify and use their own reinforcers. This kind of self reinforcement will obviously vary for different clients, but often activities which are calming or relaxing are effective in most cases. One client, a middle-aged woman, suffered from a condition called 'Obsessive Compulsive Disorder' or OCD, which in her case took the form of persistent tidying and checking. In conversation with her counsellor she mentioned that she used to love playing the piano, and later on she returned to this interest and used it as a calming self reinforcer which helped her to break the tidying and checking compulsion.

Physical exercise and nutrition

In recent years a great deal of attention has been given to the importance of exercise and diet in the maintenance of individual fitness. Although the link between physical health and these two factors has always been accepted, the significance of diet and exercise in relation to psychological health was traditionally less emphasised. This situation is currently changing, and nutritional experts now focus almost equally on the importance of a well-balanced diet for physical and psychological health. Clients often eat less or more while under stress, and it is a good idea to address this aspect of their behaviour with them,

CASE STUDY — Diet and exercise

One client, called Jeanette, described the depression and feelings of tiredness she experienced at work. During counselling she revealed that she regularly skipped breakfast, and then snacked on convenience food for the rest of the day. She also worried about her weight, and took no exercise because she felt she was too busy to do so. Through a process of self monitoring Jeanette was able to chart her mood swings in diary form, and afterwards to see that her depression was certainly exacerbated by dietary neglect and inertia. In behavioural counselling clients should be encouraged to address issues of diet and exercise so that the behavioural aspects of both are highlighted. It is possible to 'unlearn' patterns of behaviour which contribute to feelings of depression, stress and tiredness, and it is also possible for clients to 're-learn' healthier habits, though they do need encouragement, feedback and support in order to do this.

Clients who benefit from this approach

Clients with a wide range of problems respond well to behavioural counselling. Several of these problems – phobias, certain aspects of depression and lack of assertiveness for example – have been highlighted in this chapter. However, any psychological difficulty manifest through observable behaviour is likely to respond well to this approach. Clients who suffer from obsessions and compulsions often find that behavioural counselling enables them to deal more effectively with their problems. People with sexual difficulties often seek help through behavioural therapy and counselling, and clients with speech problems such as stammering or an inability to speak publicly can also be helped. Behavioural therapy is widely used in stress management and assertiveness training, and its principles are applicable in the management of childhood behaviour problems, and very often care of the elderly. Behaviour therapy is widely available, both within the NHS and privately. It is a highly adaptable approach which makes efficient use of time, and results are easily measured too.

Some limitations

We have noted that the behavioural approach is especially helpful in dealing with problems manifest through overt behaviour. This strength is, in fact, also its weakness, since often the problems often stem from deeper and hidden origins which need to be addressed in the long-term. A client who has a phobia about the dark, for example, may well respond to a behavioural approach in counselling, but unless the hidden insecurity which prompted the phobia in the first place is identified, lasting cure of the problem is unlikely. On the other hand, even temporary alleviation of the phobia might give the client sufficient inclination to look at less obvious issues, so that overall real progress is made and insight gained.

Clients need to be fully committed, especially at the beginning of counselling when stress levels are high and the gratification gained obtained through problem behaviour is still very attractive. Counsellors who work from a strictly behavioural perspective are at risk of adopting a mechanistic or over-simplified view of clients. This is because a basic principle of approach is that people react in an automatic way to stimuli – a view which leaves little room for the influence of thinking, or cognition in determining behaviour. However, the balance has now been redressed through the influence of cognitive therapy, which we shall consider in the next section.

THE COGNITIVE EMPHASIS

As the name suggests, cognitive therapy is concerned with the thinking and reasoning aspects of a person's experience. We have seen that behaviour therapy evolved from the theories of learning first formulated by Pavlov, Watson, Thorndike, Skinner, Wolpe and Eysenck, and from the experiments of Bandura and other psychologists interested in the effects of observation on the individual's learning experience. The behavioural approach, widely used in the 1950s, emphasised the importance of visible behaviour and its environmental context. However, this emphasis tended to ignore the thinking and feeling aspects of human behaviour and it was not until several psychologists, including Aaron Beck and Albert Ellis, began to focus on the thoughts and beliefs of disturbed or anxious clients, that the cognitive dimension came into being.

The work of these theorist highlights the way in which anxious and depressed clients contribute to their own problems through faulty or destructive thought processes and pre-occupations. In this section we shall look in some detail at the work of Albert Ellis, whose Rational Emotive Behaviour Therapy model is one of the most established and widely used cognitive behavioural approaches.

RATIONAL EMOTIVE BEHAVIOUR THERAPY

Albert Ellis (1913–)

Albert Ellis was responsible for pioneering Cognitive–Behaviour Therapy (CBT) at the beginning of 1955, and since then his own individual approach, now called Rational Emotive Behaviour Therapy, has become one of the most popular cognitive models. Ellis himself claims that Rational Emotive Behaviour Therapy was the 'original' cognitive–behaviour approach to psychological problems (Ellis, 1995).

Ellis, who was born in Pittsburg, Pennsylvania, continues to work as President of the Albert Ellis Institute in New York. His background training and experience include studies in Accounting, Clinical Psychology, writing, family and marriage counselling and psycho-analysis. Ellis trained in classical Freudian analysis, although he never wholly subscribed to many of the basic principles of that discipline. In particular, he questioned the efficacy of free association and dream interpretation as techniques in therapy, and he doubted the overall efficiency of psychoanalysis as a form of helping (Ellis, 1962). Classical psycho-analysis is an in-depth and time consuming form of therapy not suited (or available) to many clients, and Ellis was concerned to establish a more egalitarian and pragmatic approach which would address the needs of a wider range of people who sought help.

Albert Ellis has held many posts throughout his career, including Consultant in Clinical Psychology to the New York Board of Education and Vice President of the American Academy of Psychotherapists. He has also written numerous books and articles, and has served as consulting or associate editor of many professional journals.

Development of the approach

During the 1950s Ellis became interested in behavioural learning theory. He noted that psychoanalysis and learning theory have a great deal in common, since both emphasise the importance of conditioning in early life. However, he concluded that action, as well as insight, is necessary if people are to address the difficulties which stem from childhood and the early conditioning which determines so many problematic responses in adult life. In addition, Ellis identified the central place of negative thinking in the perpetuation of emotional disturbance and he was especially interested in the kind of negative thinking which reinforces early disturbing and traumatic experiences. Clients, he believed, often cling to outdated feelings of depression, anger and guilt which impede psychological growth and are, in any case, no longer applicable to the present situation. Outdated or negative thinking is often the direct result of information which has been conveyed to clients at an early stage, by parents or other important people at that time.

In Ellis' view, the language is the key to the perpetuation of emotional problems since it is through the use of language or internal dialogue that clients reinforce their fears and anxieties stemming from early life. To compound the problem even further, people frequently denigrate themselves and their efforts, demand perfection from themselves and others and exhibit what Ellis (1995) refers to as 'low frustration tolerance' towards others and the environment in general.

◆ Other influences

The importance of both language and thinking is stressed throughout Ellis' writing. References to philosophy and literature are also frequent, and indeed these two subjects have informed and helped define many aspects of his work. Ellis was especially interested in the Stoic philosophers, including Epictetus, who believed that people become disturbed, not by events themselves but by personal interpretations of those events.

◆ Development of the title

The original title of Ellis' approach was 'Rational Psychotherapy', but it soon became apparent to him that such a description did not adequately address every aspect of the work he was doing. He also wished to differentiate between his own model and other, purely cognitive approaches which had become popular in the 1950s. In 1959, two years after he abandoned psychoanalysis, he founded the Institute for Rational-Emotive Therapy, now the Albert Ellis Institute. Ellis described his model as 'Rational-Emotive Therapy' in order to highlight the emotional focus of his work. In 1993 this was again changed to Rational Emotive Behaviour Therapy, title which stresses the significance of all three components – cognitive, emotional and behavioural – of human experience.

◆ The theory of Rational Emotive Behaviour Therapy

Ellis believes that emotional and neurotic problems are generated from three important sources. These include thinking, emotional and behavioural sources, but he places special emphasis on the significance of 'cognition' or thinking in the perpetuation of psychological disturbance. Ellis refers to the views of a number of philosophers to support his thesis (Ellis, 1995) and suggest that people are 'largely responsible' for their own disturbed feelings which they either consciously or unconsciously generate. If we accept that this is the case then it follows, according to Ellis, that people have within themselves the resources and willpower necessary to effect lasting and healthy change. Ellis (1995) describes the sequence of events which lead to psychological disturbance through the use of an ABC model (see Figure 8.3).

In the first instance, people start with goals in life, and these are usually constructive and positive. What tends to happen, however, is that difficulties (or 'activating events') are

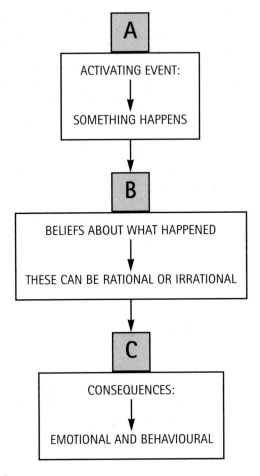

Figure 8.3   *The ABC model*

encountered at various stages which impede the individual's desire for success and comfort. After this, people construct their own largely negative 'beliefs' or interpretations of these events, and these beliefs lead to certain emotional and behavioural 'consequences.

CASE STUDY — The ABC Model

Bill, who was in his fifties, had a very good relationship with his next door neighbour Roy, who was about the same age. Bill applied to his doctor for counselling help because he suffered from increasing depression linked to several significant changes in his life. His parents had died in the previous year, and he had just discovered that his daughter's marriage was breaking up. In addition to his depression, Bill suffered from severe loss of confidence which, he said, had been prompted by his experience of early retirement, and by feelings of panic about his age. During counselling Bill talked about an incident with his neighbour which had caused him a great deal of anxiety, and had knocked his confidence even further. Roy's eight year-old grandson had come to stay for a holiday and several days later, Bill's own grandson came to stay with him too. When Bill suggested to his neighbour that they should plan some activities together, Roy responded by saying that while he would be happy to share some time as a group, he would also like to reserve most outings with his grandson and members of his own family. Bill ruminated at length about this response which he took as a personal rejection of himself and the friendship he offered. Afterwards he became even more depressed and withdrawn, and for several weeks avoided his neighbour. The Rational Emotive Therapy model, see Figure 8.4, shows in diagram form this sequence of events.

Ellis' ABC model of personality and emotional disturbance highlights the relationship between thinking and emotion. In Ellis's view (1962) it is not what happens at point A which causes emotional disturbance or distress. People form their own inferences and beliefs at point B, and reinforce them through the use of negative and 'catastrophising' self-talk and rumination. It is this internal soliloquy which then leads to the emotional and behavioural reactions which occur at point C. Bill's action in avoiding his neighbour led to a worsening situation, since after a while Roy stopped making social overtures in the mistaken belief that Bill had lost interest. This had the effect of deepening Bill's

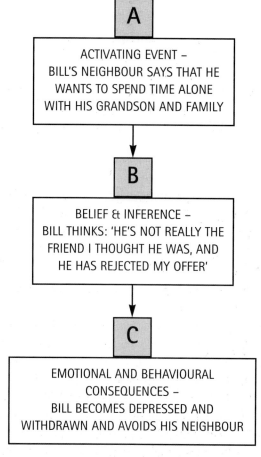

Figure 8.4 *Irrational thinking and emotional disturbance*

depression and general loss of confidence. In counselling he was helped to see how his own thinking had contributed to his problems overall. The counsellor explained the ABC model of Rational Emotive Behaviour Therapy to Bill. It should be added, however, that there were other factors in this client's life which contributed to his depression, and these were also addressed in counselling.

The following example, Figure 8.5, shows how Bill *might* have chosen to respond to the activating event described.

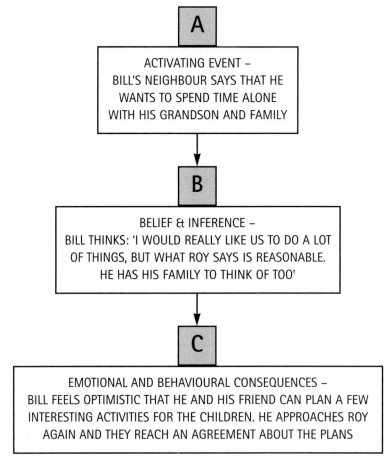

Figure 8.5 *Changing irrational beliefs*

Rational and irrational thinking

Ellis (1995) takes the view that people have a basic tendency to be irrational as well as rational in their thinking. Irrational thinking is seen as a fundamental cause of psychological disturbance. It is developed early in life and is due, in part, to biological tendencies, but it is also the result of social learning and the emotional investment we all have in our own particular beliefs. Rational Emotive Behaviour Therapy aims to help clients develop more rational, less punitive, ways of thinking, and this means encouraging them to consider the ways in which their irrational thinking of the past has contributed to numerous problems. Clients are also encouraged to work towards long, rather than short, term change, so that the ordinary (and less ordinary) difficulties of life are dealt with more effectively as time goes on.

Some irrational beliefs

According to Ellis (1962) most people subscribe to a number of irrational or illogical beliefs which lead to many of the problems experienced by clients. These beliefs, which are seldom questioned by anyone, tend to be passed from one generation to another so that they become accepted wisdom. Ellis refers to these beliefs as 'superstitions and prejudices' and he goes on to say that they can, in his opinion, only be changed through a basic 'ideational or philosophical' shift in modern outlook. The following are some of the irrational beliefs which he describes:

◆ I should always be loved and approved of by everyone.

◆ In order to be a worthwhile person, I need to be good at everything.

◆ Bad people, including myself, should be severely punished.

◆ If things are not the way I want them to be, it's a disaster.

◆ I have no real control over my problems, which are caused by external factors.

◆ I need to keep on reminding myself of the awful things that may happen.

◆ It's easier to avoid than to face problems and responsibilities.

◆ I always need someone stronger to take care of me.

◆ I can't change my behaviour because of my awful past.

◆ I should always become emotionally engaged in other people's problems.

Adapted from Ellis (1962)

< EXERCISE > — Irrational beliefs

Working with a partner, look at the above list of irrational beliefs and say how many of them you subscribe to, or may have subscribed to at certain times of your life. Discuss these with your partner, paying special attention to any beliefs you have in common. Consider the origins of such beliefs and say how you think you may have acquired your own.

Shoulds and musts

Throughout his writing on the subject of Rational Emotive Behaviour Therapy, Ellis often refers to the words 'should and 'must' which, he says are frequently used by clients who seek to impose 'absolutist' demands on themselves and others. People may, for example, express the view that they 'must' be good at certain things, or that other people 'must' always be nice to them. If these 'musts' are not realised, life is seen as intolerable, awful, or not worth living. These misleading and 'disturbance producing' shoulds and musts are irrational according to Ellis (1995), and in Rational Emotive Behaviour Therapy they are regarded as primary causes of emotional problems. Ellis also uses the terms 'catastrophise' and 'awfulise' to describe these forms of irrational thinking which tend to cause disturbed or neurotic behaviour. In addition, Ellis believes that once people accept their own or others' irrational beliefs, they are likely to produce what he calls 'secondary disturbances'. Thus people often become very anxious abut their anxiety, depressed about their depression, or self-loathing about their anger towards others (Ellis, 1995).

Helping clients to change

In Rational Emotive Behaviour Therapy clients are taught the ABC model at an early stage. Clients are also encouraged to look at the 'activating event' and the 'emotional disturbance' they have experienced. Afterwards, attention is directed to the 'beliefs' and inferences which have created such a powerful influence in the production of emotional disturbance. It is possible to teach this model effectively and quickly and most clients, apart from those who are seriously ill or confused, are able to grasp it. Clients are also encouraged to identify and dispute their 'musts' and any other irrational beliefs they entertain.

This is a highly active and directive approach which incorporates elements of teaching, persuasion, debate and even humour within its repertoire. Ellis is, in fact, notable among psychotherapists and counsellors for his support of humour as a therapeutic aid. It is not something we tend to associate with therapists who, as a group, have always been somewhat suspicious of levity and its effects on the serious business of relating to clients. There are various reasons for this reluctance to laugh when things are ludicrous or funny, and it has to be said that humour is indeed often inappropriate in the therapeutic context. However, as Strean (1994) indicates, Freud himself admired humour and freely appreciated it in his friends and in his patients. Ellis, too, appreciates it, and he recommends the use of humour as a way of helping clients to 'interrupt' their own seriousness and to separate themselves from stuffy, outmoded and 'dysfunctional' beliefs (Ellis, 1995). It goes without saying, however, that humour should never be used against clients in therapy. It also needs to be sensitively timed and appropriate to the situation. The following is an example of the way humour was used with one client who had a compulsion to check, at very frequent intervals, all the cups in the kitchen cupboard.

CLIENT: What we talked about last time did work quite well. Instead of checking the cups when I got home from shopping, I went out into the garden instead and did some work there. I felt a lot better about doing that. I think it's getting better, but I still feel like counting something.

COUNSELLOR: The saucepans and cutlery maybe?

CLIENT: Oh, God, no [laughs]. Well I am beginning to look more closely at the way I think about this checking, and I can see how I have actually been thinking the worst ... that if I don't count the cups, everything will go wrong and I'll be out of control. I actually can laugh at myself now and I think that's real progress.

Homework and other tasks

Clients may be given homework tasks to do, and they are frequently asked to read self-help books on the subject of Rational Emotive Behaviour Therapy. Homework may include self monitoring and recording of negative thoughts and self sabotaging beliefs, as well as exercises in critical thinking and questioning. Written work is sometimes included in homework exercises, and this might take the form of writing down and disputing personal beliefs which may have caused problems in the past. Imagery is another technique used in this approach, and clients are sometimes asked to 'imagine' themselves responding in positive ways to situations which have been problematic for them in the past.

Role play, which is used extensively in assertiveness training and behaviour therapy, is incorporated into the Ellis model. A client could, for example, role play some feared or threatening future event such as public speaking, a job interview, or an appointment to ask for a change of conditions at work. 'Modelling' is also used, but in this approach its application is not restricted to counselling sessions. It may be extended to models of positive behaviour which clients may have observed in others. Many clients are familiar with favourite characters in literature who display the kinds of personal qualities they would like to develop.

Ellis (1995) refers to the technique of 'cognitive distraction' as a means of helping clients deal with anxiety and depression. In simple terms, this means encouraging clients to learn relaxation procedures, yoga or meditation, but it also means teaching them how to dispute the irrational beliefs which cause problems for them. 'Semantic correction' is another interesting Rational Emotive Behaviour Therapy technique which is used with clients who overgeneralise or make sweeping statements. The following is an example:

CLIENT: People always let me down, always. Then I get depressed and fed up.

COUNSELLOR: Absolutely always let you down?

CLIENT: Well no, but quite often.

COUNSELLOR: Try changing what you first said around a bit.

CLIENT: In what way?

COUNSELLOR: Instead of the statement you made, change it to this: I allow myself to become depressed and fed up when other people let me down.

CLIENT: Like the ABC we discussed? Yes, but it takes time to change things around like that.

COUNSELLOR: That's why all the practice is important.

Dealing with shame

In Ellis' view feelings of shame, guilt or inadequacy are responsible for many of the problems which prompt people to seek help in therapy (Ellis, 1962). In order to help clients deal
with these feelings he devised what are referred to as 'shame-attacking' exercises. People
who are fearful of exposing personal weakness, or those who are inhibited about expressing themselves, are encouraged to take risks and engage in some form of activity which will
prove to them that their fears are exaggerated. A client might, for example, be asked to
become more gregarious socially, either in dress, behaviour or manner. The purpose behind
this approach is to show clients that they need not feel ashamed, nor will anything awful
happen to them if they take more risks.

◆ Contracts and commitment

Rational Emotive Behaviour can be used as a brief therapy, but it is also suited to longer
term counselling when necessary. A primary focus of the model is to help clients understand the connection between thinking and emotional disturbance, which means they also
need to understand the *purpose* of the exercises which they are asked to do. Commitment
to completion of assignments is important too, and any tasks which clients do should be
discussed in later counselling sessions. The behavioural focus in Rational Emotive Behaviour
Therapy requires that clients receive 'positive reinforcement' for any progress they make. A
working contract is always established at the beginning of therapy, the terms of which are
detailed and specific.

The therapeutic relationship

We have seen that Rational Emotive Behaviour Therapy is an active, directive and teaching
approach to counselling. It is these characteristics which set it apart from many of the other
models we have discussed in this book. However, the actual relationship between counsellor and client is just as important in this approach as it is in any other. Dryden (1990) suggests that flexibility is an essential attitude on the counsellor's part. What works with one
client might not necessarily work for another, so counsellors need to be open to the needs
of individual clients. The counselling relationship is an egalitarian one, although equality
may not be obvious at the beginning of therapy when clients are disadvantaged because of
the problems which preoccupy them. Once therapy is established however, counsellors are
frequently willing to disclose information which is seen as helpful or encouraging for
clients. This might include details of problems similar to those experienced by the client.

The Rogerian concept of empathy is problematic in Rational Emotive Behaviour Therapy,
where attitudes of detachment and understanding are valued highly. Counsellors need to
be separate from the irrational views which clients express, and this means refusing to collude or support these views when they are articulated. The concept of 'transference' is also
viewed differently in this approach. Indeed, the idea that the counsellor should encourage
a client's irrational dependence is anathema, and contrary to all the basic principles of
Rational Emotive Behaviour Therapy. 'Debate' has a central place in the model, and is meant
to encourage openness and honesty between client and counsellor.

We have seen that humour is frequently used, and this goes along with an atmosphere of informality meant to encourage creative and less rigid attitudes in clients generally. On the other hand, there are clients who prefer a more formal approach and these wishes are centrally accommodated in the model. 'Logic' and 'persuasion' are valuable skills which are also used extensively in Rational Emotive Behaviour Therapy.

Group work

Rational Emotive Behaviour Therapy is often conducted in a group setting. Although resistant to the idea of group therapy initially, Ellis later came to regard it as an effective medium for helping clients. All the advantages of group work apply to Rational Emotive Behaviour Therapy, but there is an added bonus in the sense that more people are available to dispute their own and other people's irrational beliefs and statements. Therapy can take place in single-sex or mixed groups, large groups or small groups, although Ellis himself favours a large group setting which, he suggests, tend to be more 'lively' with more interesting material available for discussion (Ellis, 1962).

Another significant aspect of Rational Emotive Behaviour group work is that all the members are taught the principles of the approach. This means that individual participants can (with the guidance of the group leader) take turns in the role of facilitator or therapist, an experience which is empowering for them. Some members of the group may also attend individual therapy sessions, and when this is the case the group can supply the extra support often needed to consolidate the progress made in the individual setting.

Clients who benefit from this approach

Clients who lack assertiveness, or those who experience problems in relation to negative thinking and depression, are likely to benefit from a Rational Emotive Behaviour approach in either an individual therapy or group work setting. Those who need specific interventions, such as family or marital therapy, may also be helped by therapists who are trained to use the model. Rational Emotive Behaviour Therapy is accessible and fairly easy to understand, which means that the majority of clients (or at least those with the kinds of problems already mentioned) can benefit from it. The principles of the approach can be applied to education and child therapy as well, and this flexibility of application is one of its main assets.

Corey (1991) makes the point that the focus on learning and teaching, which is central to Rational Emotive Behaviour Therapy, ensures that many clients regard it in a positive light, and untainted with associations of mental illness. In addition, there are many clients who welcome the stress on action under the direction of the therapist. Tasks like homework and role play may motivate those clients who would normally find it difficult to move into action without some support, initially at least. Putting ideas into action can inspire a real sense of achievement, though clients need to be committed and reinforced for all the gains they make. Rational Emotive Behaviour Therapy can also be viewed as a self help approach, since it advocates reading, listening to tapes, attendance at lectures and workshops, and generally becoming independent in the search for improvement and change. This is an aspect of the model which helps to give confidence to those clients who use it. Clients are further encouraged to view themselves as capable of making change, regardless of any past traumas they may have suffered.

Some limitations

Clients who wish to conduct an in-depth study of childhood events and attendant traumas are unlikely to seek Rational Emotive Behaviour Therapy in order to do so. This is because the approach tends to minimise the past, although this does not imply that Ellis regarded the past as irrelevant in any way. On the contrary Ellis, who trained in Freudian psycho-analysis, was aware of the influence of past events, but be came to believe that little progress could be make through dwelling on them (Ellis, 1962).

To Ellis' down surprise, the Rational Emotive Behaviour methods which he devised produced quicker and more lasting results than those gained through deep analysis. However, critics of Rational Emotive Behaviour Therapy stress the point that fast methods can produce fast results which may, in the end, be fairly transitory. The active, directive and action-based nature of the approach may not appeal to some clients, and indeed there are probably a few who might feel quite threatened by it. If certain irrational beliefs are too vigorously disputed early in therapy, clients may vote with their feet and leave. On the other hand, as Weinrach (1995) has suggested, this kind of situation can be avoided through the use of 'appropriate empathy' and the direction of attention to the client's subjective experience of the problem.

SUMMARY

Behavioural and cognitive approaches to counselling were the subject of this chapter. In the first instance we considered the evolution of Behaviour therapy, and discussed the theories of learning which informed the approach. The contributions of Pavlov, Watson, Thorndike, Skinner, Wople and Bandura were highlighted, and placed in the context of therapeutic practice. Problems which are frequently dealt with in behaviour therapy, including phobias, anxiety and social skills deficit, were discussed, and examples of techniques used were also given. The aims of therapy, the nature of the counsellor/client relationship, goals and group practice were outlined and several major behavioural methods and procedures were described in some detail. Reference was made to the cognitive emphasis in therapy, and the work of Albert Ellis and the Rational Emotive Behaviour Therapy which he pioneered was the subject of the second half of the chapter. The development of Ellis' approach was considered, along with the factors which influenced his work. The ABC model was shown, and a summary of irrational beliefs was given. Aims and objectives of therapy were included, and counsellor characteristics and examples of techniques and procedures were outlined. The nature of the counsellor/client relationship was discussed, as was the application of Rational Emotive Behaviour Therapy to group work.

REFERENCES

Avery, B. (1996)   *Principles of Psychotherapy.* London: Thorsons.

Bourne, E. J. (1995)   *The Anxiety and Phobia Workbook.* Oakland, California: New Harbinger Publications Inc.

Corey, G. (1991)   *Theory and Practice of Counselling and Psychotherapy.* California: Brooks/Cole.

Dryden, W. (1990)   *Rational-Emotive Counselling.* London: Sage Publications.

Ellis, A. (1995)   'Fundamentals of Rational Emotive Behaviour Therapy For The 1990s', in Dryden (ed.) (1995) *Rational Emotive Behaviour Therapy – A Reader.* London: Sage Publications.

Ellis, A. (1962)   *Reason and Emotion in Psychotherapy.* New York: Citadel Press.

Nelson–Jones, R. (1996)   *The Theory and Practice of Counselling.* London: Cassell.

Phares, E. J. (1988)   *Introduction to Personality.* USA: Scott, Foresman and Company.

Richards, D. & McDonald, B. (1990)   *Behavioural Psychotherapy.* London: Heinemann.

Rycroft, C. (1972)   *A Critical Dictionary of Psychoanalysis.* London: Penguin.

Skinner, B. F. (1971)   *Beyond Freedom and Dignity.* London: Penguin Books (1988).

Strean, H. (1994)   *The Use of Humour in Psychotherapy.* New Jersey: Jason Aronson, (1995).

Weinrach, G. (1995)   'Rational Emotive Behaviour Therapy: A Tough Minded Therapy for a Tender Minded Profession' in Dryden (ed.) (1995) *Rational Emotive Behaviour Therapy – A Reader.* London: Sage Publications.

FURTHER READING

Dryden, W. (ed.) (1995)   *Rational Emotive Behaviour Therapy – A Reader.* London: Sage Publications.

Trower, P. (1988)   *Cognitive – Behavioural Counselling In Action.* London: Sage Publications.

Yankura, J. & Dryden, W. (1994)   *Albert Ellis (Key figures In Counselling and Psychotherapy Series).* London: Sage Publications.

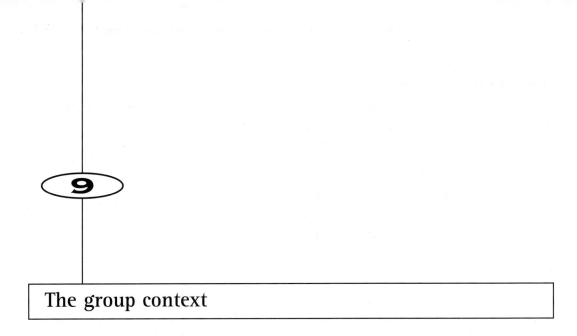

The group context

INTRODUCTION

The theoretical models of counselling described in earlier chapters are applicable to group as well as to individual counselling. Indeed it is probably true that the group approach is increasingly favoured by many practitioners, and is quite likely to supersede individual psychotherapy as a method of helping clients in the future. There are a number of important reasons for this increasing popularity and we shall consider these, along with other distinctive aspects of group counselling, in the course of this chapter. The evolution of group work and its application to psychotherapeutic counselling will also be considered, as will the variety of group settings currently in use.

Counsellors of all theoretical approaches have modified or adapted their skills so that they may be used within the therapy group setting. These include Psychodynamic, Adlerian, Existential Humanistic, Transactional Analysis, Gestalt, Behavioural and Rational Emotive Behaviour counsellors. Groups may also be used in a wide variety of settings including hospitals, out patients departments, schools, churches, day centres, children's homes and youth centres to name just a few. However, not all these settings conduct psychotherapeutic group work, although many of them do, and in some cases therapy, education and other *therapeutic* factors overlap. In this chapter, we shall look at characteristics common to all these groups regardless of their purpose or setting, but we shall also define the distinguishing features of the therapy group and its advantages and disadvantages for clients in counselling.

HOW GROUPS EVOLVED

The beneficial effects of groups have always been apparent to those who participate in them. Groups with a common purpose or goal tend to draw people closer together. After a while individual members develop a sense of loyalty – not just towards other participants but also to the concept of the group itself. This is true regardless of the nature of the group, and is just as applicable to religious groups as it is to those with a political, educational, youth, sports or indeed any other focus. However, the beneficial effects of groups for people with health or psychological problems were not always so obvious, and it wasn't until the Second World War that the true potential of the approach was identified.

Joseph Pratt

At the beginning of the twentieth century several other significant developments also took place in the history of therapeutic groups. The first of these developments was initiated in 1905 by Joseph Pratt, an American doctor who lived and practised in Boston. Pratt advocated a holistic approach to the treatment of the people in his care. His patients suffered from tuberculosis and because he felt that they needed support, instruction and encouragement, Pratt brought them together for weekly meetings. These group meetings were highly successful in the sense that the health and general well-being of the participants improved appreciably. Pratt's patients made progress because they helped each other, mainly through the sharing of information. They also, and perhaps more importantly, provided emotional support for each other, and in doing so improved the emotional and mental health of all group members. Pratt came to realise that the group was in itself therapeutic, regardless of teaching or other input.

Alcoholics Anonymous

Alcoholics Anonymous is one of the most famous and successful developments in the history of group work. The organisation was formed in 1935 in Ohio when the first meeting took place. A fundamental purpose of this group approach is to offer help and support to people who suffer from alcohol addiction. Since all members of the group have the same problem, there is an atmosphere and ethos of total equality and mutual respect. Alcoholics Anonymous is perhaps the best known example of a self help group, and its success has led to the development of many similar groups set up to help people with a wide variety of problems.

Moreno and psychodrama

We have already considered Moreno's contribution to psychotherapy (Chapter 6) but it is worth indicating again that his was a group approach to helping clients. Many of the techniques of psychodrama, including role play, have now been incorporated into other therapies and group work models. Moreno started his work at the beginning of the twentieth century and his pioneering ideas influenced many other psychologists, including Kurt Lewin, who were interested in exploring the potential benefits of working in groups.

Kurt Lewin

Kurt Lewin, a German social psychologist, was instrumental in setting up the first 'Training' or 'T' groups in America during and after the Second World War. These groups were formed in many organisations, including schools and industry, and the purpose was to facilitate the development of interpersonal and social skills among participants so that tension among racial groups could be reduced. Lewin worked with the National Training Laboratories in Washington, and a basic focus of the programmes devised by them was the training of leaders who would then pass on their newly acquired skills and knowledge to members of the organisations for which they worked. Group participants were encouraged to become sensitive to their and other peoples' needs, and to become more spontaneous in the expression of personal feelings. Many important issues relating to the organisations in which people worked were also addressed through T-group training, including issues of authority, leadership and the dynamics of change. Though the primary aim of Lewin's groups was the development of better social and relationship skills, many participants experienced other, more personal, benefits from group membership.

DEVELOPMENTS IN BRITAIN

During the Second World War many of the developments pioneered by Lewin were taken up and integrated into psychiatric practice in Britain. Bion and Rickman at the Tavistock Clinic were, for example, involved in the development of a group approach to the training and rehabilitation of army personnel who suffered from neurotic disability (Hyde, 1988). Bion, who was influenced by the work of Melanie Klein and object relations theory, was innovative and original in his approach and provided a framework for understanding group dynamics. He also identified various aspects of group mentality, and in doing so established a model which could be used by leaders and others who were involved in group participation.

S. H. Foulkes

Foulkes, who trained as a psychoanalyst in Germany, came to England in 1933 and founded the Group Analytic Society. He was also involved in the foundation of the Institute of Group Analysis, an organisation which provides training courses for therapists and others interested in group work. In Foulke's view, individuals within a psychotherapy group form a relationship network and their behaviour can, therefore, only be understood in the context of the group as a whole. The Gestalt concept of *wholeness* is applicable here since it illustrates the point made by Gestalt psychologists that the whole is greater than the sum of its parts. This approach differs from another model, popular in America, in which the individual is treated *within* the group by a therapist who concentrates on each person separately, with the other participants looking on. Many of Foulkes' most important ideas, some of which we shall consider in this chapter, have been taken up and used by a wide variety of group therapists.

Encounter groups

The success of Training groups in America led to the growth of the 'encounter' group movement, also known as 'sensitivity' groups, or 'personal growth' groups, which started first in California and then spread during the 1960s to other parts of America and eventually to Britain. The potential for self development and greater awareness through group participation became obvious to psychologists who were involved in the 'human potential' or 'humanistic' movement. The therapeutic value of groups was also apparent and Carl Rogers, whose person-centred approach emphasises personal growth and self-actualisation, became active in the encounter group movement. Rogers' groups were intended to facilitate open and honest expression of feelings, both verbal and non-verbal, within a supportive and non-judgmental environment. Catharsis, which refers to the release of pent-up feelings, was actively encouraged and became synonymous with the encounter group experience.

The original Training groups developed by Lewin did not emphasise personal growth in the way that Rogers did. However, there is an important point of similarity between the two models, in that both enhance social and communication skills through the feedback which participants supply to each other. Membership of the original Training and Encounter groups was a voluntary commitment, and those people who joined did not regard themselves as emotionally unwell or in need of remedial treatment of any kind. The humanistic dimension, derived from the work of Rogers, Fritz Perls, Abraham Maslow, Rollo May and Eric Fromm, became a strong influence in group work generally.

Self help groups

We have already noted that, in the history of groups, people with similar problems or difficulties have traditionally helped each other through a process of mutual support and the sharing of experience and information. Self help groups have, in other words, always existed in some form, though it is only fairly recently that their real benefits and potential have been recognised. The number and variety of self help voluntary organisations continues to increase. They address a diverse range of problems and situations, including the following:

◆ Bereavement
◆ Divorce
◆ Single parenthood
◆ HIV and AIDS
◆ Chemical or drug dependence
◆ Depression
◆ Gay people coming out
◆ Battered women
◆ Breast cancer
◆ Survivors of sexual abuse

This list details only a fraction of the number of self help groups now in existence. Other groups exist for any number of physical illnesses, including diabetes, stroke, arthritis, epilepsy and chronic fatigue syndrome. In addition, there are groups representing a broad spectrum of mental and emotional illness, including schizophrenia, stress and anxiety, obsessive compulsive disorder, and a myriad of addictive behaviours.

One of the most positive aspects of self help or support groups is that members feel empowered once they realise just how much they can, in fact, help themselves and others. No two groups ever function in exactly the same way, and they obviously differ a great deal in terms of structure, purpose, organisation and duration. However, there are factors common to them all, the most obvious being that members experience the same problem. This means that they are in a unique position to offer understanding, information and help to everyone else, while at the same time receiving support and assistance themselves. Perhaps the most significant aspect of self help groups is that they are 'expert free', and there is no one leader to whom people turn for guidance, authority or advice. A corollary of this is that striving for recognition or position among members is kept to a minimum, and indeed in many instances members do not even meet as a body but communicate by phone, letter or other media instead.

CASE STUDY — Oliver

Oliver, who was thirty, had suffered from anxiety and feelings of *dislocation* or *disconnectedness* for many years. In fact, in conversation with a counsellor, he revealed that he had never really known a time when he did not experience these feelings. Oliver had spent most of his early life in America, and had moved to Wales with his family when he was six. He remembered his parents telling him that he was adopted, and ever since then the strange feelings which he described became very pronounced. When he asked for details about his birth parents, Oliver's mother became evasive and assumed what he called 'a distant look in her eyes'. As a result of these responses he suppressed his curiosity (on the surface at least), but deep down he made a decision to protect, or keep separate, his *real* or inner *self* and wait until adulthood to seek details of his birth.

In spite of the control which he exercised, Oliver still felt overwhelmed with anger at times. He also went through an extremely rebellious phase at puberty and even ran away from home on several occasions. By the time he came to seek counselling Oliver had already met his birth mother, though for various reasons, the experience had not been a satisfactory one. The counsellor, with whom he established a good relationship, helped him to identify and explore many of the angry and negative feelings he had. He was especially angry about his birth mother's *abandonment* of him, but he was also furious with his parents who adopted him and withheld vital details of his personal history and antecedents. Oliver also loved his adoptive parents, and was deeply guilty about his negative feelings in relation to them. With the help of the counsellor he was able to locate and join a support group for adoptees whose problems were similar to his own. This was a very liberating experience for him, and although he continued to receive counselling for a time he derived enormous support from other participants within the group.

This is fairly detailed account of a particular client's difficulties in relation to a specific issue. However, it also serves to illustrate the point that other helping strategies (in this case a self help or support group) are often available, and sometimes more appropriate, for certain people. It is important to state once again that counselling has limitations, and although it can help many clients it cannot always provide everything clients need or seek. The counsellor who helped this client was aware that she did not appreciate fully all the complex and turbulent emotions he tried to express. The core condition of empathy, espoused by Rogers, does go a long way towards helping counsellors understand their clients, but there are some experiences which are so profound and intimate they cannot be accessed except by those who have actually been there too. An important counselling skill is the ability and willingness to acknowledge this fundamental fact.

EXERCISE — Looking at groups

Work with a partner and consider the general function and purpose of groups. Can you say exactly what a group is? Make a list of as many different types of groups you can think of. The following are some examples:

◆ Family groups

◆ Friendship groups

◆ Work groups

◆ Committee groups

◆ Creative groups

◆ Problem or task solving groups

Are there characteristics which are common to all groups? If so, what are these characteristics? Another point to consider is why people join groups. Spend about thirty minutes on this exercise, write your ideas down and then share and discuss them with other members of your own (training) group.

PSYCHOTHERAPY AND COUNSELLING GROUPS

In contrast to both Training and encounter groups, counselling and psychotherapy groups exist to help people who experience emotional, relational or psychological difficulties. Patients or clients who joined these groups are likely to need the extra support and help this model of therapy offers them. Many of the people who come into group counselling have had some previous experience of individual counselling too, and indeed some of them may receive both individual and group counselling concurrently. Clients may also be hospital patients, or they may be out-patients attending a psychiatric day centre. Sometime these clients are referred for group counselling so that specific problems, such as drug or alcohol relapse, eating disorders, bereavement, sexual abuse and difficulties relating to anger control, can be addressed. However, counselling groups are often set up by trained counsellors who work privately and accept clients on a paying basis. It goes without saying that these initiatives need careful planning, commitment, regular supervision and, above all, specialised training in group theory and practice.

Some overlap

In many instances there is an overlap between a support and counselling focus within these groups. One reason for this is that a designated trained leader is likely to act as a facilitator with responsibility for conducting sessions and the overall administration of the group. Support, therefore, comes from the trained leader, as well as from other participants within the group. Along with the many groups which are meant to address specific problems, there are also those set up to help clients remedy specific deficits which are usually directly related to the emotional problems they have. Such deficits include, for example, social skills and assertiveness, and there is an increasing emphasis on helping people access skills they already possess but do not know how to use.

Relationship problems

Many of the relationship problems people experience originate within their own families. The group situation is effective in recreating many of the tensions, conflicts, dynamics and issues which exist in all families. This means that the group is also an ideal medium through which clients can be helped to examine their personal interactional styles. Through observation of themselves and others, and with the support and accurate interventions of the leader, clients can then be encouraged to consider, and if possible change, their problem behaviour. A major benefit of group work is that members can participate themselves, while having the added advantage of watching others participate too. As Whitaker (1992) indicates, it is not unusual for seemingly passive group members to watch, listen and them take notes of events which have personal relevance for them. Counselling groups are therefore effective in promoting individual growth and awareness, but they also encourage members to remedy any emotional or relationship difficulties which may have caused problems for them in the past.

CASE STUDY — Wayne

Twenty-six year-old Wayne agreed to join an anger management group which had just been set up at the out-patients department of the local hospital. He was committed to working hard in the group, but found it difficult at first to identify exactly what his problem was. During each group meeting he sat near the door, and slightly away from the other members. Often, when someone else spoke, he showed signs of impatience by lowering and shaking his head, and sometimes he appeared not to listen at all. Wayne made no attempt to contribute to discussions, and in place of his usual tendency to become angry he displayed a great deal of passive aggression instead. During the third session one of the group members, called Frank, confronted him:

FRANK: I wish that you would join the group. If you don't want to be with us, why did you come?

WAYNE:	I'm listening. I'm here.
FRANK:	[becoming irritated] Yes, you're here, but you look as if you know better than the rest of us.
WAYNE:	Well, I reckon with some of the stories I've heard here, I don't have the level of anger some people have.
GROUP LEADER:	Being in the group has shed some light on your own feelings?
WAYNE:	My anger is not as bad as some people's …
GROUP LEADER:	Could it be that you are showing yours in a different way here?
WAYNE:	In what way?
GROUP LEADER:	Well I'm just thinking … People have different ways of being angry. Some people show it by disapproval and lack of involvement with others.
WAYNE:	That's not what I had a problem with. My problem was losing my temper.
FRANK:	Well, I can tell you I would lose my temper with someone who disapproved like you do. You could make someone else mad, and that *would* start a fight. Maybe that's what's been happening to you.

Following these exchanges and further clarifying comments from the Group Leader, Wayne began to recognise a pattern in his interactions with other people. When he was not openly angry with others, his passive and sullen aggression tended to act as a catalyst for bitter confrontation and rows. Once these confrontations were set in motion, Wayne then usually lost all control of his temper. In the group setting he learned how these triggers worked, and afterwards he set about the challenging task of changing his behaviour. An important point to make here is that Wayne's membership of the group was entirely voluntary. Clients should never be put under pressure to join a group, or indeed individual counselling, and if clients do feel under pressure they are unlikely to give the commitment necessary for real change.

Benefits of group counselling

Both individual and group counselling have their own particular advantages for clients. Perhaps the most significant advantage of group work is that it enables clients to develop and broaden their range of social skills. The interaction which takes place among participants means that skills are constantly being tried out, observed and often emulated by less outgoing or inhibited members of the group. In the same way very gregarious or dominant members often learn to modify their approach, especially when alternative, more reflective, communication styles are welcomed by other participants. Yalom (1995) includes 'the development of socialising techniques' among the therapeutic factors he lists in relation to group work. He refers to several other factors, including the following:

- Clients see that other group members have experienced similar problems and have dealt effectively with them. This inspires hope that they too will recover.
- Clients receive teaching instruction on any number of topics including, for example, the stages of bereavement or the effects of depression, from the Leader of the group.
- Clients learn to help each other. Yalom (1995) points out that people with low self esteem often believe they have nothing of value to give. When they have the experience of giving, their confidence increases.
- Clients are helped, through feedback from others, to identify and change distorted views of the self. A client who believes that she does not express herself well might, for example, be told by others that she is, in fact, very articulate when she decides to speak in the group.
- In the context of a safe and supportive group, clients may express strong (often negative, but sometimes very positive) feelings like anger, resentment or deep empathy for someone else. For certain clients, especially those who are cut off from their feelings, such expressions involve great personal risk. The fact that others continue to accept and support them means that these clients learn to trust their own emotions, and in many cases they learn to express them more appropriately too.
- Clients learn that most human problems stem from faulty or disturbed interpersonal relationships. The therapy group, which resembles a family, allows them to develop more positive and effective ways of relating to others.
- Through participation in the group, clients also learn to confront their existential anxieties, especially those concerning death, suffering, loneliness and isolation. Group discussion facilitates such considerations, and as a result clients often learn to take more responsibility for themselves and to dispense with needless, materialistic or trivial concerns.

(Adapted from Yalom, 1995)

The social microcosm

Once a group is established and members know each other well, each person's habitual interpersonal style will begin to emerge. This happens despite the fact that people often try to *control* or mask their customary styles of behaviour in relation to others. For some members, customary transactions are revealed at an early stage, while for others habitual styles take time to emerge. The group is a microcosm of society in general, and within it each participant will display, at some point, those attitudes, feelings, needs or patterns of behaviour evident in other social contexts.

The ways in which people draw attention to themselves is especially interesting, though it should be remembered here that we all need attention and we all have our own ways of getting it. For some people, however, the method of gaining attention, may be such that it actually alienates others in the long term. One example of this is the group member who is excessively vocal and dominant; other people may use humour, flirtation, drama or even lateness in order to capture the recognition they need. There are those who display disparaging attitudes towards others, but regardless of the various individual relationship styles, participants are in the group to learn more about themselves, and for this reason must be given specific feedback about their behaviour. In addition to feedback, members should also be encouraged to observe their own behaviour, to experiment with new, more open, communication styles, and to transfer the learning which takes place in the group to social and family situations outside. In the case study described earlier, Wayne was encouraged to consider the negative way he expressed his anger, but he was also encouraged later on to talk about his aggressive feelings and to consider less harmful ways of expressing these.

Group members as therapists

An outstanding advantage of group counselling is the sense of community which is established among participants. By supporting and helping each other, group members become additional therapists who, in some instances, may prove more effective than the Group Leader or facilitator. When members of a group share a common problem, they offer a degree of empathy, trust, openness and understanding which is very therapeutic for everyone concerned. Participants also learn about different, more creative, ways of tackling problems, and when membership is drawn from a variety of occupations, cultures and backgrounds there is unlimited potential for learning, acceptance, creativity and support. Personal insight tends to be gained more readily in groups, especially when several people are offering help and contributing ideas. It should be emphasised though, that direct advice giving is not helpful in either individual or group counselling, but participants in a group can, by relating and discussing their own experiences, shed light on the problems other members have. Advice giving among members is, as Yalom (1995) indicates, common in the early stages of group work. Later on, however, when the group has reached a more sophisticated and cohesive stage of development, direct advice giving is less likely to occur.

Transference in groups

Since more people are present in group therapy, transference responses are obviously wider and more varied than they are in the context of individual counselling. Interpersonal distortions (which is what transference responses are) involve not only the relationship of each individual member to the Leader, but also the wide diversity of relationships which exist among group members themselves. The Group Leader or facilitator is, as Yalom (1995) suggests 'the personification of parental images'. These parental figures include teachers, people in authority, established values and, of course, the *actual* parents of each participant. Group members expect the Leader to make decisions for them, in the early stages at least, and one of the aims of group counselling is to help clients realise that they too are capable of making decisions and taking responsibility for themselves. The distortions which exist among participants in relation to the Leader are often quite exaggerated, though there is less likelihood that the intense and dependent transference distortions of individual therapy will flourish in the group work context.

We noted that relationships among group participants may also be clouded by outdated unconscious ideas which are wholly irrelevant in the present situation. Here are some examples of how this can happen:

◆ An older woman in a group is perceived by younger members as stuffy and old fashioned. This opinion is formed early on, regardless of the fact that the older woman has not yet spoken or expressed a view.

◆ A twenty year-old female participant is regarded as immature by older group members. Again, she hasn't said or done anything to warrant this opinion.

◆ A middle-aged man is unaccountability irritated by, and defensive towards, a middle-aged woman in the group. Later he realises that she reminds him of his bossy and controlling mother.

◆ A thirty year-old woman feels drawn to another, slightly younger, member of the group. Later she realises that the younger woman reminds her of a much loved sister who died two years previously.

◆ A middle-aged woman feels intense dislike for a member of the group who is a nun. Later she analyses the feeling and realises that her perceptions are clouded by her childhood experience of being taught by a very strict order of nuns.

Comment

It should be added that the feelings, perceptions and views described in these examples were not necessarily articulated. In fact, one of the problems with transference distortions is that they are often not clarified so people continue to relate to each other as if they were somebody else. Within a supportive and cohesive group setting, however, clients are given the opportunity to explore and challenge outdated perceptions so that more realistic and reflective modes of communication are fostered. Clients can also learn, often through observation of other group members, how to respond more realistically, and with greater self assurance, to the Leader. If the Leader is challenged by confident members, for example, then less confident participants may find the courage to do this too. The same principle of modelling applies to those clients who are demanding, manipulative or excessively idealising in relation to the person leading the group. When more confident group members are seen to communicate as equals with the Leader, and without resorting to manipulation or excessive demands, their attitudes prompt others to become more open too. Once these new and more confident attitudes are developed, participants are also in a position to use them in other relationships exist outside the group.

Countertransference and groups

We have noted in previous chapters that counsellors, like clients, may have unresolved issues stemming from their own childhood or early experiences. Even when personal development and therapy are integral to counsellor training, there is no guarantee that certain areas of vulnerability or sensitivity will be comprehensively examined or dealt with. In any case, it would be impossible *not* to experience a wide range of emotional responses in relation to clients, and when so many clients are present in one group, problematic or puzzling responses to some of them at least are almost sure to develop. The following example illustrates this point.

> **CASE STUDY** — Countertransference

Eleanor, a Group Leader, acted as facilitator for a number of students who were completing a group work module as part of their training. This was an experiential course and Robert, another trainer, acted as Co-Leader. Right from the beginning of the course Eleanor felt some antipathy towards a female member of the group called Polly, who was about her age and also quite similar in appearance. These feelings made a difference to the way Eleanor related to this particular student, and on quite a few occasions she found herself 'switching off' when Polly contributed to group discussion. Eleanor talked to her Co-Leader about her responses during their processing sessions which took place between meetings. These sessions are a necessary part of group work, and provide an opportunity for Co-Leaders to analyse what has happened in individual sessions. They also provide what Conyne (1989) refers to as 'ongoing mutual supervision'. The open sharing of feelings, information and feedback is essential if Co-Leaders hope to work successfully together.

In both Eleanor's and Robert's case these processing sessions were invaluable. Through discussion with her partner, Eleanor was able to identify the basis of her antipathy towards Polly. It took some courage for her to admit it, but Eleanor felt some rivalry towards her student who, in fact, reminded her of herself. Polly exhibited some of the characteristics which Eleanor disowned and disliked in herself. Included among these characteristics was a tendency to over-intellectualise and show off. Once she acknowledged these feelings, Eleanor gained control over them. She also, of course, realised that her attitude to her student had been irrational, prejudiced and unfair. As Corey (1995) indicates, Group Leaders need to be vigilant about detecting their own unresolved conflicts, especially those which could impede the effective functioning of the group. It should be emphasised here that transference and countertransference responses occur in all groups, though therapists and counsellors who work from a psychodynamic perspective regard these concepts as key issues and are more concerned to identify their presence within the group.

Defence mechanisms in the group

The ego defence mechanisms discussed in previous chapters are relevant in the context of both individual and group counselling. However, a group offers greater opportunity for the observation of a wide variety of defences at work. On the other hand, defence mechanisms are less likely to be sustained in a group setting, because participants will, at some stage, challenge them. Accountability to the group also ensures that members are under some pressure to observe agreed rules – when these rules are ignored by an individual member someone else in the group will certainly ask why.

Some participants may show *resistance* to personal involvement in the group, and they can do this in a variety of ways. Arriving late and leaving early may indicate resistance; such activities can also represent statements of specialness or separateness on the part of the group member responsible. Indifference, hostility, distrust and lack of cooperation are attitudes which betray resistance, while verbally dominating the group or silently withdrawing from it are resistant strategies too. A member who talks too much fails to listen to others, while the member who remains silent fails to engage with or place trust in others. An important Group Leader skill is to help individual members recognise and understand their own defences, and to discuss the ways in which certain aspects of defensive behaviour help to shield us from the anxiety which is often elicited in a group context. Identification of defences should, of course, be done with the client's best interests in mind, and should never be accompanied by blame or accusation. A client in one group described her defences like this:

I wasn't consciously aware of my tendency to arrive late and to stay silent while everyone else contributed to group discussion. If anyone had asked me directly why I did this, I would have given the answer that traffic was slow on my way to the session. As it was, another member of the group simply commented that he noticed some reluctance on my part to fully participate in the life of the group. A group discussion followed his comments, and the leader highlighted the importance of looking at all aspects of our behaviour in (and outside) the group.

For the first time I was able to talk about my memories of growing up as an only child. I felt I had to be everything to my parents, and I was constantly on the receiving end of their attention. To

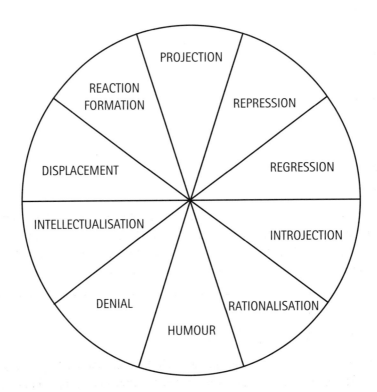

Figure 9.1 *Defence mechanisms in groups*

make matters worse, there were no cousins to divert attention away from me, so all my adult relatives expected a great deal from me too. I remember being stared at and scrutinised when I was taken to visit relatives, and often there seemed to be dozens of them claiming my attention. All their hopes were invested in me, and I felt I had to fulfil all their ambitions, accept all the responsibility for their future happiness, and provide all the entertainment and love which they needed. At some stage I rebelled against the pressure, and though on the surface I was still the 'good' only child, deep down I resolved to resist any attempts to make me the centre of group expectations.

Bringing these things to light in the group helped me a great deal, and for the first time I was able to see how my past affected my present behaviour. I could see that my attitude was a defensive one, and I was able to recognise that I often behaved like this in social situations too. On some level, I must have experienced the group members as family members, and this perception gave rise to my defensive behaviour.

> ### ⬭ EXERCISE ⬭ — Defences in the group
>
> Working in pairs, look at the following list of defence mechanisms and discuss the ways in which these might be used by members of a group. What purpose might each defence strategy serve, and what are the underlying dynamics which prompt these behaviour patterns?
>
> ◆ Denial
>
> ◆ Rationalisation
>
> ◆ Humour
>
> ◆ Intellectualisation
>
> ◆ Displacement
>
> ◆ Reaction formation
>
> ◆ Projection
>
> ◆ Repression
>
> ◆ Regressing
>
> ◆ Introjection
>
> These defences, which are discussed in the chapters dealing with psychodynamic theory, are evident in both individual and group counselling. Discuss with your partner the ways in which clients can be helped to understand and acknowledge them, bearing in mind that any help given should be free of censure, labelling or blame.

Counselling skills in group work

The basic counselling skills, which are central to individual counselling, are used in group counselling too. These include the skills of listening, paraphrasing, asking questions and summarising. In addition to these basic skills, however, a Group Leader needs to be in possession of specialised theoretical knowledge, as well as thorough experiential and practical training. This means that counsellors who wish to work with groups should gain as much experience as possible as *participants* in groups. The specialised skills of *coordinating*, *linking* and *monitoring* contributions from group members need to be seen in action, and personal experience of self disclosure is necessary too. It is unreasonable to expect clients to make themselves vulnerable through self disclosure, when Leaders themselves have had no experience of doing so. The benefits of self disclosure and trust in others needs to be familiar to Leaders, and both these essential areas of competency (self disclosure and the development of trust in others) can only be gained through personal experience and training. Other skills used by group leaders include the following:

Clarifying	This involves simplifying and illuminating statements clients make, so that confused feelings or thoughts become clearer for the speaker and for other group members.
Interpreting	This means offering tentative explanations for what is happening at various stages of group interaction. Well considered interpretations encourage clients to look more closely at their own and other peoples' behaviour. They also serve to present new perspectives and enhance possibilities for change.
Confronting	This means challenging clients when they give conflicting messages, or when there is evident discrepancy between their words and their actions. Sensitive confrontation helps clients to challenge themselves so that personal contradictions are highlighted and dealt with.
Showing support	Group Leaders need to ensure that members feel supported, valued and respected. Encouragement, feedback and reinforcement help to foster an atmosphere of trust and support
Reflecting feelings	In addition to the skill of paraphrasing (which means re-phrasing what clients have said) group leaders need to communicate to clients that their feelings are understood as well. To reflect feelings accurately it is important to listen carefully to the words clients use, but it is just as important to note the emotional content of the verbal message.
Activating	At various stages of group experience, the Leader will have to act as initiator so that communication is started and participation of all members encouraged. Unless this is done occasionally, group momentum may come to a halt. Information, suggestions and new ideas are frequently offered by the Group Leader as well, and these interventions are designed to encourage creative thinking and alternative courses of action.
Ensuring a safe environment	All group members should be told in advance that certain risks are involved in group participation. These risks include, for example,

feelings of discomfort, sadness and catharsis to name just a few. However, it is the Leader's task to ensure that members are not subjected to abuse or damaging psychological experience as a result of being in the group.

As well as the skills listed above, group leaders should also possess the skills of monitoring and evaluating process. Clients need to know what is happening in the group, and they need to understand the goals and directions towards which they are working. To work effectively with clients in this way, the Group Leader must experience a high level of empathy for individual group participants. In order to achieve this some measure of self disclosure is necessary on the Leader's part. This does not mean talking about personal problems to the group: what it does mean is that the Leader should reveal her reactions to events taking place in the group at any given time. Self disclosure done in this way is effective as a model of openness and trust. Finally, the Leader should prepare the group for its final meeting together so that the experience of ending is placed in context and linked to other ending experiences clients may have had. The ending of a group can be anticipated well in advance, and this can be achieved when individual sessions focus on and acknowledge their time constraints.

SETTING UP A GROUP

Leadership

Successful group work depends on scrupulous planning and attention to detail. This is true regardless of whether the group is being led by one person or by two. If the group is to have two leaders, they need to know that they can work effectively together, and there should be a high level of communication and commitment between them. Co-leadership of a group has major advantages over individual leadership for several reasons. In the first place, two leaders can lend each other support while sharing overall responsibility for the running of the group. In the second place, two leaders can spread themselves out more, which means that individual group members are likely to receive a higher degree of attention and support. Additionally, it is much easier to monitor a group when two leaders are present to do so, and the feedback which leaders give each other between sessions means that countertransference distortions, and any other problems, are dealt with quickly.

At an unconscious level, leaders also represent parental figures, and when one is male and the other female group members are given an ideal medium in which to explore their own relationships with parents and with authority figures in general. When one leader is less experienced than the other, co-leadership provides a safe context in which the learner is able to acquire and develop group work skills. This means that clients are unlikely to suffer, as they might do at the hands of one inexperienced person working without direction or support.

However, disagreement between two leaders is almost inevitable, though this is not necessarily an impediment in the context of co-counselling. Indeed, it is difficult to imagine how two people working in such close proximity could possibly concur on every issue. What is important is a willingness to discuss and explore differences between sessions, so that unresolved tensions are not harboured and then transmitted to clients during group meetings. It is important to remember that clients can identify acrimony between leaders, and when such feeling is present it interferes with the therapeutic function and purpose of the group. In other words, clients are in group therapy to receive help, so they should not be side-tracked into needless worry or resentment about their leaders. Co-leaders should be sure about roles and responsibilities beforehand, and all aspects of group planning should be shared and agreed between them.

Leadership styles

Group leaders obviously differ a great deal in terms of individual approach, manner and style. Various writers have identified broad categories of leadership style, although it should be emphasised that their description cannot totally encompass the diversity of personality differences which exist among people who facilitate groups. Benson (1987) describes what he calls the 'directive' , the 'permissive', the 'facilitating', and the 'flexible' styles of leadership. The directive leader is one who takes overall responsibility for group organisation tasks and goals, while the permissive leader assumes that members can make most decisions for themselves. A flexible leader will, as the term suggests, adapt to suit the needs of members and the group, and the facilitating leader sees himself as both a 'member' of the group and the person with the knowledge and skills needed for group functioning. Benson also makes the point that it is possible to pinpoint a style of leadership which will suit the needs of specific group memberships and goals.

In addition to this, the leader's own theoretical training and preference needs to be considered (Benson, 1987). We can see from this that Group leaders need to take account of membership composition and requirements: a group of adolescents may benefit from a directive approach for example, while a group of adults might adjust more easily to a facilitating or permissive style. The point to be emphasised here is that leadership style should always be geared to the needs of the group and its members, but it must also be congruent with the leader's personality, preference and training.

EXERCISE — Leadership styles

Working individually, think of occasions when you found yourself in the role of leader, either at work, at home or socially. What was your preferred leadership style, and how successful were you in helping others to define objectives, set goals or complete any tasks required of them?

Practical planning

We have already seen that careful planning is essential for successful group work. In order to plan successfully the reasons for setting up the group, and its purpose, need to be examined in some detail. Libemann (1991) suggests that the main purpose of a group is 'to provide a warm, trusting environment' in which members will feel respected and sufficiently safe to talk about personal feelings and confidential matters. The physical environment should be such that members do indeed feel safe and free to talk with confidence, and to that end the following questions need to be considered:

◆ Where will meetings be held?

◆ How convenient is it for group members?

◆ Is the room large enough, and is the area quiet?

◆ Are there liable to be any interruptions?

◆ Is there suitable access for members with physical disability, and are toilet facilities available?

◆ Are heating and ventilation adequate?

◆ Are there enough chairs, and are they comfortable?

◆ Is the lighting adequate, and are there power points for use if required?

◆ Does the environment conform to health and safety standards?

Since all groups have differing requirements, it is impossible to give a totally comprehensive list of factors to be considered when planning a group. However, there are several other important issues which need to be addressed in the planning stage of any group. These include:

◆ Purpose and composition of the group – who and what is it for?

◆ Pre-group interviews – will members receive some preparation beforehand?

◆ Size of the group – how many members?

◆ Frequency of meetings – how often should they take place?

◆ Dates of meetings – when will they take place?

◆ Duration of meetings – how long will they last?

◆ Open or closed – will new members be allowed to join at any stage, or is this group closed to additional members once it is started?

◆ Number of Leaders – one or two?

◆ Supervision for Leaders – is this available and adequate?

◆ Activities and resources – how will the group operate and what resources are needed?

◆ Monitoring and evaluating – how is progress to be monitored, and what form of evaluation should be used?

In addition to the factors listed, special attention should be directed to the first meeting of the group. The issue of confidentiality is important here, since clients need to know that what they say will not be repeated outside. In a therapeutic or counselling group there should be an emphasis on honesty, respect, caring for others and confidentiality. The subject of confidentiality can be addressed in pre-group interviews, but it should also be discussed along with other ground rules during the first meeting with group members.

The establishment of clear ground rules is essential if clients are to feel safe and supported within the group. Ground rules refer to those aspects of group behaviour which are defined by the Leader for the benefit of the group as a whole. In other words, a code of conduct, explicitly stated, is described by the leader, and this can also be discussed with clients in a pre-group interview. Members of a group need to know, for example, why it is important to attend all sessions if possible. They should also be aware of the value of starting and finishing on time, and of the detrimental effects that breaching these rules can have on others. When people arrive late or leave early, others in the group tend to resent it; on the other hand, good time-keeping ensures that members experience the group as a trustworthy environment to be in. For some very vulnerable clients, this sense of trust is essential if they are to derive any real benefit from being in a group.

EXERCISE — Setting up a group

Working in pairs, think of issues which might benefit from a group work approach. The following are some examples:

◆ Stress management at work

◆ Teenagers and drug awareness

◆ Assertiveness for women

◆ Carer's support

◆ Health awareness for men

Having selected your group, answer the questions listed below:

◆ What are your aims and objectives for the group?

◆ Who will lead the group, and where will meetings be held?

◆ Is the group open or closed? For example, can other members join after the first meeting?

◆ How many meetings should there be, and how long will they last?

◆ How many members in the group, and how should they be selected?

◆ What are the ground rules, and when are these discussed with group members?

◆ Is there a set programme of activities for the group and if so, what is it to be?

◆ How is group progress to be monitored and evaluated?

◆ What are your plans for the first meeting?

◆ How can you help group members get to know each other?

When you have completed the exercise (which should take about 45 minutes) discuss it with your trainer and other members of the training group.

STAGES OF GROUP LIFE

Although not all groups conform to an exact pattern, it is possible to identify certain key stages through which they commonly progress from the beginning to the end. Various writers, including Tuckman (1965), Bion (1961) and Benson (1987) have focussed on these stages, and Yalom (1995) describes three:

◆ Stage One – Orientation

◆ Stage Two – Conflict

◆ Stage Three – Cohesion

It is important to consider these phases of group life, and to recognise them as they appear in different groups. Unless leaders are aware of group stages it is impossible for them to offer effective leadership, or to intervene appropriately when members need them to do so.

During the initial phase participants are concerned to establish their place in the group, to form relationships and to clarify the purpose of being there. Group members tend to ask many questions in their first session, and there is often some confusion about the goals and purpose of group therapy. Most people silently wonder if they will be liked in the group, and as Yalom (1995) observes, there is a common fear of rejection by others as well.

In the second, conflict stage, members jostle for roles and position within the group. Sub-groups may form in this second phase and there is often criticism of the Leader, whose authority is challenged. Participants also tend to be judgmental, critical and advice is freely offered without any real understanding of the problems which people have.

During the third, cohesive, stage, members of the group draw closer together; there is a marked shift in mood and morale and mutual trust is increased. This last phase accommodates greater self disclosure, although as Yalom (1995) points out, negative feelings may be suppressed at the beginning of it. Later, however, conflict again emerges, but unlike the conflict of the initial stage, it is more constructive and mature.

Another model

As a result of my own experience with different groups, I have identified five stages which seem to occur frequently (see Figure 9.2). The stages are as follows:

Anxiety | Group members are anxious and very dependent on the Leader. They want to know the rules and what is expected of them. The Leader is assumed to know all the answers. Members engage nervously in verbal exchanges, but since people are unlikely to know each other the conversation lacks depth and intimacy.

Discord | Differences of opinion emerge in the group. Aggressive criticism of the Leader and other members is common at this stage. Competitiveness, antagonism, lack of co-operation, poor time keeping and absenteeism may also be evident.

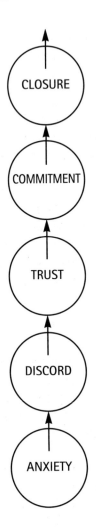

Figure 9.2   *Stages of group development*

Trust   A sense of community develops in the group, and common rules are
               accepted. People now feel they belong and become more authentic and
               natural in their responses to each other. The Leader is seen in a more real-
               istic light too: thus the person who was viewed in the conflict stage as
               either wholly competent or wholly incompetent, is now seen as a real and
               fallible person like everyone else.

Commitment   During this important stage group members feel sufficiently safe to talk
               intimately about themselves and the problems they have. There is a high
               level of commitment and self disclosure, and participants show genuine
               attitudes of support and caring.

Closure   Issues of separation and loss are highlighted in the final phase, and these
               feelings may be reminiscent of other losses or experiences of bereavement
               group members have had. Members may also be reluctant to leave the
               group, and plans may be made to meet socially in the future. Group coun-

sellors need to be sensitive to the needs of clients at this stage, and sufficient time should be allocated to preparation for group closure.

Comment

As we noted earlier, it is important to be familiar with the stages of group development if we are to be effective in helping clients to work through them. We need to understand, for example, the complex range of emotions which people experience when they first find themselves in a group of strangers. For some people, including those who come from large overwhelming families, or only children who have been sheltered or isolated, this initial stage may be more threatening than for others. However, these are often the very people who benefit most from group therapy in the long term. The stages of discord, trust, commitment and closure also present their own characteristic problems and difficulties for group members, and it is only through identification and awareness of these stages that we can hope to offer appropriate helping strategies for clients.

WHAT PEOPLE CONTRIBUTE TO GROUPS

In considering the way groups work, it is useful to look at them from two perspectives: group life, and individual roles in groups. Group life refers to the way the group functions as a *whole*, while the term *roles* describes the range of characteristics which individual group members display at any given time. In the section entitled 'the social microcosm', we highlighted certain aspects of individual behaviour which can cause problems within the group, though it should be added that people seldom make a conscious decision to create problems for others. However, the fact remains that unconscious forces often prompt members to behave in certain ways, and this effect tends to be enhanced when people are under stress in a group. Behaviour need not always, of course, be problematic, and it is often the case that contributions are made by group members which serve to facilitate the work of the whole group. In this section we shall look at a number of positive contributions made by group members which are generally helpful to the group as a whole, bearing in mind that some people take on several roles in the life of any group.

Interactive process analysis

Bales (1950) describes a range of behaviours which are shown by members in almost any group situation. Through what he described as 'interactive process analysis', Bales observed the behaviour of small groups in a laboratory setting, and in doing so provided a useful way of measuring group dynamics and structure. According to Bales' research, group members' verbal and non-verbal behaviour can be listed under two broad headings:

The task area

Some group members are more concerned than others to get the job (as they perceive it) done. To that end they will engage in a number of behaviours meant to clarify the situation and move forward towards a successful conclusion. These behaviours include:

◆ Asking questions

◆ Giving opinions, suggestions, direction and information

◆ Asking for direction, suggestions, information and opinion

◆ Repeating, clarifying and confirming what others say

Group members who contribute to the task area seldom worry too much about other people's feelings. This does not mean that they are deliberately insensitive, however, but it does imply that their first priority is to move ahead without too much focus on emotions. Task roles are very important in a group, and Leaders need to understand and appreciate their contributions. It would be easy to view the persistent questioner as troublesome or critical, for example. But the group does require answers to many questions, so the person who asks can be an invaluable asset to the other members.

The socio-emotional area

The range of socio-emotional behaviours can, according to Bales, be described under two headings: positive and negative. Positive contributions include the following:

◆ Showing solidarity

◆ Making jokes and laughing

◆ Showing satisfaction and giving help

◆ Showing understanding, acceptance and agreement

People who contribute in positive ways to the socio-emotional life of the group help to foster cohesion and a feeling of solidarity among the members. They also help to lessen tension, and this is largely achieved through the use of humour at appropriate times. There is an acknowledgement among contributors to this area that people's emotions are just as important as the rational, practical aspects of the group's existence. Task roles and socio-emotional roles complement each other and both types are necessary in any group. On the other hand, some negative socio-emotional contributions may prove problematic in a group, although even here they may prove positive in the end if they succeed in promoting self-awareness and learning.

Aspects of negative socio-emotional behaviour include the following:

◆ Becoming withdrawn

◆ Showing antagonism or rejection of others

◆ Refusing help and putting others down

◆ Disagreeing

It should be emphasised that a group requires a range of contributions, no matter how objectionable some of them may seem at first glance. The task for the Group Leader is to help members understand the meaning of different kinds of behaviour, and to encourage all participants to value what others have to offer. It is essential that task orientated people should recognise the importance of feelings, for example, while those members who shun task contributions need to consider their value in the group too. People who display negative socio-emotional traits can be helped to understand the effects they have on other members of the group. Once this understanding is achieved, it often serves to illuminate the difficulties certain people have in other contexts, especially those involving close relationships outside the group (adapted from Bales, 1950).

THEORETICAL APPROACHES TO GROUP WORK

Psychodynamic

Psychodynamic group therapy is usually conducted in closed groups. Once the group has started there is little opportunity for anyone else to join. Sessions usually take place once a week, and last for an hour and a half on average. There is a recognition that group communication takes place at two levels: the conscious and the unconscious. The concept of transference is important in psychodynamic group work, and members are given the opportunity to experience and work through a range of transference feelings. These feelings may be directed towards the leader or other participants, or both. Individual defence mechanisms become obvious in groups, and these can be examined and replaced by more open, less defensive, forms of communication. Influences from the past, and the effects of childhood experience on current reality, can also be examined in group therapy.

The Jungian perspective

Jungian therapy has been, until fairly recently, an exclusively individual approach. However, some Jungian therapists are now interested in the benefits of group work. Boyd (1994) describes the ways in which personal change may be facilitated in small groups. He refers to the composition and structure of such group, stipulating that membership should be no more than twelve, and no fewer than eight. Groups are closed, and members must give a commitment to attend all sessions. The ideal number of sessions is sixteen to twenty, and ten sessions is an absolute minimum. The leader must be clear and explicit about the group's aims and objectives, methods and procedures used, and the kinds of interactions likely to occur. Themes of Jungian group work include the identification of archetypal images among members, recognition of the collective unconscious, focus on critical life issues and the reassessment of early experience.

Adlerian group work

Because of its emphasis on relationships and social influences, Adlerian therapy is ideally suited to group work. Groups may meet on a weekly basis, and sessions last for one and a half hours to two hours. Adler believed that human behaviour could best be understood in a social context. He also rejected Freud's psychic determinism, and highlighted instead the individual's desire and ability to grow, develop and accomplish goals. In the context of the group, members both give and receive help which fosters a sense of belonging and achievement. The role of the leader is an active one, and involves challenge, interpretation, setting guidelines for behaviour and giving support. The nature of the relationship between thera-pist and clients is important, and qualities of honesty and mutual respect are valued.

The person-centred approach

Person-centred group therapy also usually takes place on a weekly basis. Sessions may last for one and a half to two hours, though groups are sometimes conducted over a weekend period. Group members are presented with very few rules by the Leader, and those which evolve come from consensus among participants. Groups may be open or closed, though once again decisions about this are generally discussed among group members. The person-centred Leader should demonstrate the Rogerian core conditions of respect, unconditional positive regard and genuineness. In addition, the Leader should accept the humanistic view that each person has the potential for growth and self actualisation.

Gestalt therapy in groups

Gestalt groups may meet on a weekly basis, though therapy is sometimes conducted in blocks of two to three days. An interesting aspect of the Gestalt approach is its application to large groups of more than fifty members. Philippson and Harris (1992) offer some useful ideas about the benefits of working in large groups. Gestalt groups are usually closed, and members may be selected on the basis of their interest in this particular approach. Perceptual and bodily awareness are central ideas in Gestalt therapy, so too is the experience of the here and now. The Leader's task is to challenge participants to assume responsibility for themselves, and to create an environment conducive to creativity, exper-imentation and change. Members say what they need and want, and they enlist the help of other group participants. There is an emphasis on the expression of feelings, and on the use of verbal and non-verbal language. Gestalt group methods also include working with dreams, fantasy exercises, changing language from passive to active, using exaggeration and experimenting with dialogue.

Psychodrama

Psychodrama is essentially a group approach to therapy. Both the theory and the tech-niques used were discussed in an earlier chapter. It is a specialised form of group work and is not widely available, though it is sometimes offered within the NHS. Groups are closed and sessions tend to be limited in number. Meetings may take place over a period of six to eight weeks, and occasionally therapy is conducted in a weekend block.

Transactional analysis

Transactional analysis therapy frequently takes place in groups. It is an educative and experiential approach which is widely available. Sessions are conducted on a weekly basis, though once again concentrated blocks of therapy are also sometimes used. Participants need to be committed to attending all sessions, and meetings are usually closed. Group members agree to work on specific issues; contracts are stated and personal goals set. This means that participants are given a great deal of responsibility, though feedback and support are provided by others in the group. The leader is both a teacher and therapist whose role is to explain theoretical concepts and the way these apply to human experience and behaviour. The leader also interacts with individual group members rather than with the group as a whole. This means that the leader's presence is a pivotal and dominant one, though the intention is always to help members become self reliant and achieve whatever change they require.

Behaviour therapy in groups

Behaviour therapy is also suited to group work and, like transactional analysis, is fairly widely practised. While it is available privately, behaviour therapy in groups often takes place within the NHS. Meetings may be open or closed, and usually takes place on a weekly basis of approximately two hours. Group therapy tends to be short term (six to ten sessions) and members are taught a variety of coping strategies and given assignments to do at home. It is a highly adaptable approach which is time efficient, and results can be easily measured. Therapy aims to help people get rid of undesirable overt behaviour and the group provides support and reinforcement for change. The leader acts as a teacher, model, supporter and reinforcer, as well as using a variety of techniques and methods whose effectiveness can be measured and objectively evaluated. Behaviour therapy has application in many areas, including social skills training, assertiveness training, and stress management to name just a few.

Rational Emotive Behaviour Therapy

Although initially unconvinced of the effectiveness of groups, Ellis came to value it as a suitable medium for therapy. Cognitive Behaviour Therapy (which is what REBT is) is usually available within the NHS, though it is also widely available privately. It is a well focused approach which is easy to understand and use. Meetings may be closed or open, and are likely to take place over a period of six to ten weeks, though it is also ideally suited to brief therapy. Sessions usually last one and a half hours, and often start with one person presenting a problem for consideration. The leader's role is a didactic and teaching one; books are recommended and participants are given homework exercises to do. The emphasis is on action, and on confronting the irrational beliefs group members hold. The group provides feedback, support, suggestions, reinforcement and challenge. Self help is encouraged, and a wide variety of audio-visual materials is now available for use either individually or in groups. REBT can be used in schools to educate young people in personal growth and development, and according to Ellis (1997) its potential in this context is vast. It can also be used in business management and communications, as well as in therapy.

Clients who benefit from group work

Earlier in this chapter we looked at some of the advantages of group counselling and listed the positive aspects of it for clients in general. However, certain clients are likely to benefit more than others, and these include people with relationship difficulties or those with problems in relation to authority. In both these instances the group can be used to spot-light and clarify the exact nature of the problem, and later on new styles of relating to others can be tested and used. Because the composition of a group is so varied, it is an ideal medium in which to identify problems of communication. Prejudice and irrational thinking are also exposed: attitudes to our own, or other people's sexuality can be re-assessed, and more open and respectful styles of communication adopted. In symbolic form, the group represents a family, which means that members who experienced problems in their own families are given the opportunity to receive the support they may have missed in the past. Groups are also beneficial for clients with specific problems of addiction, either to alcohol or tranquillisers. Reasons for addiction can be explored in a group setting, and it is often the case that common themes and underlying problems emerge in discussions. From a prac-tical viewpoint, group therapy may be cheaper and more readily available for some clients. Accessibility is an important consideration for many people, and when a number of people can be helped together, time and resources are saved too.

Some limitations

Group counselling has some disadvantages and is certainly not suitable for everyone. One disadvantage is that in a group setting it may not be possible for the therapist/leader to give every client the amount of attention needed. In addition, highly anxious clients may find groups too threatening, and those who are deeply depressed are unlikely to benefit in the acute stage of their illness. Some people are also just too afraid to try group therapy, while others may be too vulnerable to cope with all the interactions which groups entail. People who are very out of touch with reality, including those who suffer from psychotic illness, are unlikely to benefit either. However, mental illness is not in itself a barrier, but clients with this kind of experience need to recover from the acute phases of the illness before entering the group. Many of the problems relating to suitability of clients can be resolved through the simple expedient of pre-group assessment, interview and selection. In addition, people can be *matched* to specific groups where special attention is directed to helping members deal with a particular kind of problem. Groups function at their best when there is diversity of membership, because such composition mirrors the mix in society as a whole. On the other hand, if clients are mentally ill, their level of functioning may exclude realistic and meaningful participation with a very mixed or heterogeneous group of people.

SUMMARY

This chapter dealt with both the theory and the practice of group counselling. Areas covered included the evolution of groups, with special reference to the proliferation of self help and specific focus groups, and to the development of group therapy in Britain and abroad. The advantages of group work were highlighted and the concepts of transference and countertransference were discussed in the context of the group approach. The use of defence mechanisms in groups was also considered, and the skills needed for successful leadership were outlined. Leadership qualities and styles were described, along with the requirements for group planning. The stages of group development were considered, and

Yalom's model (1995) was used as a starting point for discussion. Another model, based on personal experience, was also presented for discussion, and comments were added to stress the importance of understanding stages of group development. An adaptation of Bales' interactive process analysis (1950) was included in the section dealing with individual contributions to groups. Theoretical approaches to group work, including psychodynamic, person-centred, Jungian, Adlerian, transactional analysis, psychodrama, behaviour therapy and cognitive therapy were described. The benefits and limitations of group counselling were indicated.

REFERENCES

Bales, R. F. (1950)   *Interactive Process Analysis: A Method for Study of Small Groups.* Cambridge, Massachusetts: Addison Wesley.

Benson, J. (1987)   *Working More Creatively with Groups.* London: Tavistock.

Bion, W. R. (1961)   *Experiences in Groups and Other Papers.* New York: Basic Books.

Boyd, R. D. (1994)   'Facilitating Personal Transformations in Small Groups', in Boyd (1994) *Personal Transformations in Small Groups.* London: Routledge.

Conyne, R. K. (1989)   *How Personal Growth and Task Groups Work.* London: Sage Human Services Guides, vol 55.

Corey, G. (1995)   *Theory and Practice of Group Counselling.* California: Brooks/Cole.

Ellis, A. (1997)   'The Future of Cognitive Behaviour and Rational Emotive Behaviour Therapy', in Palmer and Varma (eds) (1997) *The Future of Counselling and Psychotherapy.* London: Sage Publications.

Hyde, K. (1988)   'Analytic Group Psychotherapies' in Aveline and Dryden (eds) (1988) *Group Therapy in Britain.* Milton Keynes: Open University Press.

Liebmann, M. (1991)   *Art Therapy for Groups.* London: Routledge.

Philippson, P. & Harris J. B. (1992)   *Gestalt: Working with Groups.* Manchester: Manchester Gestalt Centre.

Tuckman, B. W. (1965)   'Development Sequences in Small Groups', *Psychological Bulletin*, 63, pp. 384–99.

Whitaker, D. S. (1992)   *Using Groups to Help People.* London: Routledge.

Yalom, I. D. (1995)   *The Theory and Practice of Group Psychotherapy.* New York: Basic Books.

FURTHER READING

Aveline, M. & Dryden, W. (eds) (1988)   *Group Therapy in Britain.* Milton Keynes: Open University Press.

Bertcher, H. J. (1993)   *Group Participation (Techniques for Leaders and Members)* (2nd edn) London: Sage Human Services Guides, volume 10.

Reichard, B. D., Siewers, C. M. F. & Rodenhauser, P. (1992)   *The Small Group Trainer's Survival Guide.* London: Sage Publications.

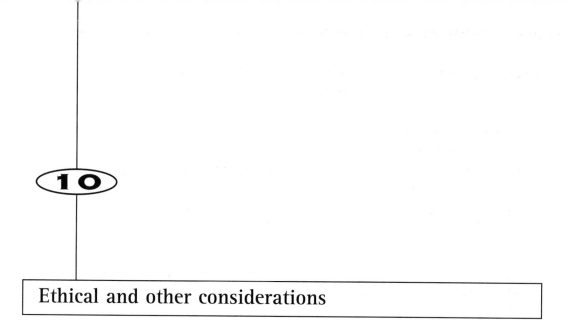

Ethical and other considerations

INTRODUCTION

In this last chapter we consider a range of ethical and other issues central to all the theoretical models discussed in previous chapters. These include the importance of adequate training for counsellors, the need for ongoing supervision and personal development, as well as issues relating to transference and countertransference. Potential problems will also be discussed, including those concerning the emotional, financial and contractual aspects of the counsellor's work. The word 'ethics' refers to the study of right and wrong behaviour, and in the counselling context this has special relevance. This is largely because of the close nature of the therapeutic relationship, and the possibility of abuse which exists within it. Indeed the actual counsellor/client relationship is perhaps the most important topic in this section, and many of the other issues, like confidentiality for example, are impossible to separate from it. The subject of confidentiality will be discussed at some length in this chapter, its limitations identified and some examples will be given to highlight the difficulties it might present. Client/counsellor contacts, good practice, counsellor limitations and knowing when to refer will also be taken up and discussed.

CONFIDENTIALITY

Confidentiality is one of the most important aspects of the counselling relationship. It is also a subject which generates a great deal of interest and discussion when it is raised in training groups. This is because it is a topic about which most people have very firm views. It is often seen as an absolute right for clients who, after all, trust counsellors with some of their most intimate thoughts, feelings and desires. The information clients disclose in counselling may never have been spoken to anyone before, and indeed it often takes clients a very long time to summon up the courage to approach helpers in the first place. For this reason clients need to have confidence in the professional integrity of helpers, and in their ability to keep private anything they discuss.

Clients may take some time to arrive at a state of complete trust in counselling. One indication of this initial reticence and caution is the way in which clients often focus quite extensively on secondary issues before they feel secure enough to reveal themselves fully. This could be seen as a way of testing the counsellor in order to ascertain just how unshockable, non-judgmental and discreet she is likely to be. Clients who do not get these assurances may retreat from counselling, but once trust has been established they should feel sufficiently confident to disclose more about themselves. The following are some general guidelines relating to confidentiality.

◆ Confidentiality is a subject which needs to be addressed as early as possible in counselling, although in crisis situations this may not be immediately feasible.
◆ Even in crisis situations the issue of confidentiality should be addressed at some stage.
◆ An atmosphere of trust is just as important as an explicit statement of confidentiality.

Some limitations

Some clients address the issue of confidentiality straight away, and when this happens the counsellor has an ideal opportunity to discuss the concept and clarify any limitations which may have to be stated. Those clients who do not address the subject of confidentiality may be reluctant to do so for fear of questioning the counsellor's professionalism. When this is the case, it is important not to assume that such clients are disinterested or unaware of the issue. They may simply be waiting for the counsellor to provide the necessary information, and if it is not provided they may lose faith fairly quickly. Sometime absolute confidentiality cannot be guaranteed in counselling, and when this is the case clients should be aware of any limitations to it. There are certain situations in which clients disclose information which, because of the guidelines stipulated by the agency or health care organisation in which the counsellor works, cannot remain confidential. These usually include some of the following:

◆ a client threatens to injure another person
◆ a client discloses details about abuse of children
◆ a client expresses strong suicidal tendencies
◆ a client develops severe mental illness

Perhaps the most important point to make about limitations to absolute confidentiality is that counsellors should be fully aware of rules pertaining to these, long before they are encountered in counselling. Counsellors who are well informed about the rules of the organisation in which they work are obviously in a better position to deal with emergencies as they arise. Regular supervision is also essential where issues of confidentiality and its limitations are covered. Occasionally, aspects of confidentiality are far from clear cut, even when guidelines have been stated. In these instances supervision can help the counsellor get a clearer picture of what needs to be done. However, clients should be told about supervision too, although they can be assured that their name or identity will not be revealed. When absolute confidentiality cannot be guaranteed to clients, they should be told this as soon as possible in the counselling process. The following case study highlights this point.

CASE STUDY — Confidentiality

Andrea, who was twenty-four, received counselling over a period of six weeks because she was depressed. The counsellor who helped her was a trained psychiatric nurse, who had also completed a counselling skills course. Andrea had been referred by her doctor who had prescribed antidepressants for her. However, he felt that she would benefit more from psychological support and Andrea herself agreed with this. During the first session the counsellor talked about confidentiality and added that she could not guarantee this absolutely if Andrea became severely depressed or suicidal. If either of these two situations arose, then she, the counsellor, would need to speak to Andrea's doctor about it. Andrea seemed to be reassured by this and, in fact, during a later session wtih the counsellor she admitted to having suicidal thoughts.

ANDREA: I think I began to feel worse after the recent rows with my boyfriend. There have been times when I wished it was just all over.

COUNSELLOR: These feelings of wishing it was all over ... tell me about them.

ANDREA: Well, ... I have felt like killing myself at times ...

COUNSELLOR: Strongly enough to make a plan?

ANDREA: Yes I had a plan. I thought of driving my car along the motorway and crashing it.

COUNSELLOR: And that feeling ... is it still with you?

ANDREA: Not so much ... but yes, sometimes.

COUNSELLOR: You remember how we talked about confidentiality ... about how I would need to speak to your doctor ... it might be that your medication needs changing or adjusting.

ANDREA: Yes, I do remember. That's alright. I don't know if these tablets are the right ones for me anyway. I don't know if they have done me any good.

You can see from this example that clients can experience great relief when they know that their problems are monitored and taken seriously in the way that the counsellor demonstrated. The issue of confidentiality had been openly discussed at the outset, which meant that further discussion flowed naturally from there. In situations where 'absolute' confidentiality is guaranteed to clients, counsellors must be prepared to respect such assurances.

Whatever the arrangement between client and counsellor however, discussion is essential if misunderstanding and confusion are to be avoided.

EXERCISE — Confidentiality

Working in groups of three to four, discuss your individual areas of work, highlighting any special rules regarding confidentiality. Ask one person in the group to write these down under individual headings, for example:

◆ Social work

◆ Nursing

◆ Teaching

◆ Citizens Advice Bureau (CAB)

◆ Samaritans

◆ Childline

◆ Cruse

◆ Women's Aid

◆ Alcohol concern

◆ Care of the elderly

◆ HIV and AIDS counselling

◆ Drugs counselling

Some of you will probably be involved in other areas of work apart from those listed above. The aim of the exercise is to generate a discussion about the issue of confidentiality generally, and to consider the ways in which guidelines differ among professions and organisations.

Talking about clients

In student training groups there are frequent discussions about problems encountered in professional work. The usual practice is to refer to clients indirectly and never by name. It is difficult to see how ideas and issues can be shared without these discussions, but there is a case for saying that every casual reference to clients, however indirect, is bound to devalue the integrity of the counsellor/client relationship to some extent at least. There is the added possibility that a member of the group will identify some of the details under discussion, and in doing so come to recognise the person discussed. This may be a remote possibility, but nevertheless it does exist. This is not to suggest that clients are damaged by indirect discussion about problems and issues which could, after all, belong to anyone. However, we all need to be circumspect when talking about work, because even though clients have no knowledge of these discussions, the effects of the way the counsellors treat them behind their backs do become manifest during counselling. Weinberg (1996) highlights this phenomenon and points to the possibility of the therapeutic 'alliance' being weakened as a result of this indirect loss of confidence. In other words, clients do pick up unconsciously transmitted messages during counselling, and when these attitudes convey casual attitudes about confidentiality real trust will never develop.

The client's responsibility

Another aspect of confidentiality concerns the client's obligation (if any) towards maintaining it. Some therapists, including Weinberg (1996) take the view that clients do have responsibilities in this regard. As far as Weinberg is concerned, the issues should be discussed early in the first session with the client. When clients find the request for confidentiality difficult in some respect, then the difficulties are explored and discussed too. It is my view that there are probably quite a few clients who would, in fact, experience anxiety if requested to make a pledge of confidentiality in counselling. These include people who have been traumatised in childhood as a result of keeping 'secrets' relating to sexual or other forms of abuse. Clients in this position would certainly need to be given the opportunity to voice their anxieties about any request for confidentiality, and if such a request is made, the reasons for it should be comprehensively explained. In spite of potential difficulties, however, confidentiality on the client's part could be considered important for the following reasons:

◆ When clients discuss their sessions freely with other people, the beneficial effects of counselling are often negated. This is because others tend to offer conflicting opinions and even advice which may prove confusing for the client.

◆ Facts are very often distorted when they are discussed outside counselling.

◆ Other people may feel the need to tell the client what to say in counselling. Clients who lack basic confidence might well lose sight of their thoughts, feelings and opinions as a result of such pressure. This goes against the whole ethos of counselling, since a basic aim of therapy is to help clients identify their own needs, and to become more autonomous generally.

◆ Discussions which take place outside counselling tend to weaken the client/counsellor relationship. This is an important point to consider since the quality of the relationship is, as Rogers points out, central to effective counselling (Rogers, 1991).

◆ A client may choose a confidant, or confidantes, who will support their reluctance to change. When this happens counselling may prove to be a waste of time.

◆ If a client knows that he will talk to relatives or friends about counselling, he may become more inhibited about what he actually says in sessions. Moreover, once other people are included, however indirectly, in the client's therapy, they are given the right to monitor progress and comment accordingly (Weinberg, 1996).

All the above points do not, of course, mean that clients should be encouraged to be totally silent about receiving counselling. Clients need to feel free to be open about this, just as they need to feel free to be honest about any other aspects of their lives. Counselling should not be something which clients have to hide, but detailed accounts of what is discussed in sessions are probably best avoided. Clients often know this instinctively anyway, but when outside discussions do become an issue in counselling, helpers need to address this as they would address other significant aspects of the client's behaviour. The following is an example:

CLIENT: I talked to my friend Angie about some of the things I said last week. She said I should never have mentioned the abortion … that it's better to keep some things quiet … now I don't know.

COUNSELLOR: You don't know what to think now that your friend has given her opinion …?

CLIENT: I suppose it's made me worried about anyone else finding out …

COUNSELLOR: Perhaps you are worried about confidentiality …

CLIENT: I don't know … yes maybe.

COUNSELLOR: What you say to me here is confidential … what you told me last week is confidential.

CLIENT: Yes, I know. It's just that Angie made me feel I shouldn't have said it.

COUNSELLOR: This is something which obviously worries you. And Angie … her views matter to you a lot?

CLIENT: Well sometimes … though she does irritate me … I just wish she would keep her opinions to herself at times.

COUNSELLOR: And your own view … about what you said last week … are you regretful that you mentioned it?

CLIENT: No [slowly] No I'm not. I've never told anyone before … it was a great relief even though Angie doesn't approve [laughs].

COUNSELLOR: Maybe we could look at why you ask for her approval … why you don't trust your own judgment more.

The example just given illustrated another point, which is that clients sometimes seek further assurances of confidentiality apart from the one which has been given early in counselling. In instances like this clients should be given the assurances they need, though the underlying reasons for repeated pledges of confidentiality need to be discussed. This is because clients who lack trust in this important area may well lack trust in any relationship. For these clients the development of trust is crucial, and over a period of time they need to learn to express trust in order to foster and promote it.

> **EXERCISE** — Developing trust
>
> Working individually, think of a time in your life when you confided in another person. What were your feelings beforehand about revealing personal information? What were your feelings afterwards when you realised you had given another person important information about yourself? Write down the feelings you experienced, and afterwards discuss these with other members of the training group. It is not necessary to discuss the nature of the problem you disclosed, but you should focus on your reactions to the disclosure itself.

THE COUNSELLING RELATIONSHIP

People are usually affected by some degree of emotional stress when they first seek counselling. This fact alone makes it imperative that they receive the best possible help, with the lowest possible risk of exacerbating any of the problems they already have. The difficulties clients experience may have been with them for a very long time. These include problems of depression, faulty relationships, marital problems, anxiety, phobias, difficulties at school or university – to name just a few. One of the factors which prompts people to seek help through counselling is the realisation that it might be impossible to continue to cope alone. When people feel helpless like this, they frequently look for someone who is 'expert' in a particular field. Though trained counsellors do not regard themselves as experts in this way, they nevertheless need to be aware that vulnerable people may have such a perception of them.

The majority of clients have a basic trust in a counsellor's ability to help them deal with the problems they experience. In fact, it is probably true that many clients over-estimate any helper's prowess, and may actually ascribe to a counsellor exaggerated or magical powers which are, of course, unrealistic. It is important that clients do in fact trust the counsellors who help them, but excessive expectations can work against clients unless counsellors are aware that they do exist. When there is this awareness on the counsellor's part, then it becomes possible to help clients become more autonomous and self directed over a period of time. Such a position of autonomy cannot, of course, be achieved until clients are given the opportunity to explore their problems and to consider what it is they need to do in order to effect change. The following example illustrates some of these points.

CASE STUDY — Mr Black

Mr Black was sixty-eight when his wife died. Apart from the grief which he suffered, he was also distressed by the many new and unfamiliar tasks he now had to perform. Mr Black's wife had been his best friend as well as a loving partner, and their relationship was a traditional one in the sense that both had clearly defined roles throughout their marriage. Mrs Black had taken care of the home and children, while Mr Black had gone out to work, earned the money and generally looked after all the financial aspects of their lives together. When Mr Black retired this pattern continued, and after his wife's death he found himself unable to cope with the basic tasks of shopping for food and cooking. The tasks which his wife once fulfilled now seemed incredibly daunting to him, and in a fairly short space of time he became depressed and neglected to care for himself generally. Through his GP Mr Black was persuaded to attend a day centre one day a week, and here he received counselling help from a nurse who was trained to give this kind of support. Mr Black's initial response was to abdicate personal responsibility for his diet and other practical aspects of his care. Over a period of time, however, he was encouraged to discuss the problem which he now experienced, and to consider ways in which he might become more independent and self reliant generally. Mr Black confided that he always liked the idea of cooking, but his wife had opposed this ambition and always seemed to be threatened by it. With the help and encouragement of the nurse who worked with him, Mr Black attended basic cookery classes, and after a while became proficient in many of the skills he had previously lacked. This gave him the confidence to tackle other practical problems, and his depression lessened as he acquired new skills and became more independent.

Mr Black's case study highlights the point made earlier concerning the vulnerability of clients, and the tendency they often have to place all their expectations and trust in the person who is designated to help them. The nurse who helped Mr Black did not encourage him to become dependent on her, although she accepted some measure of dependence in the initial stage of their relationship since this is what he needed at the time. Having reviewed his life, however, and the current problems which affect him, Mr Black was then encouraged to identify his own personal resources and to develop these in ways which would enable him to become more independent and confident about his own ability to cope. If the nurse had encouraged his dependence (in many ways an easier option for her) she would have acted unfairly towards the client, even though this is probably what he would have liked her to do initially.

TRANSFERENCE AND THE COUNSELLING RELATIONSHIP

The subject of transference is one we considered in some detail in Chapters 3 and 4, in the context of psychodynamic counselling. However, transference and its twin concept countertransference are not unique to psychodynamic theory, and the concepts have been discussed in connection with other theoretical approaches described in this book too. Because of their significance within the counselling relationship, transference and countertransference also deserve extended consideration in this section dealing specifically with the subject of the counselling relationship. We know that transference refers to the client's emotional response to the counsellor (or to any other helper) and we know that it is based on much earlier relationships, especially those formed in childhood with parents and other important people in the client's life. Transference, therefore, is by definition unrealistic since it stems from outdated information which people carry with them and apply to others who help them (as parents might have done) in times of emotional upheaval or distress. When people are distressed they are, of course, vulnerable and it is this vulnerability which makes them open to abuse, however unintended.

Unconscious feelings

Unconscious transference feelings may be either positive or negative, idealising, loving, erotic, envious or antagonistic. Though these (and many other possible responses) may not be obvious at the beginning of counselling, they tend to emerge once the client/counsellor relationship is established. In other words, clients may respond to helpers in totally realistic ways to start with, but later on they may respond in ways which are inappropriate or out of date. When Freud first wrote about psychoanalysis he fully expected his patients to co-operate with him in saying what was on their minds. After a while, however, he discovered that despite their conscious wishes to participate in therapy, various transference feelings tended to interfere with the ability of these patients to produce material which would be beneficial to their recovery. Freud referred to this phenomenon as 'transference resistance' (Freud, 1909).

The counsellors' response

One reason for highlighting these unconscious transference feelings is to show how important it is to be aware of their emergence in counselling. It is also important to realise that transference feelings are, as we have already indicated, unrealistic and inappropriate. This may be easier said than done, however, and it often takes another person to help us see this more clearly. Regular supervision is essential as an aid to monitoring both transference and countertransference feelings, and without this facility counsellors are quite likely to make serious mistakes in respect of their own feelings and those of their clients. The word countertransference describes the counsellor's emotional response to the client's transference. A counsellor who is, for example, cast in the role of critical parent, may well be drawn into responding in the way that a critical parent would respond. This kind of unconscious role play situation might continue unproductively and indefinitely, unless and until it is identified and changed either through spontaneous insight or with the aid of supervision.

Lack of objectivity

The point to make here is that clients do not benefit when a counsellor's judgment is clouded because of counter-transference feelings and residual complexes stemming from unresolved problems of his own past. Any distorted view of the client/counsellor relationship will inevitably get in the way of objectivity when dealing with clients and their problems. When counsellors experience counter-transference feelings towards clients, they need to be able to 'contain' these, rather than acting on them in a way that clients act on their transference feelings.

Apart from regular supervision, counsellors also need to develop habits of self scrutiny if they are to identify the roles which are often unconsciously forced on them by clients. In addition, counsellor awareness of both transference and countertransference feelings can prove to be an invaluable asset to therapy, especially when it provides information about the client's emotional problems. However, it is important to remember that not all responses to clients come under the heading of countertransference. Counsellors frequently perceive their clients as they really are, and often the responses elicited by clients in counselling are similar to those elicited in any other situation or relationship. On the other hand, it is often difficult to differentiate between what is real in our responses to clients, and what is countertransferential. The following are some indications of counter-transference reactions which may be experienced by counsellors:

◆ Strong sexual or loving feelings towards the client
◆ Inexplicable feelings of anxiety or depression

◆ Feelings of over-protectiveness towards the client

◆ Feelings of guilt in relation to the client

◆ Extreme tiredness or drowsiness

◆ Feelings of anger towards the client

◆ Loss of interest in the client

◆ Inability to make proper interventions when necessary

◆ Dreaming about clients, or thinking about them outside sessions

Several other countertransference reactions have been highlighted in Chapter 4, and the point was made there that every imaginable feeling, prejudice or bias may present itself in this form. One way in which counsellors can monitor their own counter-transference feelings is to ask the following questions in relation to work with clients:

◆ Do I experience any strong feelings at this moment which seem inappropriate or out of place?

◆ Are my interventions geared to the client's needs, or do they stem from my own needs?

It is not, of course, always possible to answer these questions, which is why regular supervision is needed for all counselling practitioners.

The possibility of exploitation

Any discussion about exploitation in counselling tends to focus on the more obvious forms, including those relating to the sexual and financial abuse of clients. It is true (and unfortunate) that these forms do indeed occur, but there are other, less obvious forms which counsellors can, either knowingly or unknowingly, inflict on clients. It is fairly easy to see how sexual involvement with clients can arise, especially when we consider the heightened emotions which clients often experience in relation to counsellors, as well as the imbalance of power which exists within the relationship. Such responses can be seductive and irresistible to those helpers who currently experience some problems in their own lives, especially if these are relationship problems or problems of loneliness. Once again this emphasises the point that counsellors need to know how to take care of their own needs without involving vulnerable clients. In Chapter 1 we looked at the issue of personal therapy, and discussed its inclusion or non-inclusion within counsellor training programmes. Whether or not it is a part of training, however, it should certainly be undertaken later on, when and if personal problems arise. Some of the other, possible areas of abuse within counselling and therapy include the following:

◆ Failure on the counsellor's part to undertake adequate supervision

◆ Arriving late for sessions, or leaving too early

◆ Encouraging clients to become dependent

◆ Being unclear or inconsistent about financial arrangements

◆ Premature termination of counselling, and lack of consultation with clients

◆ Failure to maintain confidentiality

What clients should know

There are, of course, other ways in which clients may be exploited by the people who claim to help them. Perhaps the best safeguard of all for counsellors, apart from supervision, is accountability within a team of professional workers. With back up, support (and scrutiny) helpers are less likely to engage in inappropriate or damaging behaviours towards clients. Counsellors who work in private practice, or those who charge direct fees for their work, need to be especially careful about the quality and standard of their service. However, all counsellors, regardless or their work setting, should ensure that their clients are aware of certain important aspects of counselling. These include clear details about the following:

◆ Financial terms, if these apply

◆ How payments should be made

◆ Confidentiality

◆ Arrangements concerning missed appointments

◆ Any special concessions for people on low incomes or those unemployed

◆ Length of sessions and the number likely to be needed

◆ Counsellor qualifications and training

◆ Counsellor's theoretical orientation and details about any specific procedures to be used

◆ Counsellor supervision

◆ Any records or notes the counsellor may keep

Clients should also be given information about any research the counsellor may be engaged in. It is obviously unethical to use any explicit or recognisable information gleaned from clients without asking for their permission to do so.

Contracts

One way of providing explicit and clear guidelines for clients is to establish contracts with them. Establishment of a contract ensures that both client and counsellor understand the nature of the commitment between them, and that they work together in harmony. In Chapter 3 we considered the subject of contracts, with special reference to their significance in a psychodynamic framework. However, contracts are an important component of all approaches to counselling and should be made at an early stage. In the first instance it is useful to clarify certain points with clients, especially those relating to the nature of counselling itself. Many clients believe that counselling includes advice, for example, while others may expect to receive friendship or a more intimate relationship. Culley (1991) highlights the importance of letting clients know the exact nature of the counselling relationship. When contracts are made in this way confusion is less likely to arise, especially when objectives and desired outcomes are also clarified and priorities discussed. Many of the factors already mentioned in this chapter, including those listed under the heading 'what clients should know', would form part of the client/counsellor contract. Among these are issues relating to number, frequency and length of sessions.

> **EXERCISE** — Making contracts
>
> Working in groups of three to four, draw up a list of factors which, in the opinion of group members, should be included in counselling contracts. Members of the group may have differing views about this, depending on individual areas of work or experience. What are the factors which emerge as the most important in relation to client/counsellor contracts?

ENDING COUNSELLING

We have noted several times throughout this book that the main objective in counselling is to help clients become more independent, self reliant and capable of dealing with any present or future problems. This means, in effect, that the counselling relationship, unlike many other relationships, is meant to end. Termination of therapy is, therefore, always implicitly present. Endings can be difficult for all of us however, and clients in counselling are no exception in this respect. Many people experience a variety of conflicts about endings in general, and this is especially true of those people who have been traumatised by separations in the past. The ending of any relationship is obviously much more difficult for someone who has lost a parent in early life, for example, or indeed for anyone who has been bereaved in later life too. Each new ending in an individual's life tends to reactivate memories of previous separations, endings or loss. Clients need to be able to talk about these experiences and what they mean to them, and counsellors can help by encouraging expression of all these feelings.

Looking ahead

When contracts are established at the beginning of counselling clients should ideally, be aware of the number of sessions they will attend. When the number of sessions is limited to a very few, and in many organisations and agencies this is currently the case, clients may also be more motivated to make whatever changes are necessary to help them deal more effectively with the problems they have experienced. A good beginning is often the key to a satisfactory ending in counselling, and for this reason clear, explicit goals discussed at the outset will tend to lessen some of the more negative aspects of the latter stage.

Often a client's newly acquired confidence becomes obvious towards the last stage of counselling, and this may show itself in different ways. One way in which this new confidence is visible is in the client's attitude to counselling itself. What was once the most important focus of the client's life is now placed in perspective and becomes secondary to other relationships and interests. Clients may also be less shy than they were originally, and they may find it more difficult to think of subject matter during sessions. For those clients who have had very specific problems, like phobias or addictions for example, there may be clear identifiable gains which indicate a readiness to cope independently of counselling. Feelings about ending counselling may also surface in dreams. The following case study describes one client's experience of this.

CASE STUDY — Endings

A client called Terry received counselling over a period of eight sessions. Terry, who was twenty-five, had been accused of assault by a colleague at work. Although he was acquitted of the charge he suffered panic attacks and agoraphobia as a result of his ordeal. During counselling he was able to explore all the angry feelings he felt about the accusation, and he was later able to discuss the development of his other symptoms. The exploration of his feelings was a great relief to Terry, because the nature of the accusation made against him meant that he was extremely reluctant initially to acknowledge his anger to anyone. He felt that if he admitted to feelings of anger this would be taken as proof of his guilt in relation to the incident with his colleague. Over a period of time Terry came to see that his feelings were a part of the ordeal he had been through, and once he had acknowledged and expressed them his panic attacks diminished in frequency and his reluctance to go out decreased too. Terry had formed a good relationship with the counsellor (a man) who worked as a volunteer helper at his local health centre. He had specifically asked to see a man, because he felt inhibited about relating the incident to a woman. A contact had been agreed between client and counsellor when they first met, so Terry was aware of the number of sessions there would be. Towards the end of his counselling Terry had a dream in which he was leaving school, but was unable to tell the teacher that he wanted to go. He related this dream to the counsellor and together they discussed it. Terry felt that the teacher in the dream would be hurt if he stated his intention to go. As a result of discussing the dream and the issue of endings and what they meant, Terry was able to place the dream in context, and to identify the counsellor as the teacher in it.

OTHER CLUES

The end of counselling, like the end of any close relationship, involves some degree of mourning. However, it should also involve internalisation of the process itself by the client, so that the experience of counselling becomes a useful guide for more productive ways of dealing with any difficulties which may arise later on. Following a successful experience of counselling clients may continue their own internal dialogue, similar to that conducted with the counsellor. In addition to the factors mentioned earlier, readiness to end counselling may also be indicated in other significant ways. The client is likely to feel more independent, for example, and as a result of this independence will see the counsellor as a 'real' person rather than an object or a transference figure. Increased understanding of 'self' is another aspect of client development, and often clients will demonstrate more assertive attitudes as a result of this.

From the counsellor's point of view this change is often 'felt' in the sense that the client's transference is no longer experienced, and the counsellor becomes more relaxed. When client and counsellor actually do separate, they do so as two 'equal' adults who have worked together toward a goal (Soloman, 1992). Additionally, they may both have a sense of sadness that the relationship has ended, although clients are sometimes offered the opportunity to attend another session in the future in order to discuss progress.

EXERCISE — Looking at endings

Working individually, make a list of all significant endings you have experienced in your own life. These might include some of the following:

◆ End of school holidays

◆ End of summer

◆ End of childhood

◆ End of college or university

◆ End of friendship

◆ End of working life

◆ End of single life

◆ End of childbearing years

◆ End of marriage or intimate relationship

Can you identify the range of feelings you had on any of these occasions? Discuss these, and any other thoughts you have about endings, with other members of the group.

REFERRAL

Clients receive counselling in a wide variety of contexts, some of which have been discussed in this book. In addition, clients may be helped by people who work in a variety of helping occupations, and many of these people would not describe themselves as counsellors. On the other hand, there is an increasing tendency for helpers and carers to undertake counselling skills training, and this trend (though welcome) can cause some confusion for those people seeking assistance with personal or psychological problems. One of the difficulties which helpers themselves can have as a result of these trends, is to determine the limits of their own capabilities in providing the right support for clients. An important aspect of training, therefore, is identification of specific problem areas which might require other forms of help or support. Obviously helpers differ in terms of professional training and background, and it is these very differences which necessitate discussion of the subject so that proper guidelines for referring clients can be defined. Some helpers may not, for example, have the specific skills needed to deal with clients in crisis, or those with severe depression or other forms of psychological illness. We all need to know what our own limitations are, and the first step is to look for these and then acknowledge them. The next step is to know 'how' to refer clients so that they receive the appropriate help when they need it.

Kennedy (1989) stresses the importance of anticipating referral in advance, if possible, so that clients are not taken totally by surprise. He makes the further point that referral should be integrated into the counselling relationship itself, so that it follows naturally from the experience which client and counsellor have shared together (Kennedy, 1989). Referral may be difficult for clients for a number of reasons; some may have experienced rejection in the past, while others may come to believe that they (or their problems) are just too formidable for anyone to cope with. On the other hand if referral is left too late, clients will not receive the kind of support or specialised help they need. This last point emphasises the importance of good communication with clients from the outset, so that the possibility of referral is identified early on. Kennedy's suggestion that referral should be anticipated in advance is also relevant here. Clients should be given the opportunity to discuss their feelings about the prospect of referral too. If they are not given this chance to express feelings, they may experience resentment and anger in relation to the whole process.

Reasons for referral

At every stage of the counselling process, however, helpers need to ask themselves what is the best course of action for specific clients. The reasons for referral are obviously very varied. A counsellor or client may, for example, be in the process of moving away from the area, in which case referral might be necessary if the client is to receive ongoing help. Certain clients may require psychiatric support, or other specialised health services. There are clients whose problems are specific to certain areas, for example adoption, recovery after surgery, disability or language difficulties, who might well benefit from contact with a helper specially trained in one of those areas. Whatever the circumstances, and regardless of the problem, it is essential that clients are given the opportunity to participate in any decisions which are made about them. The counsellor's task is to inform clients about any specialised services which are available to them, and it is then up to the client to accept or decline.

Occasionally clients may ask to see either a male or female counsellor. This request is usually made for very good reasons and counsellors should respect them. A woman who has been physically abused, for example, might feel more comfortable with a female counsellor, while a man who has sexual problems may well feel more at ease with a male counsellor. Occasionally clients who receive individual counselling are given the chance to participate in group work too. This necessitates referral of a different kind, since the client is not being asked to forfeit one kind of support for another. Another reason for referral is indicated when the particular theoretical approach which another counsellor uses is considered more appropriate for an individual client's needs. Financial constraints may also have a bearing on the kind of help available to a client; a client who cannot afford the services of a particular helper might benefit from referral to a voluntary agency for example.

The following is a list of factors which may impinge on your ability to help certain clients:

◆ Your level of expertise of lack of it

◆ Time: you do not have sufficient time to offer the client

◆ Your theoretical orientation and training: this may not be right for the client

◆ Information: you lack the kind of information the client needs

◆ Confidentiality: you may not be able to offer this to certain clients
◆ Relationship: your relationship with the client is difficult or compromised
◆ Distance: the client may receive appropriate help nearer home

---

> **◁ EXERCISE ▷** — Referral
>
> Working in groups of two to three, make a list of the reasons for referring clients to other people or agencies. Do these reasons vary for different members of the group? Discuss the counselling skills necessary for successful referral, and indicate how early or late in the counselling process you would do it.

Resources for referral

Preparation is probably one of the most important aspects of referral. All helpers, including those whose work is part of other occupational responsibilities, need to be well informed about all the resources available to them within the community, and indeed beyond. The names, addresses and telephone numbers of other professional workers who might be in a position to help clients with specific needs should be kept on record. Good liaison and consultation with other professionals is essential too. However, ongoing personal development and training is also needed for counsellors who wish to remain in touch with new developments in all the helping and allied professions. Continuing education has the added advantage of keeping counsellors in contact with as many people as possible, either locally or nationally, who might be able to help clients. Subscribing to professional journals and periodicals is also helpful and informative, since these can provide vital information about changes and trends in the helping professions generally.

CLIENTS IN CRISIS

In Chapter 1 we noted that clients often seek help when they experience a crisis. We also noted that each person's interpretation of crisis is quite subjective, which makes it difficult to list the experiences which might fall into that category. However, it is not just the client's response to a perceived crisis that we are concerned with here. The counsellor's response to the person in crisis is important in this context, and there are certainly a number of grave situations which are familiar to most experienced practitioners. These include those circumstances in which clients threaten suicide or violence towards other people. We have already considered the issue of confidentiality in relation to such expressed intentions, and the point has been made that many agencies have very specific guidelines about them. Apart from the practical steps which counsellors can initiate, however, the emotional impact on them needs to be considered too. In this respect, discussion and preparation are vitally important, since issues discussed openly in this way tend to be less threatening when they are actually encountered. Suicide and violence are not subjects which people readily talk about, but we need to address them in order to identify our own feelings in relation to them. We could start by looking at the following points:

◆ Some people take the view that as far as suicide is concerned there is no ultimate preventative.

◆ Other people take the view that clients who say they feel suicidal are, in fact, asking for positive intervention from helpers.

Helping clients in crisis

These two points are likely to generate a great deal of discussion in any training group, and you need to be clear about your own responses in relation to them. The view taken here is that clients should be offered whatever support and help we can possibly give. It seems to me that clients who reveal themselves in this way, are, in fact, seeking the reassurance that someone else cares sufficiently to intervene. It should be added that intervention does not necessarily mean dramatic action; what is usually needed is identification of all the client's feelings and plans so that a realistic assessment of risk can be made. When this is done, clients are frequently relieved to be taken seriously. Afterwards, practical steps can be implemented to lessen the suicide risk. These steps may include consultation with the client's doctor so that medication can be prescribed or adjusted, though none of this can be done without the client's permission. Helpers are sometimes reluctant to address the subject of suicide openly, on the grounds that to do so would encourage the client's action. This is an entirely mistaken belief, and one with immense potential for causing harm to clients. More often than not people are very relieved to articulate their worst fears and impulses in the presence (or hearing, as in telephone counselling) of someone who is supportive and calm. In order to determine the extent to which a person is serious about suicide it is useful to establish the following:

◆ Has the person made a plan?

◆ Is the plan specific?

◆ Does the person have the means to commit suicide?

◆ Is there a past history of suicide attempts?

Without looking closely at these factors it is impossible to establish the level of risk to those clients who may refer to suicide in oblique terms only. Counsellors and helpers should also be aware of some other factors which may accentuate the risk of suicide.

◆ History of depression

◆ Alcohol or substance abuse

◆ Mental illness, for example schizophrenia

In addition to these factors, there are also certain groups of people who appear to be more at risk than others. These include:

◆ Young men: suicide is three times as common in men as in women.

◆ People who are in trouble with the law are also a risk.

◆ Those people who experience conflict, either socially or within their own families, because of their sexual orientation.

◆ Divorced people, and people who are unemployed.

◆ Older people who have been recently bereaved are particularly vulnerable.

◆ Some occupational groups are high risk; these include farmers, doctors and vets.

◆ Professionals who work in the prison service are aware of the high incident of suicide among prisoners (Dept of Health Publications, 1996).

When helping clients in crisis counsellors need to be prepared to look at the underlying causes. Suicidal feelings are usually precipitated by a number of accumulating factors, and it is these factors which need to be identified and discussed with clients. Once this is done clients tend to experience relief of pressure, and with ongoing support and therapy they may be able to deal with their problems. Counselling can be continued with those clients who are referred for medical help, and often it is this combined approach which proves most beneficial for them.

Threats of violence

Sometimes clients express violent feelings or impulses towards other people. In these circumstances helpers need to assess the degree of actual danger involved and act accordingly. This is much easier said than done, since all of us have probably experienced antagonistic and negative emotions occasionally, as a result of conflict with others. Most people hide these feelings, for fear they will cause unnecessary alarm or upset. However, clients in counselling may express their negative feelings more readily, especially when they know they will not be judged for doing so. On rare occasions, though, clients may be serious in the threats they make, and in these instances helpers need to adhere to the guidelines set down by the agencies in which they work. Clients who threaten violence to others, like those who threaten violence to self, may in fact wish to be stopped. It is unlikely that they would verbalise their impulses if they did not expect some intervention. However, counsellors, in common with other responsible citizens, have a duty to safeguard vulnerable people who might be at risk of violence. Support through supervision is probably the most effective way for helpers to deal with problematic issues of this kind.

Other crisis situations

Suicide and threats of violence are not the only forms of crisis which counsellors and other helpers may hear about from clients. Others include:

◆ Sudden death

◆ Rape and assault

◆ Accident and injury

◆ Discovery of child abuse

◆ Acute illness

◆ Diagnosis of terminal illness

◆ Unexpected break-up of a relationship

◆ Burglary or loss of belongings

◆ Sudden financial problems

◆ Loss of a job

SUPERVISION

Throughout this book we have emphasised the central place of supervision for counsellors. Some of the issues just discussed, especially those relating to crisis and its management, should highlight even further the need for regular support of this kind. Many professional agencies make their own arrangements for supervision, and helpers who work in these settings are aware of the benefits of professional assistance and backing. However, the concept of supervision may be relatively new to some trainees, and although its importance has been stressed in preceding chapters, it merits further consideration in this section.

What supervision means

The word supervision refers to the practice of giving support and guidance to counsellors who work with clients. It is, in fact, mandatory for anyone, including trainees, who work with clients in a therapy or counselling context. The British Association for Counselling makes its view quite clear on the subject of supervision, and it is important that you read their Code of Ethics and Practice in order to acquaint yourself with this and other requirements. Supervision is, of course, not a new idea, for it has been in existence for a very long time. Freud and his followers supported one another in a similar way; supervision has been used ever since, though not just by counsellors and therapists but also by helpers in a variety of other caring roles. This kind of support is essential for counsellors and helpers because it affords an opportunity to discus all aspects of work with another trained person. More than anything else, however, it is the benefit to clients which is of primary importance.

Support for counsellors

Supervision is of benefit to counsellors for a number of reasons. These are:

◆ It provides a more objective view of the counsellor's work.

◆ Loss of confidence and 'burnout' are less likely when supervision is regular.

◆ It gives the counsellor a clearer picture of transference/countertransference issues.

◆ It allows the counsellor to appraise the skills and approaches used with individual clients.

◆ It provides support, guidance, encouragement and differing perspectives.

◆ It affords time for reflection and thought.

◆ Aspects of the relationship between client and counsellor are often mirrored in the supervisory relationship. This can provide important information abut the counsellor's work.

◆ It is rewarding for counsellors, both intellectually and emotionally.

◆ It can help counsellors to clarify and modify any negative emotions they may experience in relation to certain clients.

◆ Personal problems which counsellors have may be identified through supervision, although these are not directly dealt with by supervisors.

◆ It serves to identify the counsellor's own need for personal therapy.

◆ It enables counsellors to increase and develop their range of therapeutic techniques.

What supervision is not

Supervision is not the same as counselling, and the supervisor/counsellor relationship is quite different also. In the first place supervision is not therapy, although it can have therapeutic benefits. The supervisor's principal task is to improve the counsellor's relationship with her clients. This means that a supervisor is never directly involved in helping a counsellor to deal with personal problems, although evidence of these sometimes appears in the course of supervisory sessions. It may even be difficult to distinguish between the counsellor's personal problems and those of the client. One of the supervisor's duties is to help the counsellor differentiate between the two, and to recommend therapeutic support for the counsellor when necessary. Although supervisors do not give counselling, therefore, they nonetheless encourage counsellors to consider personal issues and to look at the way these impinge on their relationships with clients.

CASE STUDY — Jenny

Jenny worked as a student counsellor in a university. One of her clients, an eighteen year-old student called Tamsin, had been dieting over a long period of time and had requested counselling when she realised that she had developed problems in relation to this. Jenny had also been overweight as a teenager, and this had caused her a great deal of anxiety and stress at the time. Because of her experience, Jenny felt deep empathy with her client, but sometimes this identification threatened to cloud the true nature of the counselling relationship. On several occasions Jenny was tempted to offer advice and to steer Tamsin towards certain courses of action. She also found herself worrying a great deal about her client outside counselling sessions. In supervision Jenny was able to identify her countertransference feelings, and to separate her own memories and experience from the client's experience. Afterwards her relationship with Tamsin was much improved, and certainly less controlling than it had previously been.

Confidentiality and supervision

One point of similarity between the supervisory and counselling relationships is that both are confidential in nature. This means that supervision should be independent of other relationships which might be in conflict with it. One example of such a conflicting relationship is that which exists between manager and employer. Employees are obviously accountable to managers for a variety of work related reasons, and the nature of the manager/employee relationship may mean that true confidentiality cannot be guaranteed when supervision is also taking place. Another example of a relationship which might compromise the supervisory function is that of trainer and trainee. Teachers and trainers are required to assess their student and this might inhibit those trainees who are concerned with receiving satisfactory grades. Some elements of teaching are certainly contained in supervision, but as Page and Wosket point out, supervisor and supervisee are (or should be) 'fellow participants' within the relationship (Page and Wosket, 1994). Regardless of the relationship between supervisor and supervisee, however, absolute confidentiality may not always be guaranteed. Contexts in which it is not assured are similar to those which obtain in counselling, and include situations in which threats of violence or examples of bad practice are revealed.

Finding a supervisor

It is still the case that in some agencies people in managerial roles also act as supervisors for other employees. Additionally, in some training establishments trainers may still take on the role of supervisor to students. We have seen that these are not ideal arrangements, so a question arises concerning the best way to find a competent person outside these categories to fulfil the role of supervisor. The answer probably lies in co-operating with your trainer, so that any suggestion you make for supervisory arrangements is discussed and agreed between you.

How much and how often?

The amount of supervision needed by individual counsellors varies according to volume of work undertaken and the experience of the counsellor (BAC Code of Ethics and Practice for Counsellors, B.6.3.3, 1988). You should check with your trainer, and the agency you work with, about the level of supervision needed. The BAC Code of Ethics and Practice is updated on a regular basis, so it is always a good idea to check with them too if in doubt.

Other methods of supervision

In a one-to-one context, supervision is provided for the counsellor by a person who is usually more experienced. Other methods include co-supervision in which two people provide supervision for each other. In this second instance roles are alternated, so that participants take turns to be counsellor/supervisor. Peer group supervision is a third method which utilises the expertise of a number of trained counsellors who supervise each other. In contrast to this, the next model (group supervision) uses a designated supervisor/leader to facilitate the group, and ensures that each participant is given sufficient attention. A variant of this method is used when the supervisor/leader acts as a 'consultant' or technical resource within the group. A final model eclectic supervision, is favoured by some counsellors who take advantage of combined methods of supervision.

The relationship

It is obvious that the relationship between counsellor and supervisor needs to be based on trust and mutual respect if it is to work effectively. This means that supervisors should be prepared to discuss their qualifications, training and theoretical approach with their supervisees. Similarity of approach and training are important considerations too, since any substantial discrepancy in training and approach is likely to work against the effectiveness of the relationship. All administrative and practical details of the supervisory contract should be openly discussed and agreed upon by both counsellor and supervisor. Details about the boundaries of confidentiality should also be clarified.

<< **EXERCISE** >>— Experiences of supervision ——

Working in groups of three to four, discuss the benefits of supervision and identify the methods which are used by members of the group. How often do members of the group receive supervision and how long do sessions last?

EDUCATION AND TRAINING

In Chapter 1 we discussed a range of issues relating to counsellor training, and most of these are common to many programmes. However, individual programmes do still vary a great deal nationwide. Differences in training provision are even more marked if we look at the wider European context. At present the Professional Training Standards Committee (PTSC) of the European Association for Counselling is conducting research into training and standards, and the British Association for Counselling is also involved in setting new standards for counselling. These developments represent real progress in counsellor training and general accountability, and anyone interested in the subject of training and standards should monitor them closely. Finally, it is worth emphasising that counsellor training does not stop when you have completed a recognised course. If you intend to practice as a counsellor you need to continue your education and professional development at various stages throughout your career.

SUMMARY

In this chapter we considered a range of ethical issues in counselling. These included the subject of confidentiality, and its central place in the therapeutic relationship. The limitations to absolute confidentiality were discussed, and examples were given of situations in which it might not be guaranteed. The counselling relationship was an important focus of this chapter, and we examined the twin concepts of transference and counter-transference in this context. Contracts in counselling were discussed, and the subject of 'endings' and its attendant difficulties was considered too. The subject of referral and reasons for it were also detailed. Crisis, and its effects on both client and counsellor, was addressed in this section. The necessity for regular supervision and ongoing training was stressed, and the different models of supervisory support were described.

REFERENCES

BAC (1993)   *Code of Ethics and Practice for Counsellors.* Rugby: The British Association for Counselling.

Culley, S. (1991)   *Integrative Counselling Skills in Action.* London: Sage Publications.

EAC (1996)   *Newsletter.* Rugby: European Association for Counselling, June 1996.

EAC (1997)   *Newsletter.* Rugby: European Association for Counselling, July 1997.

Department of Health (1996)   *Mental Illness.* Lanes: Baps Health Publications Unit.

Freud, S. (1909)   *Five Lectures on Psychoanalysis.* London: Penguin Books.

Kennedy, E. (1989)   *On Becoming a Counsellor.* New York: Gill and MacMillan.

Page, S. & Wosket, V. (1994)   *Supervising the Counsellor.* London: Routledge.

Rogers, C. (1991)   *Client Centred Therapy.* London: Constable.

Solomon, I. (1992)   *The Encyclopedia of Evolving Techniques in Dynamic Psychotherapy.* New Jersey: Jason Aronson Inc.

Weinberg, G. (1996)   *The Heart of Psychotherapy.* New York: St Martins Griffin.

FURTHER READING

Daines, B., Gask, L. & Usherwood, T. (1996)   *Medical and Psychiatric Issues For Counsellors.* London: Sage Publications.

Dryden, W. & Feltham, C. (1992)   *Psychotherapy and its Discontents.* Buckingham: Open University Press.

Dryden, W. & Thorne, B. (1991)   *Training and Supervision for Counselling In Action.* London: Sage Publications.

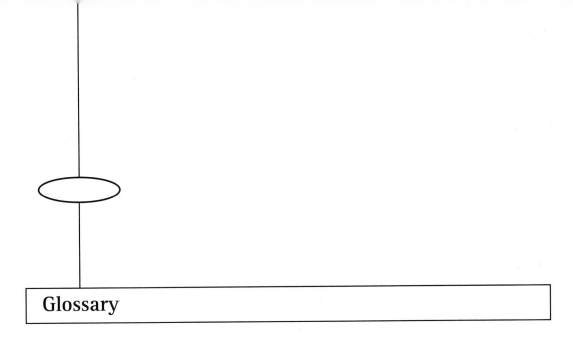

Glossary

Abnormal psychology	The study of behaviour disturbance, including the causes, classification and description of abnormal types of behaviour
Abreaction	A term used in psychodynamic theory to refer to the process of reliving, either in speech or in action, a previously repressed experience. It also involves the release of the emotions associated with the experience.
Actualising tendency	A propensity described by both Rogers and Maslow. It refers to the human urge to grow, develop and reach maximum potential.
Acquisition	The process whereby a conditioned stimulus begins to produce a conditioned response.
Adaptation	The ability to function effectively in the environment. Adaptations are helpful changes which enable people to cope with others and with their surroundings.
Addiction	A pronounced physical or psychological dependence on, or need for, a chemical substance.
Adlerian	Referring to Adler, who was an early follower of Freud. Adlerian counselling and therapy is based on the theories developed by Adler.
Affect	Refers to feelings and emotions.

Affective disorder   Mental disturbance characterised by mood changes. Depression is one example, while extreme excitement (mania) is another.

Agoraphobia   An abnormal fear of being alone or in a public place where escape might be difficult. The term is derived from two Greek words: Phobos (Fear) and Agora (Marketplace).

Ambivalence   Conflict of feelings or emotions (love and hate) towards another person or object. There may be contradictory impulses as well, and often one of the ambivalent feelings is conscious, while the other is unconscious.

Anal stage   According to psychoanalytic theory, this is the second stage of psychosexual development. Gratification and conflict are experienced in relation to the expulsion and retention of faeces. Control of bodily function and socialisation of impulses are major tasks at this time.

Anima/animus   Jungian terms referring to unconscious opposite sex images. The anima is the unconscious female image in the male psyche, while the animus is the unconscious male image in the female psyche.

Anxiety   Feelings of dread associated with physical symptoms including raised pulse and sweating. According to Freud, anxiety is related to unconscious mental conflicts stemming from childhood.

Archetypes   Unconscious images, ideas or patterns of thought which, according to Jung, are inherited from our ancestors and are universally present in all of us.

Aversion therapy   The use of punishment to remove undesirable behaviour such as alcoholism. Has been used in the past as part of behaviour therapy to treat a range of problems, but is less popular now.

Basic needs   A term used by Maslow (1954) to describe a range of needs which all humans experience. These include physiological, safety, belongingness, esteem and self actualisation needs. Maslow arranged these needs in a hierarchy, and although it is often assumed that they are in a fixed order, he did not intend that it should be interpreted so rigidly.

Basic trust   A fundamental attitude derived from positive early experience. The term is used by both Erikson and Winnicott and refers to the feelings about *self*, which are formed as a result of an infant's relationship with the primary care giver.

Behaviourism   The scientific study of behaviour based on observable actions and reactions. The focus is on analysing the relationship between behaviour and the environment, and on the way that stimuli provokes responses.

Behavioural counselling	An approach to counselling which focuses on observable behaviour. (See *Behaviour therapy*).
Behaviour therapy	A term first used by Skinner to describe a method of psychotherapy based on learning principles. Also sometimes called 'behaviour modification'. Clients are taught, through a variety of techniques, to modify problem behaviour.
Belongingness need	A term used by Maslow (1954) to describe the human need to give and receive acceptance, affection and trust.
Biofeedback	A technique which allows individuals to monitor and control their physiological processes, including blood pressure, pulse and temperature. This is achieved through the use of electronic equipment.
Biological determinism	Freudian concept which states that sexual and aggressive forces govern human experience and behaviour.
Bipolar disorder	Describes two emotional extremes of depression and mania which a person may experience on a daily or even hourly basis.
Blind spots	A term often used in counselling to describe characteristics, behaviour or areas of personal experience which are (temporarily at least) outside our awareness. One aim of counselling is to help clients shed light on these blind spots, although it should be emphasised that counsellors have blind spots too.
Bulimia nervosa	An illness characterised by recurrent episodes of binge eating alternating with self induced vomiting, abuse of laxatives and diuretics. Strict dieting is also a feature, so too is a rigorous exercise regime designed to prevent weight gain.
Burn–out	The outcome of accumulated stress characterised by physical, psychological and behavioural dysfunction.
Case history	Material or information which is recorded for the purpose of understanding a patient's (or a client's) problems. Case histories are often used to help plan treatments or helping strategies, though they are sometimes kept for research programmes too.
Castration complex	In Freudian theory, an unconscious fear of genital mutilation or loss, as punishment for sexual attraction to the opposite sex

parent. The concept applies to women as well as to men, and should be interpreted in a symbolic rather than a literal sense. Men may, for example, *fear* a loss of power or potency, while women may *actually experience* disempowerment because of their relative lack of status or opportunity in society.

Catastrophising	A term used by Albert Ellis to describe a tendency to dwell on negative events or possibilities. An over-emphasis on the worst possible scenario or outcome.
Catharsis	Release or elimination of repressed emotions, usually achieved through crying or verbal expressions of anger or resentment. The word is translated from Greek and means to *clean*. It is used in both art and drama where release of emotions can occur vicariously. See also *abreaction*.
Cathexis	A term used in Freudian theory to describe the attachment of emotional energy or libido to mental representations of other people (object catharsis) or to aspects of oneself (ego or id cathexis).
Censor	A Freudian term used to describe an unconscious mechanism used by the ego in the production of defence mechanisms. Also used to denote the mechanism whereby dream content is distorted to make it more acceptable to the ego.
Character disorder	A long-standing pattern of deviant or socially unacceptable behaviour, for example criminality.
Clairvoyance	The ability to foresee events or objects other than through sensory experience. Sometimes called extrasensory perception.
Claustrophobia	An abnormal fear of enclosed spaces.
Clinical Psychologist	A psychology graduate who specialises in the understanding, assessment and treatment of emotional or behavioural problems.
Cognition	The experiences of thinking, reasoning, perceiving and remembering.
Cognitive dissonance	Conflicts in attitude or thinking, which lead to feelings of uneasiness. These feelings then motivate the person to seek ways of achieving consistency.
Cognitive restructuring	The process of replacing stress producing thoughts with more positive or constructive cognitions. Often taught as a therapeutic technique to clients in counselling.
Collective unconscious	A Jungian concept which postulates that all human beings,

have, at an unconscious level, shared memories, ideas and experiences, based on the knowledge acquired through time by our common ancestors.

Compensation	The development of personality traits designed to overcome other inadequacies or imperfections. In Freudian terms, a defence mechanism.
Complex	Unconscious ideas and associations which influence behaviour.
Condensation	The representation of several complex ideas in a single symbol. Used in Freudian theory to describe aspects of dream imagery.
Compulsion	An overwhelming drive to repeat certain actions or rituals. See also *obsessive compulsive disorder*.
Conversion reaction	Turning a psychological problem into a physical one so that anxiety is transformed into a tangible form.
Counselling	A form of psychological helping which values, and seeks to identify, each client's innate (though perhaps temporarily obscured) internal resources, coping abilities and strengths.
Crisis intervention	The procedures used in an immediate response to any psychological emergency.
Daydreaming	Indulging in fantasy or dreaming while awake.
Death instinct	A concept introduced by Freud in 1920 to describe aggressive or destructive forces, which are directed against *self* rather than against others. Certain self destructive forms of behaviour, drug taking or alcoholism for example, could theoretically be prompted by the death instinct.
Defence mechanism	A method of coping with the threat of anxiety. A pattern of behaviour designed to obscure unpleasant emotions.
Déjà vu	A strong feeling that a present experience has in fact been experienced before. May be an unconscious association of forgotten past events with current experience.
Delusion	A false belief or conviction which is firmly held and defended.
Denial	Defence mechanism, which is often used in situations of extreme stress. For example, a person with terminal illness might simply deny the diagnosis in order to reduce intolerable anxiety.
Depression	A feeling of hopelessness, apathy or despair. A mood (or affective) disorder, see also *affect*. May include physical

	symptoms, loss of self esteem, sleep disturbance, loss of appetite and tiredness.
Depressive position	The second of Melanie Klein's developmental positions (age 3 months) characterised by a recognition that the object (mother) who was hated is also loved and is, in fact, a 'whole' object rather than just disjointed parts. This is accompanied by depressive anxiety, feelings of guilt, concern and a desire to repair the (imagined) damage done to the object.
Developmental Psychologist	A psychology graduate who specialises in the study of development throughout the lifespan. There is a special emphasis on the relationship between early and later behaviour, and on the experiences of childhood and adolescence.
Displacement	A defence mechanism whereby unacceptable motives or impulses are directed towards another target or object.
Dissociation	A lack of integration or connection between mental processes. Loss of contact with reality which may occur during sleepwalking, hypnosis, loss of memory or severe illness.
Divergent thinking	The use of creativity as an approach to problem solving. Instead of a single answer, many possible solutions are generated.
Dreams	Mental images which occur during sleep. According to Freud, dreams originate in the unconscious, have psychological meaning and can be interpreted. In psychodynamic theory, dreams are said to have a manifest content and a latent content. The former refers to that which is remembered by the dreamer, while the latter refers to the deeper meaning, which can only be accessed through interpretation.
Eclectic	An approach used in counselling and psychotherapy characterised by adherence to one preferred theoretical school, while using methods belonging to other schools when appropriate to the needs of individual clients.
Ego	The 'I' or conscious part of personality. In Freud's tripartite theory of personality the ego mediates between the impulses of the id and the strict demands of the superego.
Ego boundary	The imagery line which separates *self* from others. A person who lacks ego boundaries finds it difficult to maintain a separate identity from others.
Ego ideal	How each person would like to be. Often used interchangeably

with the term superego. Refers to the parental and other influences which set guidelines for civilised behaviour.

Ego integrity Refers to the last of Erikson's eight psychosocial stages, for example ego integrity v despair. Indicates equanimity and acceptance of both life and death in old age.

Ego psychology A branch of psychodynamic theory which stresses the positive, autonomous and creative functions of the ego. This is in contrast to strict Freudian theory, which limits ego function to the arbiter in disputes between the id and superego.

Elecrtra complex A Freudian term used to describe the psychosexual stage of development at which girls are said to experience a constellation of impulses similar to the Oedipus complex in boys.

Endogenous Originating from within the person, for example endogenous depression.

Environment All outside influences, including other people, which affect the individual.

Environmental determinism The idea, enshrined in behaviourism, that people are influenced by external forces.

Esteem needs From Maslow's hierarchy, where the need for respect for oneself and others is described.

Eros Used by Freud to denote the life force or sexual instinct. See contrast with the death instinct or 'thanatos'.

Extravert Personality type described by Jung. Refers to people who are inclined to direct mental energy and interests outwards towards other people and events. The term was also used by Eysenck (1991) to describe the outgoing personality type.

False memories Memories recalled during therapy or hypnosis, which may in fact be dreamlike creations prompted by suggestion (spoken or unspoken) from the therapist.

Family therapy A psychotherapeutic approach in which the whole family is involved so that common problems can be dealt with.

Fantasy Daydreaming to fulfil a psychological need. A defence mechanism which may be used as a substitute for harsh reality.

Fetish An object worshipped by certain cultures for its magical qualities. In Freudian theory the word refers to an object or piece of clothing which is necessary for sexual gratification.

Fixation	In Freudian or psychoanalytic theory, arrested development at an early stage of life. Failure to progress through the stages of psychosexual development, for example oral fixation.
Flight into health	Describes the way in which clients in therapy sometimes seem to recover rapidly. May be viewed as a defence against introspection or self analysis.
Flooding	A method used in behaviour therapy to treat clients with phobias. The person is encouraged to stay in the feared situation, and to experience all the anxiety it evokes. For example, a client with a phobia about snakes might be encouraged to visit the snake house at the zoo and to stay there until the anxiety is lessened.
Free association	A procedure originated by Freud and used in psychodynamic therapy. The client is encouraged to say whatever comes to mind in the hope that unconscious ideas and conflicts will surface.
Free floating anxiety	Anxiety of unknown origin or cause.
Freudian slip	A mistake, either verbal or action based, which indicates some underlying meaning. One example is the student who misses the bus on the way to sit an important exam.
Fugue	A dissociative reaction which usually stems from a desire to escape an intolerable situation. The person wanders off or sleepwalks and afterwards is unable to remember what happened.
Genital stage	The last of Freud's psychosexual stages of development. It is characterised by an interest in the formation of sexual relationships.
Gestalt psychology	That branch of psychology concerned with the way in which human beings perceive things as whole patterns rather than just collections of individual parts.
Gestalt therapy	An approach to therapy devised by Fritz Perls. Therapy usually takes place on a one-to-one basis in a group setting, but it is also practised by therapists working with individual clients. A goal of therapy is to help clients become more integrated and aware of themselves in the 'here and now'.
Ground	The background in our visual field. The term is used in Gestalt theory along with the word figure (figure and ground) to describe a whole or pattern which is known as a Gestalt.

Group dynamics	The study of the ways in which group members interact.
Group polarisation	A tendency, present in groups, to make decisions which are more extreme than those made by individuals.
Group think	A tendency among group members to lose the ability to be objective and realistic in their evaluation of decisions.
Growth motive	Described by Maslow as a human motive to develop and grow, even when there is no obvious need to continue striving.
Guidance	Advice and help given to people with educational, vocational or work related problems.
Halo effect	A belief in the total goodness of a person possessed of one outstanding quality. May also apply when a negative quality is taken as evidence of general negativity.
Hallucination	A sensory perception which may be visual, auditory, olfactory or tactile. Experiences which are not present in reality, but are nevertheless believed to be real by the individual. Common in certain forms of mental illness, including psychosis. May also occur after bereavement when the hallucination is seen as evidence of the dead person's presence.
Hallucinogens	Drugs which produce hallucinations and other perceptual changes. LSD is one example of an artificial hallucinogenic substance, although there are others which are derived from natural sources.
Hierarchy of needs	The order of importance which Maslow ascribes to human needs. Lower order needs must be fulfilled before higher order needs can be experienced.
Holistic	An approach which stresses the connection between all areas of experience, including the physical, the emotional and the environmental.
Homeostasis	An organic tendency to maintain a constant state or an optimum level of functioning. One example is the physiological mechanism which ensures a uniform body temperature. In Jungian theory, psychological homeostasis or automatic self regulation also occurs, and is achieved when there is a balance between the conscious and unconscious aspects of the psyche.
Horney, Karen (1885–1952)	A German psychiatrist and psychoanalyst who moved to America in 1932. Emphasised the role of cultural and environmental factors in the development of neurosis, especially those affecting women.

Humanistic psychology	A psychological approach which emphasises subjective experience and the uniqueness of human beings. Sometimes referred to as the 'Third Force' in psychology, after psychoanalysis and behaviourism.
Hypnagogic images	Images which occur during the drowsy state just before sleep.
Hypnosis	The trance like state resembling sleep. Artificially induced state during which a person's perception, voluntary actions and memory may be altered, and susceptibility to suggestions is heightened.
Hypnotherapy	The treatment of problems or illness through the use of hypnosis.
Hypochondria	An exaggerated concern with the body and with health. The presentation of physical symptoms with no underlying cause. Usually linked to psychological problems which need to be addressed if overall health is to improve.
I	The subjective experience of self similar to the word ego. However, I is a personal pronoun whereas the word ego is used as an objective description of the self.
Id	Refers to the primitive pleasure seeking part of the personality described by Freud.
Ideal self	A Rogerian concept describing the kind of person one would really like to be. Conflict often arises between the 'ideal self' and the 'false self', especially when the former cannot be expressed or fully acknowledged.
Identification	A process of modelling personal behaviour on the behaviour of someone else. In extreme cases, a person's identity may be totally merged with that of someone else. In psychoanalysis, primary identification refers to a relationship in which the mother is the object, whereas secondary identification refers to a relationship where the object is seen as having a separate identity. See also *projective identification*.
Identity	The sense of being separate and different from others. May be poorly developed when there is trauma or disruption in childhood, and may even be lost when there is severe mental illness at any stage of life.
Identity crisis	A term used by Erikson to describe the turmoil which accompanies certain developmental stages, especially the stage of adolescence. Young adults are faced with the task of separating from parents and of finding a suitable place in

society. Erikson also describes the tendency to form peer groups at this stage, so that individual identities become totally merged.

Illusion	Mistaken perception of reality.
Imago	A term used in psychoanalytic and Jungian theory to describe unconscious object representations. Similar to Jung's concept of the Archetype.
Incorporation	In Freudian theory this refers to a fantasy of having taken in or swallowed an external object or person.
Individuation	A Jungian term which refers to the process of psychic development and growth. A lifelong process which is particularly significant in middle age when existential issues appear in sharp focus.
Inferiority complex	A term coined by Adler to describe a constellation of ideas and feelings which arise in response to personal deficiency. The term is now more commonly used to denote feelings of worthlessness and inadequacy which often lead to lack of self esteem or aggression.
Insight	In psychoanalytic terms, the capacity to understand mental processes, personal motives and the meaning of symbolic behaviour.
Instinct	Innate, unlearned, goal directed behaviour arising from a biological source.
Intellectualisation	A defence mechanism which is used to ward off emotionally threatening material.
Internal reality	A person's own subjective experience of events.
Internalisation	The process of acquiring mental representations of people or objects in the external world. Often used in object relations theory to describe the way in which an infant builds up an inner world of images which are derived from relationships, especially the relationship with mother. These representations are then used to form an image of *self* which can be either good or bad depending on the quality of early relationship experience.
Intrapsychic	Refers to mental activity and the processes which occur between the id, the ego and the superego.
Introjection	A term used in object relations theory and similar to internalisation. However, strictly speaking, introjects are the

result of internalisation. Objects (or other people) are internalised and become mental representations. These internal objects then form the subject's values, beliefs and attitudes and are the basis of the superego.

Introversion A psychological type described by Jung. Refers to a human tendency to withdraw inwards or to become introverted especially at times of stress. Eysenck (1975) also used the term to describe a melancholic personality type. (See also *extraversion*.)

Isolation A defence mechanism used by people to separate thoughts from emotions. Experiences are deprived of *affect* or feeling and can be viewed in a wholly detached way.

James, William (1842–1910) An American psychologist who wrote the two-volume book *Principles of Psychology* in 1890.

Latency Freud's fourth stage of psychosexual development (age 6–12 years approx.) during which sexual interests become dormant.

Latent content Referring to dreams, see *dreams*.

Law of effect Refers to a law stating that any behaviour which is followed by reinforcement is strengthened. Responses which are not rewarded are less likely to be performed again.

Lay analyst Psychoanalyst, a person who is not a trained psychiatrist and who treats clients through the use of psychoanalysis.

Learned helplessness Refers to a state of apathy or helplessness described by Seligman (1975) which develops when a person is unable to escape or avoid a situation in which there is discomfort or trauma.

Levels of consciousness Different levels of mental activity, some of which may be outside awareness.

Libido In Freudian theory refers to a person's basic life instincts.

Longitudinal study Research method used to study people over a period of time taking measurements at different stages of development.

Lucid dreaming Being aware that we are dreaming while the dream is actually in progress. This indicates that sleep may not always involve a total loss of consciousness.

Maladjusted behaviour Behaviour which is socially inappropriate and causes difficulties for the individual and others.

Mania An elevated expansive mood with increased levels of restlessness or irritability. There may also be a sense of grandiosity, flights of ideas and a marked reduction in the need for sleep. Frequently accompanied by alternating periods of depression.

Manifest content
(See *dreams*.)

Marital therapy
Therapy which aims to help both members of a couple to resolve their relationship problems.

Masochism
A desire for pain, humiliation or suffering which is inflicted either by oneself or by others.

Maturation
The process of growing and becoming fully developed both mentally and physically.

Medical model
Sometimes called a biological model. An approach which states that mental illness and behaviour disorders are due to physical causes which can, therefore, be treated by medical means.

Meditation
An altered state of consciousness induced by intense concentration or the repetition of certain words or actions, and resulting in feelings of inner peace and tranquillity.

Moral principle
Refers to the influence exerted by the superego whose purpose is to restrict free expression of id impulses. Guilt is reduced when such impulses are restricted through the moral principle.

Multiple personality
A dissociative disorder in which a person appears to possess more than one identity, all acting and speaking in different ways.

Multidisciplinary approach
A team approach to working with patients or clients. Counsellors working in the public sector frequently liaise with other professionals including doctors and social workers.

Narcissism
A form of self love in which there is an investment of energy or libido in oneself. In other words, the subject is preferred to the object. In Freudian theory the term 'primary narcissism' refers to the infantile love of Self, which is then followed by 'secondary narcissism' when love of Self is replaced by love of an introjected other person or object.

Need satisfying object
An object or other person who is valued for an ability to satisfy one's basic or instinctual needs, without any regard for the needs or personality of the object.

Negative therapeutic reaction
A term used in psychoanalysis to describe a negative response whereby a client's general condition worsens as a result of interpretations offered by the therapist.

Neo–Freudian	A term describing a group of American theorists who re-interpreted Freudian theory and emphasised the influence of society and relationships, on people and their behaviour. Included in the group are Eric Fromm, Karen Horney and Harry Stack Sullivan.
Neurasthenia	An outdated Freudian term to describe a condition similar to Chronic Fatigue Syndrome.
Neurosis	A pattern of behaviour, including fear and anxiety, with no organic basis. Possible psychological causes include past event or traumas, relationships and sexual difficulties.
Nightmare	A frightening or terrifying dream which may be prompted by trauma or conflict in a person's working life.
Norm	Average, standard or common. A learned and accepted rule of society which dictates behaviour in various situations.
Object	In psychodynamic (and especially object relations) theory, this refers to another person to whom emotional energy, including love and desire, is directed. However, an object can also be a part of a person or a symbolic representation of either a person or part of a person
Object cathexis	Investment of emotional energy in another person. Contrast with narcissism. (See *narcissism*.)
Object constancy	The tendency to adhere to a specific lasting relationship with another person. In infancy, object constancy refers to the baby's preference for, and strong bond with, the mother.
Object, good	May be internal (as a mental representation) or external. An object who is perceived as reliable, dependable, trustworthy and loving.
Object permanence	The knowledge that objects exist even when they are hidden from view. Such knowledge results from the ability to form mental representations of external objects.
Object relations therapy	Psychoanalytic theory of relationships which stresses the significance and dynamics of the bond between mother and infant, and later between mother, infant and father. The infant's need to relate to objects is paramount, and the nature of object relationships affects personality development.
Object, transitional	A substitute for another person or for an important relationship. Winnicott (1988) uses the term to describe soft toys, dolls and pieces of cloth or blanket which children value

because of the symbolic link to mother. These objects are effective in helping children move gradually from dependence to independence.

Object, whole
The object or other person who is seen as separate and existing in their own right, with feelings and needs similar to those of the subject.

Observational learning
The process of observing, and learning from the behaviour of others.

Obsessive Compulsive Disorder (OCD)
Persistent thoughts, ideas and impulses which are inappropriate and intrusive, and which lead to anxiety and a compulsion to do certain things. The goal of such compulsive behaviour is to prevent or reduce anxiety, and when the sufferer tries to interrupt obsessive thinking or behaviour, severe anxiety and agitation follow. Cleaning rituals and checking are examples of OCD, and onset of problems tends to occur in late adolescence (Lemma, 1996).

Oedipus complex
In Freudian terms, the phallic stage of psychosexual development when a young boy is sexually attracted to his mother. There is accompanying hostility towards the father who is seen as a rival. Fear of retaliation ensures that these incestuous desires are repressed, and the eventual outcome is identification with the father and the adoption of male sex role behaviour by the son.

Omnipotence
A Freudian concept which indicates a belief that thoughts can alter the environment or events. At an early stage, infants are said to experience omnipotence of thought, and only late come to realise, through frustration of everyday living, that reality prevails.

Operant conditioning
The process whereby an animal or person learns to respond to the environment in a way which produces a desired effect. In laboratory research, B. F. Skinner trained animals by immediately rewarding them for correct responses. He later applied the same concept to human learning.

Oral stage
In psychoanalytic theory, the first of Freud's stages of psychosexual development is characterised by the infant's pleasure in feeding and dependence on the mother.

Panic disorder
Sometimes referred to as panic attacks. Terrifying recurrent anxiety which appears without warning and is not associated with a specific phobia. There is a sudden onset of fear accompanied by a fast heart rate, sweating, shortness of

breath, trembling, dizziness or faintness and sometimes nausea. During an attack people often feel they may go crazy.

Paranoia	A mental disorder in which delusions of persecution or grandeur are common.
Paranoid–schizoid position	The first of Melanie Klein's position which occupies the first three months of an infant's life. It is characterised by feelings of persecution and threats of annihilation, along with splitting of the ego and the self into good and bad. In Klein's view, the paranoid-schizoid position precedes the depressive position and represents the infant's attempts to deal with destructive impulses which are projected on to the object (mother). Failure to negotiate the paranoid-schizoid position results (according to Klein) in a range of later difficulties, including schizoid and paranoid conditions.
Paraphraxis–Freudian slip	Describes unconscious mental processes which prompt certain unintended faulty actions or mistakes in speech. In Freudian terms, these errors are seen as evidence of unconscious conflicts or wishes.
Parapsychology	That branch of psychology which studies supernatural phenomena, including clairvoyance, telepathy and extrasensory perception.
Perception	Refers to awareness of the external world through the use of the senses.
Persona	Jungian term which means a mask, and describes the characteristics which people assume as part of their roles in everyday life.
Personal construct	A personality theory proposed by the American psychologist George Kelly (1905–1967) which suggest that people *construe* their own worlds. According to Kelly we interpret things and try to understand them, and to do this we employ *personal constructs*. These represent our own private logic, and include deductions and conclusions which determine personality and guide behaviour. When events accord with our expectations we feel comfortable and our personal constructs are validated. If however we anticipate wrongly, then we are obliged to *reconstrue*, a process which causes discomfort and threat.
Personality	General patterns of behaviour and thought which are characteristic of an individual. Major theories have been forwarded by Freud, Adler, Jung, Klein, Sullivan and Erikson, though other writers have contributed to the field as well.

Personality disorder	Psychological disturbance in which personality traits or behaviour interfere with social functioning. (See also *character disorder*.)
Phallic stage	The third of Freud's psychosexual stages of development, preceded by the oral and anal stages. Characterised by the Oedipus complex. (See *Oedipus complex*.)
Phantasy	Refers to unconscious mental activity and differs from fantasy, which takes place at a conscious level. The word is used in object relations theory to describe much of the psychic activity occurring in infancy.
Phobia	Irrational fear of a specific object or situation. An anxiety disorder which interferes with daily life. In psychodynamic theory, the phobic situation or object represents an unconscious fear or impulse which the person is unable to face.
Pleasure principle	In psychodynamic theory this is the operating principle of the id which prompts people to seek immediate satisfaction of desires and needs.
Post Traumatic Stress Disorder (PSD)	The development of symptoms following an extremely stressful experience or situation. It differs from other anxiety disorder because of its specific causation. The traumatic event is usually experienced through recurrent and intrusive recollections, images, thoughts or perceptions. Distressing dreams and nightmares also occur, and there is often persistent avoidance of anything associated with the trauma.
Precognition	The ability to perceive events which have not yet occurred.
Primary process thinking	A Freudian concept to describe a primitive form of thinking which is characteristic of early infancy. A very basic form of wishful thinking through which the id can access images of a desired object (mother).
Projection	In psychoanalytic theory, a defence mechanism in which people ascribe unacceptable desires or feelings to others instead of to themselves. The result is a reduction in guilt and discomfort. In Kleinian terms, projection has a different meaning, and refers to a normal developmental strategy used in early infancy. In this sense, impulses, including good and bad feelings, are projected by the infant on to the object (mother).
Projective identification	Kleinian term which describes the way in which clients in therapy may force aspects of their internal world onto the

therapist. These aspects include a range of feelings and anxieties. The concept of projective identification is used to illustrate the way in which shifts in transference and counter-transference occur in therapy. The purpose of projective identification varies but may include control, ingratiation, sexual communication or dependency.

Psychiatrist A medical doctor with specialised training in the treatment of mental or emotional disorders.

Psychoanalyst A psychiatrist or psychologist who is trained in psychoanalysis. (See also *Lay analyst*.)

Psychodynamic Referring to schools of therapy and counselling which are derived from Freudian theories and which emphasise the unconscious mental process which influence human behaviour.

Psychologist A person who has obtained a general degree in psychology. May also specialise in different areas of psychology including clinical, developmental, educational, industrial and abnormal psychology.

Psychotherapist A person who helps others with psychological or emotional problems, usually by verbal means. There are various schools of psychotherapy, and the length of training varies. It is possible to train as a psychotherapist without any specific prior qualifications, although training establishments have well defined entry criteria and are selective in their choice of students. Psychotherapy tends to differ in length of training from counselling, and usually takes longer. The words psychotherapy and counselling are often used interchangeably now, and in many instances it is difficult to identify any appreciable difference between them.

Psychopathology The study of mental illness.

Psychosis A severe mental illness in which a person loses contact with reality and is unable to manage daily living. May include delusions and hallucinations.

Psychosomatic disorder Physical illness with psychological cause.

Rapport Harmonious communication between people. Especially important in a relationship between client and counsellor.

Rationalisation Freudian defence mechanism which offers false reasons for unacceptable behaviour. A person who steals might, for example, overcome feelings of guilt by saying that the people he steals from have too much money anyway.

Reaction formation	Another Freudian defence mechanism in which a person's views, impulses and behaviour are directly opposite to what he or she really feels.
Reality principle	Describes the operating principle of the ego in Freudian theory. The reality principle is acquired through development and experience, and is that part of personality which seeks to compromise between the unreasonable demands of the id and the demands of the real world.
Regression	Returning to an earlier less mature stage of development when stressful conditions prevail. One example is the small child who starts to thumb suck or use baby language after the birth of a sibling.
Reinforcement	In classical conditioning, strengthening responses through a system of rewards. Rewards increase the likelihood that a person will behave in certain desired ways.
Reparation	A Freudian defence mechanism which involves a process of repair. Guilt is reduced when action is taken to atone for imagined damage to internal objects. One way of doing this is to re-create the object which has been destroyed in phantasy. In Kleinian theory, reparation is a normal part of the developmental process and is used by the infant to resolve ambivalent feelings (feelings of love and hate) towards the mother.
Repetition compulsion	A Freudian term which describes the tendency to repeat certain patterns of behaviour derived from early experience. Since much of this early experience is based on relationships with parents and other significant figures, later repetitions also tend to occur in the context of relationships.
Repression	Freudian defence mechanism which involves pushing unacceptable emotions or feelings into the unconscious. This ensures that deeply distressing impulses or emotions do not cause anxiety.
Resistance	A word used in psychoanalytic literature to describe the client's opposition to the process of therapy. It is especially evident in relation to interpretations offered by the therapist. These interpretations may be rejected for fear that unconscious material will surface and so have to be faced. Resistance may also be present when sessions are missed or when clients arrive late or talk about totally irrelevant topics.
Rorschach Test	A personality test devised by Swiss psychiatrist Hermann

Rorschach (1844–1922). The test uses a series of ink blots which the subject is asked to interpret. Answers are meant to provide evidence of the subject's fantasy life and personality structure.

Sadism	A pathological need to obtain pleasure by inflicting pain on others. (See also *masochism*.)
Safety need	From Maslow's hierarchy of needs: the human need to be safe from physical and psychological danger.
Schizophrenia	A severe mental illness characterised by delusions, hallucinations, disorganised behaviour, incoherent speech and withdrawal.
Secondary gain	Any advantage which can be derived from an illness or condition, or positive side effects which accompany a negative event.
Secondary process thinking	In contrast to primary process thinking, this refers to logical and realistic thought processes. (See also *primary process thinking*.)
Self	The way in which a person experiences him or herself. This is in contract to the concept of ego which is a descriptive term used in psychodynamic theory to refer objectively to a *part* of human personality. (See also *ego*).
Self actualisation	A Rogerian concept describing an innate tendency towards personal growth and self realisation.
Self concept	A person's view of self.
Self fulfilling prophecy	Ideas or beliefs about people which influence our attitudes to them. These ideas and beliefs are then reinforced when peoples' responses fulfil our expectations.
Sibling rivalry	The competition for parental attention which occurs between children in the same family.
Social psychology	That branch of psychology which studies social interaction, including the thought processes and behaviour of individuals, pairs and groups.
Somatisation	The expression of emotional distress through bodily symptoms. Such expression of emotional distress may occur with people who are unable, or unwilling, to feel deeply about trauma or conflict.
Stereotyping	Preconceived ideas and expectations about certain groups of

people, and about male and female behaviour and roles. Such ideas and expectations may act as a defence against intimacy and closeness, since they excuse the believer from establishing any real contact with the stereotype group or individual.

Sublimination	A defence mechanism which involves the conversion of instinctual impulses into socially acceptable activities.
Sullivan, Harry Stack (1892–1949)	An American psychiatrist who emphasised the importance of social factors in the development of personality.
Superego	In the Freudian tripartite structure of personality, the superego is the component which guides ethical and moral behaviour.
Syndrome	A group of signs and symptoms typical of a specific illness or disorder.
Telepathy	Communication between minds without use of the senses.
Thanatos	Greek god of death. The term was used by Freud to describe the aggressive instinctual forces which, in his view, motivated human beings towards destructive behaviour and death. (See also *Eros*.)
Thorndike, Edward Lee (1874–1949)	An American behavioural psychologist famous for his research in animal learning and his studies in educational psychology. He established that mental abilities are independent so that, for example, a person with an aptitude for verbal skills might lack an aptitude for maths.
Token economy	A procedure used in behaviour modification for rewarding desired behaviour with tokens which can be exchanged for privileges. These tokens include snacks, gifts, access to television or trips. Sometimes used in institutions including hospitals.
Transference	In pyschodynamic theory this refers to the process of directing feelings, attitudes and conflicts experienced in childhood, to people in the present. The term is used to refer specifically to a client's response to the therapist, but the phenomenon is evident in many other relationships.
Trust v mistrust	The first of Erikson's eight psychological stages which corresponds roughly to Freud's oral stage of development. When early experience is positive and supportive, a child is likely to develop a sense of basic trust and confidence in self. When early experience is negative, however, anxiety, estrangement and mistrust of self and others is the outcome.

Type A personality	A person who is competitive, aggressive, driven and achieving. Such people are believed to be susceptible to certain forms of illness including heart attack.
Type B personality	A person who is able to relax and enjoy life even when conditions are pressured.
Unconditional positive regard	An attitude described by Carl Rogers in his client centred approach to therapy. It refers to the way in which the counsellor should value the client unconditionally, and accept him exactly as he is.
Unconditioned Response (UCR)	A term used in behavioural psychology to describe the automatic or unlearned response to a stimulus.
Unconditioned Stimulus (UCS)	A term used in behavioural psychology to describe the stimulus which elicits an automatic response with learning or conditioning.
Unconscious	That area of mental activity which, according to Freud, is outside immediate awareness. Contains feelings, memories and motives as well as sexual and aggressive impulses which, although hidden, nevertheless affect behaviour.
Unconscious motive	A motive of which a person is unaware. Some motives have both conscious and unconscious components, and occasionally a motive is discernible in distorted or disguised form
Wish fulfilment	A term used in Freudian theory to suggest that dreams may express unconscious wishes or desire. Clearly not all dreams could be described as wish fulfilment, since many of them are frightening or disturbing.
Working through	A term used in psychodynamic theory to describe the process whereby a client in therapy gains insight, becomes independent and prepares to change. The process also involves some degree of mourning for the past.

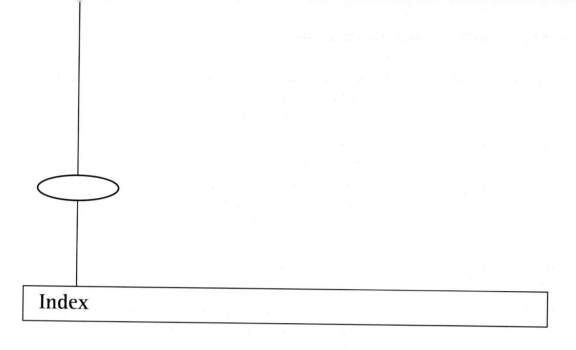

Index